God's BIG Idea

Also by RosAnne C. Tetz:

Love Letters From Jesus

To order, call 1-800-765-6955.

Visit us at www.reviewandherald.com for information on other Review and Herald® products.

God's BIG Idea

Primary Devotional

RosAnne C. Tetz

R

REVIEW AND HERALD® PUBLISHING ASSOCIATION
HAGERSTOWN, MD 21740

The author assumes full responsibility for the accuracy of all facts and quotations
as cited in this book.

Unless otherwise noted, Bible texts are from the *International Children's Bible, New Century
Version,* copyright © 1983, 1986, 1988 by Word Publishing, Dallas, Texas 75039. Used by permission.
Bible texts credited to Amplified are from *The Amplified Bible,* copyright © 1965 by
Zondervan Publishing House. Used by permission.
Texts credited to KJV are from the King James Version of the Bible.
Texts credited to NIV are from the *Holy Bible, New International Version.* Copyright ©
1973, 1978, 1984, International Bible Society. Used by permission of Zondervan Bible Publishers.

This book was
Edited by Kathy Pepper
Copyedited by James Cavil
Designed by Genesis Design
Cover illustration by Robert Papp
Typeset: Sabon 12/16

PRINTED IN U.S.A.

07 06 05 04 03   5 4 3 2 1

R&H Cataloging Service
Tetz, RosAnne C., 1953-
    God's big idea.

    1. Children—Religious life.   2. Devotional literature—Juvenile.   3. Devotional
calendars—Seventh-day Adventist.   I. Title.

                      242.62

ISBN 0-8280-1762-X

Dedication

**This book is dedicated
to Raymond.**

Dear Boys and Girls,

There are ideas grown-ups like to pass on to children. For instance:

• Don't play with matches.
• Use a tissue. Not your finger. Not your sleeve.
• A triangle has three sides.

Grown-ups think these ideas are important. As you get older, they give you bigger and bigger ideas. Chances are that since you've been little, grown-ups have been teaching you ideas about God. We take you to church. We've taught you to pray.

We love you very much, and there are some things we want you to know. Really important things. There are more big ideas we want to pass on.

That's why we wrote these ideas down and printed them into a book and got this book for you. That's why we're planning on reading it together (or hoping that you'll read it). That's why we're asking you to think hard about these ideas.

We want you to believe.

We want you to know about God's Big Idea, about His plan for our world.

Dear Caring Adult,

It's possible that Bible Docs was not your favorite class in school and that you were hoping for something a little more upbeat in a primary kids' devotional. That's only reasonable. So were we.

It's possible that when it comes to primary-age kids, some of the fundamental beliefs are more fundamental than others. That's why we spend a month on "The Bible Is the Word of God" and considerably less on the investigative judgment.

It's possible to make the fundamentals interesting, relevant, vital. Because they are.

It's possible that when you and your child have finished this book, your child will know what it means to be a Seventh-day Adventist. But even more important, it's possible that your child will have the peace that comes from knowing that God has a plan for this world, the joy that comes from knowing that God has a plan for his or her life, and the love that comes from knowing Jesus.

It's possible. And it is our deepest, dearest hope.

God's Message to You

Does your family have an answering machine? It's a handy gadget. If friends are trying to reach you by phone, they don't have to keep trying and trying until you're home. They can just leave a message on your machine. Once you get used to it, it's hard to imagine living without it.

It really is God's message. And that message works in you who believe.
1 Thessalonians 2:13.

God has a message for you. It's right in the Bible, waiting for you, whenever you're ready. God wants to talk to you.

After God created Adam and Eve, He would come to their garden and talk to them, face to face. Sin put a stop to that.

But God still wanted to communicate. He didn't just say "Good luck!" and walk away.

God wants to be a part of our lives. He wants us to be a part of His plan for this world. God wants us to know Him.

So He gave us the Bible. The Bible tells us what God is like. It tells us how He wants us to live. The Bible is one of God's best ways of communicating with us.

And once you get used to it, you can't imagine living without it!

Treasure Hunt

Cry out for wisdom. Beg for understanding. Search for it as you would for silver. Hunt for it like hidden treasure. Then you will understand what it means to respect the Lord. Then you will begin to know God. Proverbs 2:3-5.

Have you ever been on a treasure hunt? It can be a lot of fun, especially if you play in teams. Your team gets a clue on a piece of paper, and when you solve it, it leads you to another clue, which leads to another clue, until you finally reach the treasure. The treasure is wonderful, of course, but the hunt itself is wonderful too.

Our Bible text talks about a treasure really worth looking for—learning to know God. God wants us to know Him. He wants us to know how much He loves us. He wants to tell us about His plan to save the world from sin.

That's why He gave us the Bible. We can't see God, but we can find out about Him if we read the Bible.

Do you want to learn about God? Search the Bible. Do you want to know what God is like? Hunt in His Word.

And the more you search, the more there is to find. The more you hunt, the greater the reward.

There is no better hunt. There is no better treasure.

Imagine That

Are you good at imagining? Try this. Imagine that no one ever tells you what to do. At home, no one tells you to clean up your room or turn off the TV or practice the piano. At school, no one tells you to listen carefully or line up or get busy on that worksheet.

You probably will need a powerful imagination to imagine such a thing.

So how are things going in your imagination? Pretty good? Lots of recess? Lots of video games? Candy, anyone? Jumping on the furniture?

Ah, but think a little deeper. What's your imaginary classroom really like? Very noisy, no doubt. Lots of arguing, maybe even some hitting. Does someone want your sandwich at lunch? No one says "no." No one says "don't." No one says "play nice."

I don't imagine that would be so great after all.

We need to know how to behave. We need to know what to do and how to do it. Or else we won't be happy, and neither will anyone else.

That's another reason God gave us the Bible. The Bible tells us how God wants us to live. It is "like a lamp for my feet and a light for my way" (Psalm 119:105). When things seem dark and confusing, the Bible can help you figure out the right thing to do. The Bible can help you make good choices.

Using the Scriptures, the person who serves God will be ready and will have everything he needs to do every good work. 2 Timothy 3:17.

The Word of God

God's word is true.

Psalm 33:4.

Have you ever heard some say this? "I give you my word." What do they mean? Is a word something that you can pick up and hand to someone? Of course not. You can't see or touch words that are spoken. You can't give a word to someone the way you'd give them a piece of candy.

When you say you are giving your word, you mean that you are making a promise. It's usually a rather solemn promise. For instance, you might say, "If you let me have a puppy, I give you my word that I'll take good care of it."

You have probably heard that the Bible is the Word of God. The Bible gives us God's messages: It tells us what God is like, how He wants us to live, His plan for the world.

And in the Bible God gives us His Word. The Bible gives us God's promises. He promises to take care of us. He promises to save us from sin. He promises to bring us to heaven.

The Bible is full of stories that show that God keeps His word. When God makes a promise, it happens.

The Bible is full of God's promises. The Bible is God's Word.

The Ideas of God

Have you ever said, "I'm starving"? Did you mean that you were actually dying of hunger? Of course not. And the people you were talking to knew what you really meant: you were very, very hungry.

All Scripture is given by God. 2 Timothy 3:16.

Pretend your mom tells you, "Stay away from these cookies. It's too close to suppertime." A few minutes later your brother comes in and reaches for the cookies. You say, "Mom says don't eat the cookies because it will spoil your appetite." Did you quote her exact words? No. But are you telling the truth? Of course. You got the idea right.

Words are important because they stand for ideas.

When we say that the Bible is the Word of God, we mean that these are God's ideas. How could the Bible have God's exact words when there are so many different versions and translations? And how could they be His exact words when we are reading in English and they were written in some ancient language?

And speaking of writing, did God actually write the words down? No (except for the Ten Commandments, which He wrote with His finger on the stone tablets).

God chose people to write His ideas. Sometimes God sent these people a vision or a dream. The Bible writers wrote what they saw. Sometimes He gave them messages. They wrote what God told them to write. Thousands of places in the Bible you can read such sentences as "The Lord spoke these words to me" or "This is what the Lord says."

The Bible is full of God's ideas.

If There Were Only One Word

Have you ever been on a team? Even though it is made up of several different people, it is one thing. Your baseball team might have 10 people on it, but it is one team. All 10 of you work together for one goal—to have fun playing baseball. (OK, so maybe there is another goal as well—to win the game.)

Because we have ideas like this, we need words that are about one thing with many parts. Team. Popcorn. Newspaper. Word.

We say the Bible is the Word of God, but if you look at a Bible you can see that there are lots of words. Nearly 800,000, actually. Obviously, when we say Word we don't mean just one word.

But if there were only one word in the Bible, what do you suppose it would be? There's really only one choice: love. The New International Version uses the word *love* 505 times.

Love seems to be God's main message. How God loves us. How we can show our love for God. How we should love each other. Love, love, love. Over and over and over.

God loves you. He doesn't want you to forget. Ever.

The Greatest

Have you ever been in a race? Maybe you were on a walk and your dad all of a sudden said, "I'll race you to the corner." Or maybe at a church picnic you got to be in a three-legged race or one of those races in which you hop toward the finish line in a potato sack.

God's word is alive and working.
Hebrews 4:12.

Races like that can be a lot of fun. But they aren't the Olympics. The Olympics are the greatest of races. To race in the Olympics, you have to be an excellent athlete—one of the best in the entire world. The fastest. The strongest. The greatest.

There are lots of books. Many of them are very good. But they aren't the Bible. The Bible is the Olympics of books. Other books can't even come close.

What's so special about the Bible? It tells great stories—but a lot of books have great stories. It gives good advice—but a lot of books offer advice. The Bible is more than stories and advice and rules and lists.

The Bible is special because it contains messages from God. Many people have written books explaining their ideas about God. But the Bible is not a person's ideas. It is God's ideas.

The Bible is special because it changes lives. Many people have written books that cause change—some books have even changed governments or started wars. But God's messages of love in the Bible offer salvation—the biggest, best change of all.

The Bible is not just words on a page. Like our text says: "God's word is alive and working." It's the greatest.

Look Closer

Take a look at a tree. What do you see? Maybe a round blobby shape with a trunk. Or maybe a longish triangle shape. Good.

Now take a closer look. Can you see the trunk? Is it tall and straight, or does it split off into a bunch of branches? Since this is winter, you may be able to see all of the trunk and branches, unless it's an evergreen tree.

Now look even closer—at the leaves or needles. What shape are they? What shade of green? Are they very thick together, or can the sun shine through them?

Do you know the tree a little better now? To know it well, you'd probably have to watch it for an entire year—see the birds build their nests and the squirrels scamper in its branches. You'd have to climb in it yourself, of course. And watch its leaves fall and see the new leaves appear. And use a magnifying glass to examine the bark and leaves and bugs. And even then, there would still be a lot to learn.

You can look at the Bible that way too. You can see an old book with a lot of words and no pictures. But what happens when you look closer? What are those words saying? What does that story mean? Read it. Then look closer. And even closer.

The closer you look, the more there will be to learn. The closer you look, the closer you will grow to God.

Jesus and the Bible

Jesus read the Bible. Of course, His Bible wasn't exactly like yours. For one thing, it was written in a different language—Hebrew. Hebrew is written from right to left, and it doesn't have vowels. If you were to write "Jesus Loves Me" that way, it would look like this: M SVL SSJ.

Jesus' Bible wasn't shaped like yours either. It wasn't a rectangle with lots of pages. It was written on long pieces of paper that were rolled up into scrolls.

And your Bible has more parts. Jesus studied the part we call the Old Testament. In those days it was called the Scriptures.

Jesus' mother, Mary, taught Him to read, and they studied the Scriptures together. He learned it very well. Probably one of His first memory verses was "Love the Lord your God with all your heart, soul and strength." (Deuteronomy 6:5). Do you remember the story in which He quoted that text to the Pharisees? (Look in Matthew 22:34-40.)

It's not surprising Jesus knew the Scriptures so well—after all, they were His ideas in the first place.

Jesus knew the reason we were given the Scriptures—so we could learn to know God. That's also one of the reasons He came to this earth—to help us know God better. Both Jesus and the Bible were sent to help us learn about God. Jesus is the Bible brought to life.

Then Jesus opened their minds so they could understand the Scriptures. Luke 24:45.

Old Testament and New Testament

*"Those are the same
Scriptures that tell
about me!" John 5:39.*

Do you know how to make a peanut butter and jelly sandwich? It's a skill worth having. You need two pieces of bread, some peanut butter, and some jelly. You spread the peanut butter on one slice of bread and the jelly on the other. When you put them together, you've got a sandwich.

A peanut butter sandwich is good, and a jelly sandwich is good—but put them together, and you've really got something.

In a way, the Bible is like a sandwich. You've got the Old Testament and the New Testament, and together they make the Bible.

The Old Testament is the Bible that Jesus read, and the New Testament tells the story of Jesus and the first Christians.

What does *testament* mean, anyway? One meaning is "telling the truth" and another meaning is "an agreement or promise."

The Old Testament tells the stories of people like Abraham and Joseph and Jeremiah. It also tells of the agreement God made with His people to send a Redeemer. The New Testament tells the story of that Redeemer and God's plan to save the world from sin.

The Old Testament and the New Testament are both important. Together they tell the whole story. Together they show God's whole plan. Together you've really got something.

The Answer

When you have a question, sometimes you just have to know where to look. If you want to know the time, you look at a clock. If you need someone's phone number, you look in the phone book or call information. If you are curious about the year Beethoven was born, you can look in an encyclopedia or use the Internet.

However, some questions are harder and deeper. Why does the world exist? What should I do with my life? Why is there so much suffering in the world? For questions like this, the best place to go for answers is the Bible.

Imagine what your life would be like if you didn't have the Bible. What is wrong? What is right? What hope is there for the future? What is the point of living? Without the Bible there would be no answers. Without the Bible we would be like a boat drifting around in the darkness.

You can find answers in the Bible. It's not always easy. The harder the question, the harder you have to search for an answer. But all that searching leads to more than just an answer. It leads to wisdom. And as today's Bible text says, that leads to salvation.

More than anything else, God wants to save you. And in the Bible He has given you everything you need to know. The Bible has the answer.

The Scriptures are able to make you wise. And that wisdom leads to salvation through faith in Christ Jesus. 2 Timothy 3:15.

God's Plan for the World

His goal was to carry out his plan when the right time came. Ephesians 1:10.

Have you ever done anything on the spur of the moment? Let's say you're riding home from school and all of a sudden someone in the car says, "Let's get some ice cream," so you all decide to stop at an ice-cream store and have an ice-cream cone. That's fun!

But spur of the moment isn't always fun. Let's say you're riding home from school and all of you, right then, decide to go on a vacation. It may be fun for the first bit. But then you get lost because you don't really know where you are going. You don't have a toothbrush or clean underwear, because you haven't packed anything. You begin to worry about your pets because you haven't arranged for anyone to take care of them.

That's not fun. That's a mess. Most things work better when there is a plan.

God has a plan for this world. He didn't just create it and stand back to watch what would happen. You can read about His plan in the Bible.

God's plan has always been to be with us. Even though things went wrong in the Garden of Eden, God had made other plans to keep us close to Him. When the right time came, God sent His Son to save us from sin. And when the right time comes, He will send His Son again to bring us to heaven.

God has a plan.

God's Plan for You

Some people don't like to think. They avoid it. And if they can't avoid it, they try and get someone else to think for them. They don't like to make choices. They'd rather let other people make choices for them.

People like that have a hard time with the Bible. They would rather have a Bible that would tell them, "Today you need to share your pencil with Katie. Next week you should take some flowers to Mrs. Jones. At summer camp you should take horseback riding class." That would be so simple.

The Bible doesn't work like that. God has a plan for your life. And you can learn about it in the Bible. But you will have to think. You will have to make choices.

The Bible doesn't say, "Today you need to share your pencil with Katie." But it does say, "Be happy to give and ready to share" (1 Timothy 6:18). You will have to look around to see who needs help. You will have to decide what you can give. You will have to think.

God has a plan for your life. But you will have to choose whether you want to be a part of it. And you will have to work to discover what it is. You will have to search God's Word. You will have to pray. You will have to live close to Him, day by day.

You must choose for yourselves today. You must decide whom you will serve. Joshua 24:15.

23

Don't Be a Baby

Then we will no longer be babies.... We will not be influenced by every new teaching we hear from men who are trying to fool us. Ephesians 4:14.

Do you think you would like to be on a jury? It seems as if it would be very difficult. First one witness tells one side of the story. Then another witness tells another side of the story. One lawyer argues that the accused person is guilty. And another lawyer argues that that person is innocent. Then you meet with the other members of the jury, and they all have different opinions. It would be hard to decide. But if you are on a jury, it's important for you to decide for yourself. You can't let someone else tell you what to think.

There are so many different kinds of churches, and they have different ideas about what the Bible means. It can be confusing. How can you know which ideas are right? How can you find the truth?

The Bible text for today says that there are even some people who twist the words of the Bible to try to fool us. What can you do?

You have to learn the Bible for yourself. You can't be a baby about it. You can't just believe everything you hear. If you know the Bible well, it is not likely that someone will be able to trick you.

And the more you know, the more you will be able to understand. As you study, your spiritual self will grow up. You will no longer be a baby.

But Don't Get Old, Either

Have you ever wondered what you'll look like when you get old? What will your face look like with wrinkles? Or your head with gray hair? Or no hair? It's hard to imagine.

It's hard to accept, too. Many people who are in their 60s or 70s say that they still picture themselves as being in their 20s or 30s. So when they catch a glimpse of themselves in a mirror, they are surprised, for a moment, at how old they look.

Today's Bible text points out that even though our bodies are getting older every day, our spiritual lives don't need to get old and tired. God wants your spiritual life to stay fresh and interesting. He will help you stay curious and eager to learn.

It is possible to look at the Bible as a dusty old book that doesn't say much about life today. But God can show you that this old Book is alive and is written just for you, right now.

Some people who talk about the Bible make it sound dreadfully boring. They just have a knack for that. But don't get discouraged. God can revive it for you if you ask Him to.

God will make you new every day.

So we do not give up. Our physical body is becoming older and weaker, but our spirit inside us is made new every day.
2 Corinthians 4:16.

"Help Me Understand"

He will lead you into all truth. John 16:13.

Do you remember what it was like when you were learning to read? Learning to read is a complicated process. It was probably easier for you if someone taught you to sing the ABC song when you were little. It was probably easier if you were lucky enough to have someone who read you a bedtime story every night. You probably learned a little easier if there was someone you could go to when you needed help with the hard words.

We all need help learning to read the Bible, too. Except that with the Bible it's not just *reading* the words—it's *understanding* the words.

You probably have many people who are happy to help you—family, teachers, people at church. That's wonderful.

God will help you too. He wants you to understand His messages. In today's Bible text He promises that He will help you find the truth.

So it's important to ask Him to be with you when you read the Bible. David wrote this prayer: " Let your word help me understand" (Psalm 119:169). You can pray the same prayer. You don't have to try to figure it out all by yourself. God wants to help you understand the Bible. Just ask.

Take It to Heart

Do you believe that the earth rotates around the sun? Most people accept this as fact.

I have taken your words to heart. Psalm 119:11.

Assuming that you do believe this, what difference does it make in your life? Probably not much. You most likely can go for any number of days without thinking about it even once.

Now imagine that they say on the news that school is canceled tomorrow because of too much snow. Is that fact going to make a difference in your life? You'd better believe it! You won't have to go to school, and there will be lots of snow to play in.

There are some things we believe that are just facts; for instance, the earth rotates around the sun. We believe these things with our minds. They don't affect our lives very much.

There are other things we believe that make a big difference in the way we live and behave. These things are a real part of our lives. They can change our lives completely.

The Bible can fall into either of these categories. You can read it as literature or as history. You can skim over every word so that you can say you've read the Bible all the way through—and yet it doesn't make a bit of sense to you.

Or you can treasure it and look deep into its words. You can take the Bible into your life so that it makes a difference. You can take its words to heart.

Prove It

*All these things have
happened to make the
Scriptures come true.*
Mark 14:49.

Imagine that you get a phone call tonight from a friend, who wants to go sledding with you tomorrow because it's a snow day and there won't be any school. This is the first you've heard about it.

It is also news to your mother. She wants to make sure that it's true before she says you can go sledding. She says prove it.

So what do you do? Do you show her a thermometer? Well, that will prove that it is cold enough to snow, but it doesn't say anything about school.

You have to find a way that will convince your mother—something that she has confidence in. How about turning on the radio or TV? That's a much better choice. The news will probably have a lot to say about the weather, and will no doubt mention that schools will be closed.

The Jewish people had been looking for their Redeemer for thousands of years. They knew He was coming to save them because God had told the prophets, and the prophets had written it in the Scriptures, and the people believed the Scriptures.

But when Jesus did come to earth, many people didn't believe that He was the Redeemer. So sometimes Jesus used the Scriptures to prove it. After Jesus went back to heaven, His followers often used the Scriptures to prove that Jesus was the Redeemer. And many people who believed in the Scriptures also believed in Jesus.

Do you want to know if an idea is true? Look in the Bible. There's proof.

Full of Hope

Your have different kinds of hope. On Christmas Eve, when you can't wait to open your presents, you hope that morning will come soon. It definitely will happen. But you may also hope that you'll get the pony on your wish list. Maybe, maybe not.

Everything that was written in the past was written to teach us, so that we could have hope. Romans 15:4.

Today's Bible text says that the Bible was written so that we can have hope. And the Bible is full of all kinds of hope.

When we feel alone, the Bible gives us hope that God is on our side: "If God is with us, then no one can defeat us" (Romans 8:31).

When we are worried about what will happen, the Bible gives us hope that God wants what is best for us. "I plan to give you hope and a good future" (Jeremiah 29:11).

When we get discouraged and things look bleak, the Bible gives us hope that things will turn out: "We know that in everything God works for the good of those who love him" (Romans 8:28).

When someone we love dies and we miss them very much, the Bible gives us hope that we will see them again (1 Thessalonians 4:16).

And biggest and best is our hope that Jesus will save us: "We have this hope as an anchor for the soul, sure and strong (Hebrews 6:19). And He will come again to take us to be with Him (John 14:3).

Because the Bible is full of hope, we can be full of hope.

Powerful Words

They celebrated with great joy. They finally understood what they had been taught.
Nehemiah 8:12.

It was a sad time for the Isrealites. Jerusalem had been destroyed about 150 years before, and the people had been captured and taken to Babylon. Finally, the king allowed the Jews to return to their homeland. But it wasn't easy for them. Everything was in ruins. There was little to eat. The Samaritans kept attacking them.

Nehemiah persuaded the king to make him governor, and he set off to help his people. First on his list was making sure that the walls of Jerusalem were rebuilt.

But that wasn't the real problem. The people had been away so long they had forgotten their history. They had forgotten the laws and how to worship God. They needed to learn how to live as God wanted.

Early one morning the people gathered in the courtyard. Ezra the priest climbed a high wooden platform, and began to read the Scriptures out loud. The people listened carefully. Teachers were there to explain things so that everyone could understand.

It was the first time some of the people had heard the Scriptures. As they listened they began to realize how wrongly they had been living, and many of them began to cry.

Nehemiah and Ezra told them that they should be happy instead, because now they knew the way to follow God. When the people realized that, they began to celebrate.

The Word of God has power to make us sad, to make us happy, and, best of all, to make us change. They are not ordinary words. They are powerful.

Some Things Don't Change

I am the Lord. I do not change. Malachi 3:6.

Do you like to eat? Let's assume that you do. Now, the Bible doesn't say, but let's assume that Adam and Eve liked to eat too. What do you imagine their favorite foods were? OK, what would you like to eat right now, if you could have anything you wanted?

There is a pretty good chance that your favorite foods are different from what Adam and Eve ate. They didn't have can openers or microwave ovens or fast-food restaurants. We eat different foods that are prepared in different ways.

However, even though we are so different from Adam and Eve in the way we eat, in one very important way we are the same: we all like to eat.

The Bible was written a long, long time ago. The people of the Bible are very different from us. Because of this, some people think that the Bible is not relevant—that it doesn't have any meaning for people in modern times.

But they are forgetting that some things don't change. Even though we don't eat the same things, we still eat. Even though we don't live in the same kinds of houses, we still need shelter. People still laugh and cry and make mistakes and worry. People still can worship and pray and seek God.

And the most important thing that will never change is God. God is the same today as He has always been. We can count on Him to be the same in the future.

The Bible that tells us about God may have been written a long time ago, but it tells us the truth about things that are still true today, and will always be true.

Food for Thought

As newborn babies want milk, you should want the pure and simple teaching. By it you can grow up and be saved. 1 Peter 2:2.

Let's talk about food some more.

What was your answer yesterday about what you'd choose if you could eat anything you wanted?

How about right now? Are you hungry for the same thing, or does something else sound good now?

Most of us don't want to eat the same thing all the time. Sometimes ice cream is what we dream of, and other times it is the last thing we'd want.

Your favorite foods probably change too. Maybe last year your favorite was pizza, and before that it was pancakes, and so on, all the way back to mashed bananas, and, even before that, milk.

The Bible is like food—it says so (Hebrews 5:12-14). When you are first learning about God, you just drink "milk." You learn the basics, like "Jesus Loves Me, This I Know." It's very important to learn this well and to believe it with all your heart.

But after a while you are ready for more than milk—you want more. And it's there in the Bible. As much as you can hold.

And it can be delicious. "Sweeter than honey" (Psalm 19:10). Enjoy!

What's the Point?

Why do you go to school?

To see your friends? Now, that would be a very honest answer and a good reason, but it's not the most important reason.

Because it's the law? Yes, it is. But why do we have that law?

To get a gold star for perfect attendance? Now, that's just sad.

You go to school to learn. And not just learn—to learn how to learn. The things you learn how to do in school (such as think!) will help you in your life.

Sometimes you have to keep looking and asking to get the real answer.

What is the point of the Bible?

To teach us history? Yes, it is history, but these stories have a point. What is it?

To tell us about God? Of course! God wants us to know what He is like. But why? Why is that important to Him?

Because He wants to save us? That's it! That's the point of the Bible. More than anything else, God wants to save us.

God gave us the Bible to tell us everything we need to know about His plan to save us.

What's the point? He loves you. He wants to be with you always. He wants to save you.

This teaching can save your souls. James 1:21.

Defense/Offense

Wear God's armor so that you can fight against the devil's evil tricks. Ephesians 6:11.

When you play team sports you need both a defense and an offense. Let's say you have a really good defense but no offense. The other team will have a hard time scoring any points, but you won't be able to score any points at all.

And imagine what would happen if you have a great offense but no defense. While you spend all your time trying to get through their defense to score, they won't have anyone stopping them from scoring whenever they get the ball.

The balance of defense and offense is one of the things that make a great team.

You need that balance of defense and offense in your life as a Christian, too. It is like a battle. We are fighting against Satan and his armies, against sin and darkness. We need a good defense.

And we need a good offense. Our assignment is to spread the good news about God's plan to save us. In order to do that, we need to be strong and brave. How can we do that?

We can't. We need God to help us. And He promises that He will help us in this battle.

What is our chief weapon? The Bible. It is our armor, which will protect us. And it is our sword—"That sword is the teaching of God" (Ephesians 6:17). The Bible is our defense and our offense.

I Hear and I Obey

Imagine that your teacher has given you a math worksheet. She says that you don't have to solve every problem; you only have to do every other one. She assigns the odd-numbered problems on this worksheet.

But you look at the worksheet and you decide that you would really rather do the even-numbered problems. You see that there are fewer even-numbered problems on this particular worksheet, plus you think that the even-numbered ones look easier. So you do the even-numbered problems instead of the odd-numbered problems.

Is this a wise decision? What will your score be?

It is important to listen to instructions. But it is even more important to follow them.

This is what the Bible says about itself. It's not enough just to listen to the words of the Bible. You must believe them and make them a part of your life. You must follow them and act on them.

Jesus told a story about this. He said, "Everyone who hears these things I say and obeys them is like a wise man. The wise man built his house on rock" (Matthew 7:24). That house was safe from the storm. However, the foolish man, who heard but did not obey, built his house on the sand. That house did not survive the storm.

God's Word can keep you safe—but only if you listen *and* obey.

> *Do what God's teaching says; do not just listen and do nothing. James 1:22.*

The Secret of Happiness

*Your words made
me very happy.
Jeremiah 15:16.*

What is the secret of happiness? Well, what would make you happy today? What if your teacher said, "Instead of practicing our handwriting today, let's have extra recess." That would probably make you happy. But that's no secret.

What if you got a letter from your grandma and she sent you $20 just for fun? That would probably make you happy. But that's no secret.

How about if you won the spelling bee or got an extra dessert in your lunch or got invited to a party? All happy, happy things.

But what if none of these things happen? (And chances are they won't. Sorry.) Can you possibly still be happy? If you can, then you must be learning the secret of happiness.

The Bible says, "The truly happy person is the one who carefully studies God's perfect law that makes people free" (James 1:25). The Bible shows the way to happiness. The Bible holds the secrets of happiness.

Yet the ideas in the Bible about happiness may seem rather unusual. At first you would not think that it could make you happier to give than to receive. But the Bible says it will. And after you try it, you can see that it's true.

Being happy is not as simple as it seems. It's complicated. The Bible holds the secrets. If you carefully search for them, the Bible can show you the way to be happy.

Word Shortage

Have you ever been through a drought? It doesn't rain and it doesn't rain, and people get worried and say, "Don't waste water," even more than usual. We need water to live.

But they will be hungry for words from the Lord. Amos 8:11.

And so do plants, so a drought can lead to a famine. You probably have never experienced a famine; if the crops fail, food can be shipped from somewhere else. But not all countries can do that, and drought or flood or war can cause a famine. Then people die because they don't have food.

The Israelites knew about drought and famine. But the prophet Amos warned them about a drought that was worse than no water and a famine that was worse than no food. Amos warned them about a shortage of words—the words of the Lord.

A regular drought and famine are terrible things, but some people will survive, and life will go on. A famine of God's words is another matter altogether. Without God's word there is no hope. There is only darkness.

Many of us are so used to the Bible. It is always there. We are free to read it whenever we want—or not. We take God's Word for granted.

But there have been famines. In some Communist countries, no so long ago, Bibles were illegal. Many people never heard God's word. They didn't even know what they were hungry and thirsty for.

Don't take it for granted. Thank God for His Word. Drink deeply. Eat your fill.

To Open, Close

Sometimes people don't mean exactly what they say. For instance, if your mom says, "You'd better watch it!" you know that you'd better behave. And if you say something like "What do you want me to watch?" you are just asking for trouble.

If you say, "I fell over laughing," you are probably speaking figuratively. You just mean you laughed really hard. If you actually did fall over, then you would be speaking literally.

The Bible often speaks figuratively. When Jesus tells the Pharisees, "You are snakes! A family of poisonous snakes!" (Matthew 23:33), He doesn't mean they are actually snakes. He means they are as dangerous as snakes.

Think about the text for today. Is it speaking figuratively? Yes. Our eyes need to be open in order to read the Bible. But this isn't talking about that. It says "Open my eyes," but it means "Help me understand."

The person who wrote this Psalm is praying for help in understanding God's teachings. When you pray you usually close your eyes. So the best way to "open your eyes" is to close them in prayer.

Open your Bible. Close your eyes. And ask God to open them.

Building Better Bible Study

T ry to imagine building the best, most glorious ice-cream sundae ever. Start with ice cream, any flavor—or lots of flavors. It doesn't have to be a normal flavor—make up your own if you want. It doesn't have to be ice cream, either. You can have frozen yogurt or mashed potatoes. It's your imagination.

But dear friends, use your most holy faith to build yourselves up strong. Jude 20.

Now add sauces. Butterscotch on the butter pecan. Chocolate on the peppermint. Gravy on the mashed potatoes. Whatever makes you happy.

What's next? Chopped nuts? Sprinkles? Candies? Are you a whipped cream fan? Is one maraschino cherry enough?

That was fun. Too bad it was only in your imagination. Or maybe it's just as well.

When you build your sundae yourself, you can appreciate all the different "layers." You understand that it is more than just a sundae.

When you study the Bible, there can be different layers. You can build the experience so that it is more than just reading words.

You start with reading it, of course, and asking God to help you understand. Then you can build it higher. You can take it to heart—believe it, feel it.

Keep building. Once you believe it, you can let it make you strong and brave. Then you can live what you have learned. What you studied has become a part of you.

And the best part is that you don't have to build any of this all by yourself. God will be with you every step, every layer.

Future Smiles

Do you think you might need to get braces? You may have them already. Some people get braces put on their teeth to straighten them or to line up their jaw. Methods have improved over the last few years, so it's not as much torture as it used to be. However, there still is some "discomfort," as they say.

Some people's teeth are so out of line that they have to get their jaws broken and reset. Talk about discomfort! But maybe you'd rather not talk about it.

What everybody has to remember is that when it is all over they will have a beautiful smile. Sometimes things have to get worse before they can get better.

The Bible can work like braces. It can be painful to read some things in the Bible: How perfect things were until sin came into the world. How often we fall short of what God asks of us. How shamefully Jesus was treated, how horribly He was killed.

It's no fun to read about how sinful we are. But sometimes things have to get worse before they can get better. We need to see how awful sin is before we will ask to be rescued from it. We need to understand our sin before we can appreciate our salvation.

When we get to the difficult, painful parts of the Bible, we need to remember that all the sad things in the Bible are covered by a miraculous hope that not only cancels out the bad, but makes everything right. We can handle the bad because we know how good the good is.

And when it is all over, we will have a beautiful smile.

Go to the Bible

Do you like to go shopping? Some people do, some people don't. There are huge stores that help make shopping a better experience for both types of people. People who hate to shop can go there knowing that the place is so big they are bound to find what they need and don't have to drive all over town looking for it. People who love to shop can walk into these enormous stores and see row after row of things to look at and compare and all those choices and colors and sizes . . . and they are blissfully happy.

The Lord will always lead you. He will satisfy your needs. Isaiah 58:11.

You can look at the Bible as being a big department store, only way bigger and with much, much more to offer—the Bible has stuff you need, stuff you can really use.

Do you have a problem you need to solve? Go to the Bible. It won't say, "Lisa, you should be a doctor when you grow up." But it will help you figure out the right thing to do.

Are you having a hard time doing the right thing? Is it way, way easier to do the wrong thing? Go to the Bible. It can help you find the strength you need to overcome temptations. It can give you the power you need to do what God asks you to do.

When you are sad, go to the Bible. Bad things happen. Every day, around the world, there is plenty of sorrow. There is comfort in the Bible, and peace. It reminds us that everything will turn out for the best. It reminds us who is in charge.

Are you lonely? Go to the Bible to meet your Best Friend. You can find Jesus in the Bible. He has everything you need.

Personal

*So you will be my people, and I will be your God.
Ezekiel 36:28.*

Do you know what PC stands for? Personal computer. The first computers were incredibly big and expensive, and you had to be a genius to use them. Now average, everyday people have computers in their homes. We use computer networks at school and work. With computers we can go on the Internet and find out just about anything. The computers are personal, and yet they connect us with others in many ways.

The Bible tells us that God is personal and is connected to the entire world.

God gave us the Bible so we could learn about Him. Let's learn a little right now.

Look at Jeremiah 32:27. "I am the God of every person on the earth." God belongs to everyone. And everyone belongs to God.

Yet sometimes the Bible says that God belongs to a country or group of people. Luke 1:68 says, "Let us thank the Lord, the God of Israel." God did belong to Israel in a special way. He chose His people to tell other nations about Him.

Sometimes God says that He belongs to a certain person. He was known as "the God of Abraham" (Exodus 3:6) because He had a special agreement with Abraham.

Mostly God wants you to know that He is your God. He is a personal God. He tells you in Ezekiel 36:28, "I will be your God." You can answer with Psalm 118:28, "You are my God, and I will thank you."

He is the God of the universe. He is the God of Israel. He is the God of Abraham. And He is your God. Personal. Connected.

Three in One

Have you ever filled out a form? Usually the first line is for your name—and under the line, the little letters ask for last, first, and middle. If you have three names, it's easy. But if your parents gave you only two names, you can't write "None," or it will look like your middle name is None. Anyway, even though the prince of England may have five or six names and some famous celebrities use only one name, most people have three names. So the forms ask for three names.

The grace of the Lord Jesus Christ, the love of God, and the fellowship of the Holy Spirit be with you all. 2 Corinthians 13:14.

Even though you have three names, you are only one person. One person, three names. It's not that difficult to understand this concept.

The Bible says that God also has three names. But it is quite a bit more difficult to understand how it works.

God's names are (1) God the Father, (2) God the Son, and (3) God the Holy Spirit. But these are not first, middle, and last names. They are three separate names. God is three persons with three names.

This is where it gets complicated. God is three persons, but He is only one God. There is only one God—one God with three names.

How can this be? How can God be three persons and one God at the same time? People have been trying to explain this for thousands of years. We'll talk about it some more in the next few days.

43

More Names

Yesterday we talked about your first, middle, and last names. But you probably have even more. If your grandma says, "Sweetheart, please get me my purse," you'll do it. You'll know she's talking to you. If your dad says, "Son, I told you to make your bed," you aren't going to answer, "My name's not 'Son.'" Not if you know what's good for you.

Your friends probably have nicknames for you—names that are short forms of your real name, or names that fit your personality or the way you look.

God has nicknames too.

God the Father has other names mainly because people felt that His name was too holy to actually say. God told Moses at the burning bush that His name was Yahweh, but people usually said "the Lord" instead. Another name is Jehovah—it combines those two names in the Hebrew language. He is also called the Almighty because that's what He is.

God the Son is most commonly known as Jesus. That's the name He had while He was here on earth—the name the angel told Mary and Joseph to give the baby. He is also known as Christ (the Greek word) or the Messiah (the Hebrew word). That name means that He is the one God sent to save His people from their sins.

Another name for the Holy Spirit is the Holy Ghost—it's just another way of saying the same thing. Jesus called Him the Helper, and He is also known as the Comforter.

There are many other names—wonderful names for our wonderful God.

Only One

Before we talk about God being three persons, it needs to be absolutely clear that there is only one God.

And we know that there is only one God.
1 Corinthians 8:4.

Let's say that you want to go to a baseball game, but you don't have a ticket. So you take a piece of paper and write on it "One Ticket to the Baseball Game." Are they going to let you in? Of course not. It's not a real ticket. You made it yourself.

You can't make up your own gods, either. It doesn't work.

God had an agreement with the Israelites: He would be their God and they would be His people. But they had a hard time keeping their part of the agreement. The countries nearby had their own gods, and the Israelites kept wanting to worship them.

These nations had lots of gods; they even "borrowed" gods from each other. For instance, when invaders took over a country, they often took over the gods, too. If the attackers saw that the people had a moon god and they liked the idea of having a moon god, they would add the moon god to the collection of gods that they worshiped.

They made idols because they wanted gods they could see. They also used their gods to try to control nature. They thought, *We need rain. Let's give the god of rain a name and make an idol. We'll worship him and bring offerings, and he'll give us rain.*

The Israelites wanted to do this too. But it doesn't work. You cannot worship the one true God and a bunch of made-up gods at the same time. You cannot control God.

God created us. We did not create Him.

Father/Jesus/Spirit

Shout with joy to the Lord, all the earth. Burst into songs and praise. Psalm 98:4.

Have you ever sung along with a round? "Are You Sleeping?" is a famous round. A round must be sung with a group, because humans can sing only one note at a time. One group starts singing, then at a certain point the next group starts, then at another point the last group starts. If you could freeze the music while the round is going in full swing, you could hear three separate notes being sung at the same time—harmony. A round is complicated and beautiful and exciting to sing and hear.

A round is one song with three different melodies going on at the same time. One song with three groups singing. A round is one song and three songs at the same time.

God is one God and three persons. One and three at the same time.

God the Father, God the Son, and God the Holy Spirit are all different. Unique. They do different things.

But they work together as one God. They have the same goals and purpose.

We have a name for this idea of three persons in one God: Trinity. The word Trinity does not appear in the Bible. But the ideas are there.

There is a lovely round you may know called "Father, I Adore You." In this song the second verse says, "Jesus, I adore You," and the third verse says, "Spirit, I adore You." So this song is like a musical illustration of the Trinity. Three songs in one round are praising the three Persons in one God.

Three working as one, in harmony.

Dimensions

Let's say you are doodling on a piece of paper and you draw a straight line. That line would have one dimension—length. We could measure how long it is, but not how high. It isn't high; it is only long.

But if you draw a box or a dog or a flower, that doodle would have two dimensions—length and height. We could measure how long your drawing is and also how tall.

You could also take that piece of paper and fold it into an airplane or a hat or an origami frog. Then your paper would have three dimensions—length, height, and depth. We could measure how long it is, how tall it is, and also how wide across.

One paper with three dimensions. One God with three persons. Can you see how God can be one God and three persons at the same time?

One problem we sometimes have is that we think of God in just one dimension. Just a straight line. Perhaps we think of God as a way to get what we want—someone to answer our prayers. Heavenly room service.

But God is so much more than that. He is so much greater than anything we can think of. There is an old song that says God's love is "so high, you can't get over it; so wide, you can't get around it . . ." We can't measure how high or how wide His love is, because it doesn't end. The dimensions of God are more than we can measure.

With God's power working in us, God can do much, much more than anything we can ask or think of. Ephesians 3:20.

47

The Parts of the Whole

*Baptize them in the
name of the Father
and the Son and
the Holy Spirit.
Matthew 28:19.*

If someone handed you a small mirror and asked you what you saw when you looked in it, you would probably say you saw your face. Or you might say you saw your eyes, your nose, and your mouth. Both answers would be right.

Sometimes the word "face" works best. If you saw a cheerful-looking person, you would probably say they had a happy face—not happy eyes, nose, and mouth.

Other times it makes more sense to talk about the different parts of your face. If you got something in your eye, you wouldn't tell someone, "I've got something in my face." They wouldn't know how to help you.

It is good to have both kinds of words so we can talk about the whole and also about the parts. Usually the Bible uses the word "God." But sometimes it talks about the individual members of the Trinity.

For instance, the Bible tells us that God the Father, God the Son, and God the Holy Spirit were all present at Jesus' baptism. As Jesus came up out of the water, the Holy Spirit came down from heaven like a dove. And the voice of God the Father spoke from heaven: "This is my Son and I love him" (Matthew 3:17).

Just before Jesus went back to heaven, He told His disciples to baptize people "in the name of the Father and the Son and the Holy Spirit." He wants His followers to understand that their God is one Whole with three Parts.

Team Trinity

Have you ever noticed that there is never just one firefighter fighting a fire? There is always a team. There are firefighters who drive the fire truck. There is one who rides in the seat giving orders, telling the driver where to turn, calling for other emergency vehicles. When they get to the fire, some of them hook up the hose, and others are ready to rescue. They all know what they are supposed to do. They all are ready to work as a team to save lives and put out that fire.

And with that Spirit we say, "Father, dear Father." Romans 8:15.

God works as a team. The three members of the Trinity have different roles; they do different things. But they have the same goals, and they work together as one God to save us.

For instance, God the Father, God the Son, and God the Holy Spirit all work together when we pray.

The Holy Spirit is the one who helps us want to pray. Sometimes we don't know how to pray or what to say. Sometimes we are too tired or too distracted. The Holy Spirit will help us.

Jesus takes our prayers to God the Father. Jesus has been here. He has lived through everything we are going through. He understands. He is on our side.

And when we pray, we pray to "our Father which art in heaven." He is listening. He wants to give us what we need and forgive us and deliver us from evil.

God is working as a team whenever you pray.

Love Branches Out

God is love.

1 John 4:16.

When you are outside today, take a look at the trees. Not the evergreens—look at the ones that have lost their leaves. You should be able to see the branches pretty well this time of year.

Notice that even though a tree might have several branches, it is still just one tree. Notice that all the branches come from one trunk.

And if you see a tree with three branches, maybe it will remind you of the Trinity.

God the Father, God the Son, and God the Holy Spirit are all one God. And these three "branches" come from one "trunk": love.

You can tell from His name that God the Father loves us. He tells us that He is our Father so that we can understand how He cares for us, protects us, gives us what we need, teaches us to do the right thing, wants the best for us, and on and on. Just like a father. Jesus tells us, "The Father himself loves you" (John 16:27).

God the Son loves us. At the Last Supper Jesus said, "This is my command: Love each other as I have loved you" (John 15:12). And He has loved us very much indeed. He loves us so much that He died for us so that we will be able to live forever.

You can tell that God the Holy Spirit loves us from the things He does: He helps us know what to say, He comforts us, He gives us power and courage. You can tell He loves us from the gifts He gives: "love, joy, peace, patience, kindness, goodness, faithfulness, gentleness, self-control" (Galatians 5:22, 23). God is love.

Love All Around

Have you ever heard of the term outer space? It's that space beyond the earth's atmosphere. Outer space is out there with the planets and stars and comets. That sounds like the way many people think of heaven, so I guess you could say God the Father lives in *outer space*.

There is one God and Father of everything. He rules everything. He is everywhere and in everything.
Ephesians 4:6.

Have you ever heard of the term *inner space?* The dictionary has two definitions for that. The first definition says that inner space is the space at or near the earth's surface. That's where we walk around and build our houses and live together. That's where Jesus lived when He came to teach us about God and save us from our sins. So I guess you could say that God the Son lived in this inner space.

There is a second definition for inner space. It can also refer to a person's "inner self." Maybe that means your thoughts and feelings—your personality. Maybe it is what the Bible calls your heart or your soul. And that is where we often say the Holy Spirit lives. So I guess you could say that God the Holy Spirit lives in this other inner space.

The love of the Holy Spirit is within us. The love of Jesus was here among us. And the love of the Father surrounds us and goes beyond us.

God's love is everywhere.

And the love within us, among us, surrounding us, and beyond us is all the same love. There is one God. God is love.

The Entire Alphabet

The Lord God says,
"I am the Alpha and
the Omega."
Revelation 1:8.

Most likely there is an alphabet above the chalkboard in your classroom. So chances are that sometimes you daydream while gazing dreamily at the alphabet.

The alphabet really is an amazing thing. With those 26 letters we can write any word, any sentence, any page. We can put our thoughts into words and use the alphabet to help us share our ideas.

But that probably isn't what you are daydreaming about.

Well, consider this about the alphabet. God says He is like the alphabet. Today's text says God is "the Alpha and the Omega." Alpha is the first letter of the Greek alphabet, and Omega is the last letter.

We say the same type of thing now. If you went to the fair and rode every single ride, you could say, "I did it all, from A to Z." That is, you could say it if you weren't too dizzy.

It means completeness. Everything. God is complete. There is nothing lacking.

God is the Alpha. The beginning. But the word the Bible uses doesn't mean just the first. It means the source. All things begin in God. Everything comes from Him.

God is the Omega. The end. But the word the Bible uses doesn't mean just the last. It means the goal. The place where things become complete. Everything is made complete in God.

Everything begins and ends in God. He is the entire alphabet, from A to Z.

Goodness

What do you mean when you say a pizza is good? You may mean that it smells wonderful, that it looks great, that it's nice and hot. But mostly you mean that it tastes delicious.

The Lord is good. His love continues forever. Psalm 100:5.

What do you mean when you say a book is good? You may mean that it taught you something, that it made you laugh, that it had beautiful pictures. But mostly you mean that you enjoyed reading it.

What do you mean when you say a dog is good? It could be many things, but mostly you mean that the dog is obedient.

Delicious, enjoyable, obedient. Good means different things, depending on what you are talking about. If we said that a book was good, we would never mean that it was tasty. And we would never say a dog was good because he was so much fun to read.

Something is good when it is exactly what it is supposed to be. A pizza is supposed to taste delicious. And when it does, it is good.

The Bible says that God is good. What is God supposed to be? Look at today's text. "The Lord is good. His love continues forever." God is love. And He's very, very good at it. Perfect, actually. Perfect love.

As you read the Bible and learn more and more about God's goodness, you will take some of that goodness with you. And the more you learn of God's goodness, the more you will want to be like Him. David sang, "Surely your goodness and love will be with me all my life" (Psalm 23:6). It's a very good song.

Icebreaker

Sometimes when people get together for a party or a meeting, they may not know each other. So the hosts have an icebreaker. An icebreaker is an activity that helps people start talking to each other; it makes it easier for people to get to know each other. Usually you begin by introducing yourself and telling a little bit about yourself.

There is sort of an icebreaker in Exodus 34. Only maybe we should call it a "stonebreaker," because Moses had just broken the stone tablets on which God had written the Ten Commandments.

When Moses went back for another set of commandments, God introduced Himself. God and Moses had been talking to each other since the burning bush. They already knew each other. God wanted Moses to pass this information on to the Israelites. Because they had been slaves for so long, they didn't know God. They needed an introduction.

Then God told a little bit about Himself. It's there in today's text. Merciful and kind. Loving and faithful. Forgiving and patient. Fair and just.

What does God mention first? Mercy. The Israelites needed it. They had just been caught worshipping the golden calf. When He explained what kind of God He was, God offered them forgiveness they didn't deserve. It was a gracious introduction.

Seeing God

When you hear a story or read a book, do you imagine what the characters look like? Do you see their houses or gardens in your mind while you listen or read? If it's a good story, and well written, it's easy. And the pictures in your mind make the story seem more real.

Teach me what I cannot see. Job 34:32.

People have always had to imagine what God looks like. Paul wrote that God the Father "lives in light so bright that men cannot go near it. No one has ever seen God, or can see him" (1 Timothy 6:16). Paul knew about that light. He saw it once, and it changed his life.

Moses wanted to see God. They had been talking together and working together. Moses had been in God's presence. He had seen God's power. But he wanted to actually see God.

God was pleased with the way Moses was leading the Israelites. It wasn't easy. God knew that if Moses could see Him, it would give him more courage. But God explained, "You cannot see my face. No one can see me and stay alive" (Exodus 33:20).

So God decided to show Moses as much of His goodness as he could take. God put Moses in a large crack in a rock. He covered Moses with His hand. Then God took away His hand and let Moses see His back. Moses remembered that the rest of his life.

We cannot see God now. He is too good. He is too holy. But someday we will see Him. When He takes us to heaven we will see His face (Revelation 22:4).

See What God Does

I recall everything you have done. I think about all you have made. Psalm 143:5.

If you've ever been sick or gotten an infection, chances are you've had to take some medicine. Once you swallow that medicine, you can't see it anymore. You know it's there because it's fighting germs or bacteria or doing whatever it's supposed to do, and you feel better.

Sometimes we describe something by telling what it looks like. Other times we describe it by telling what it does. We usually describe medicine by talking about what it does—it soothes a sore throat, it stops itching, it makes a headache go away.

Since we can't see God, sometimes it's best to describe Him by talking about what He does. The Bible often describes God that way.

God creates. There are many stories in the Bible that show God as Creator. The most obvious, of course, is the story of the creation of the world in Genesis 1. God spoke, and it appeared. Remember how God made sure the flour and oil didn't run out for Elijah, the widow, and her son (1 Kings 17). He is still creating. Every morning He creates a new day for us. Every moment He is ready to create in us a pure heart (Psalm 51:10).

God saves. He saved Noah from the flood. He saved Esther and her people from Haman. He saved Jonah by arranging for him to be swallowed by a whale. He sent His Son to save the world from sin. He is still saving. What He has created, He wants to save.

God creates. God saves. He forgives, blesses, punishes, guides, calls. We can see in the Bible what God has done. We can see all around us what He is doing. We can learn about God by seeing what He does.

Character Witness

Let's say you want to describe your grandma to a friend of yours who's never met her. What would you say? You could describe the way she looks (always smiling). You could describe the things she does (makes great cookies). And you could describe her character—the way she behaves (kind, good listener, lots of fun ideas).

The Lord is great. He is worthy of our praise. No one can understand how great he is. Psalm 145:3.

You can learn a lot about people by listening to a description of their character from someone who loves them.

David loved God. That's for sure. And he gave quite a few descriptions of God in his Psalms. Look at Psalm 145. It is a wonderful description of God's character.

David sings praises to God's majesty and glory, might and power. He knows his God is not like the gods of other nations. He has seen God's goodness up close.

He speaks of how God protects His people and takes care of all He has made. God protected David many times—from King Saul, from enemies, from his own sons.

He speaks of God's faithfulness and blessings. God kept His promises to David, even when David made mistakes. God blessed David and his reign over Israel.

David knows from experience that God is kind, merciful, patient, fair, and loving.

And David decides that, even with all these beautiful words and ideas, he can't fully describe God. "No one can understand how great he is." God is greater than we can understand. But He wants us to know Him, and He shows us His character in the Bible.

57

Metaphorically Speaking

You are my father, my God, the Rock, the one who saves me. Psalm 89:26.

Has anyone ever called you a little monkey? It happens. If they did, they didn't mean you were an actual monkey. They probably meant you were as cute as a monkey. Or maybe as lively as a monkey. Or possibly, as naughty as a monkey.

We use words that way. When we say someone we know is a princess, we don't mean she is actually a princess. We mean she looks like a princess, or acts like a princess, or thinks she ought to be treated like a princess. These are metaphors. We use a metaphor to say that something is like something else is some way.

Sometimes the Bible writers didn't have the words to describe exactly what they wanted to say about God. He was too great. He was beyond anything they could describe. So they used metaphors.

God was often called the King. The King of kings. "The King that rules forever" (1 Timothy 1:17). People understood what a king was. God was like a super king.

Sometimes the Bible writers wanted the people to remember that God was fair. "God is the judge" (Psalm 50:6) meant that God would help people who had been treated unfairly. And He would punish the guilty.

"The Lord is my shepherd" (Psalm 23:1) is a well-known metaphor. God promises to take care of His people the way a shepherd takes care of sheep.

God is also called a warrior, a lawgiver, a husband, a rock. But perhaps our favorite metaphor is to call Him our Father. It's so close to home. It's easy to understand.

An Important Thing to Know About God

Perhaps you don't read the newspaper or watch the news on TV. But you probably can't avoid hearing people talking about the news. And it's usually about something awful—a war or a fire or a flood or an accident. It can be downright scary.

Joshua was facing something very scary. Moses had been leading the children of Israel for 40 years. Now Joshua was supposed to take over and lead the people into the Promised Land. But Moses had known God so well. They talked together all the time. How could Joshua ever hope to replace him?

God wanted Joshua and the children of Israel to know that He was in it for the long haul. Their agreement didn't end when Moses died. He would be their God, and they would be His people. Forever.

Moses told them in very simple language, as clear as could be, as plain as plain, so that there could be no mistake, no misunderstanding, no mix-up: God will not leave you or forget you. Don't be afraid. Don't worry.

You don't need to read the news to know that bad things happen. They don't just happen to other people; they happen to us. Friends move away. People we love die. Things get lost and broken. People get angry and hurt. It can be downright scary.

But don't be afraid. Don't worry. He will not leave you or forget you. God is with you always. He is in control. He has a plan. Everything is going to be all right.

The Lord himself will go before you. He will be with you. He will not leave you or forget you. Don't be afraid. Don't worry.
Deuteronomy 31:8.

Jesus to the Rescue

Sometimes when there is a fire in an apartment building with several stories, people get trapped. They can't get out through their doors because of the fire raging there. They can't get out through their windows because it is too far to the ground.

Their only hope is to be rescued by the firefighters and their ladders.

God saw that we were trapped by sin. It was a hopeless situation; we could not save ourselves. So God sent Jesus to rescue us.

When we sin, we break God's law. A penalty for the sin must be paid. God the Father loved us so much that He sent His Son to take our punishment. God the Son volunteered to rescue us. That meant that Jesus had to die because of those sins. Jesus paid the penalty for our sin.

This rescue mission is called the plan of redemption. Redemption means "to rescue, to buy back, to set free." Jesus is our Redeemer, our Rescuer.

This rescue mission is greater than any burning building rescue. Human firefighters may put out a fire, but they can't get rid of fire forever. In God's plan, sin will be destroyed forever. And not only people are rescued—the entire world is rescued and made new.

Someday our Redeemer will come again to bring peace to the world and eternal life to those who believe in Him.

The Word Became a Man

What is a word? Words are what we use to express our thoughts. When we have an idea and we want to share it, we put it into words.

The Word became a man and lived among us. John 1:14.

If you know the answer to a question in school, no one will ever know if you just think it. You've got to raise your hand and use words to speak the answer. You must use words to write the answer on your paper.

A word is a way to communicate. We use words to connect with others.

So what does John mean when he calls Jesus "the Word"? Is Jesus a thought or an idea? Is He a communication?

It's a metaphor again. When John calls Jesus "the Word," he is saying that Jesus is the expression of God's thoughts. Jesus is the way that God communicates with people. Jesus connects us to God.

God communicates in other ways. He gave us the Bible. He sent the prophets. But when God sent Jesus to earth, it was more than just a message. "The Word became a man and lived among us." People could actually see Him and hear Him and touch Him. This Word they could understand.

And if the Word were just one word, what would that be? Love. Jesus says, "I loved you as the Father loved me. Now remain in my love" (John 15:9).

Jesus was both God and man. He came to earth to rescue us from sin and to teach us about God.

61

Jesus Came to Teach About God

O
K. You're at school. You've had lunch, and you've just come in from recess. What would you rather do—listen to your teacher read a story, or listen to a lecture about adjectives? The story wins; it's no contest. We all like to hear stories.

Did you know that one of the best ways to learn is by hearing stories? Jesus knew that was true; one of His favorite ways to teach was by telling stories.

The kinds of stories Jesus told are sometimes called parables. The word *parable* means placing one thing beside another. When Jesus told a story, He placed it beside a spiritual idea so people could understand the idea more easily.

Listen to His story from Luke 15:4-6: "Suppose one of you has 100 sheep, but he loses 1 of them. Then he will leave the other 99 sheep alone and go out and look for the lost sheep. The man will keep on searching for the lost sheep until he finds it. And when he finds it, the man is very happy. He puts it on his shoulders and goes home."

It's a small story with a big point. This story teaches us that God loves us.

God loves each of us. Ninety-nine sheep were not enough. One sheep was lost, and the shepherd wanted to find it and bring it home. Each of us is important to God.

God loves us enough to search for us. The shepherd doesn't wait for the sheep to come crawling home. He actively went out, calling and searching everywhere.

God's love is patient. It was the sheep's own fault that it got lost. But the shepherd doesn't lecture the sheep for getting lost. There is only joy when we are found.

62

Jesus Came to Heal

Jesus didn't use just words to teach about God's love. He also used actions. Jesus spent quite a bit of His time healing people, showing that God wants us to be whole.

Lord, we want to be able to see.
Matthew 20:33.

Blind Bartimaeus was sitting in his usual spot by the side of the road, calling, "Help the blind! Have mercy on the blind!" When he heard a crowd of people coming down the road, he started asking, "What's happening? What's going on?" Finally someone told him that Jesus was passing by.

Bartimaeus had heard of Jesus. He had heard that Jesus could heal people. He knew that this was his only hope to ever see. He was not going to let this chance pass him by. So he began to shout, "Jesus, Son of David! Please help me!" (Luke 18:38).

The people who were near him got upset. He was bothering them, and they couldn't hear Jesus. They told him to be quiet. "But the blind man shouted more and more" (verse 39). Louder and louder he yelled, desperately, frantically.

Jesus heard. He stopped and asked Bartimaeus what he wanted. And Bartimaeus said, without hesitation, "Lord, I want to see again" (verse 41). "Jesus said to him, 'Then see! You are healed because you believed.' At once the man was able to see, and he followed Jesus, thanking God" (verses 42, 43).

Bartimaeus gained more than eyesight that day. He also gained insight. He had been sitting in darkness more total than blindness. Now He had met the Messiah, and he saw the light—the light of truth and hope. And he followed that Light, thanking God.

Jesus Has Been There

He is able to help because he himself suffered and was tempted.
Hebrews 2:18.

Have you ever been stung by a bee? It hurts! If you have never been stung, it would be difficult for you to understand why someone who has just been stung is making such a fuss. It's just a little bee sting. However, if you have been stung before, you are more sympathetic. You know how much it can hurt.

Jesus is sympathetic with us because He was a man. He went through our human experience. He understands what we are going through—even better than we do.

Jesus was tempted, but He never sinned. This may sound as if He didn't suffer as much from temptation as we do. But actually He suffered more.

See, we fall to temptation pretty easily. When Satan tempts us, it doesn't take long before we fail. But Jesus didn't fail, so Satan's temptation kept getting fiercer and more terrible. Satan put everything into his attacks, and Jesus withstood it. Jesus was tempted at a level far beyond what we are.

Because of this, we know that Jesus is truly sympathetic. He really understands. He has been through it all, and more.

Because of this, we know that Jesus is merciful. We know that Jesus is willing to forgive. He can give comfort and advice because He's been there.

Because of this, we know that Jesus is able to help. We know that Jesus wants to give us the power to resist temptation and do the right thing. He knows what we need. Jesus understands.

Our Example

Handwriting is probably one of your subjects at school. Often one of the assignments in handwriting is a worksheet with some letters or words or sentences at the top; you try to copy them on the lines at the bottom of the page. As you know, some people have better handwriting than others. All you can do is try your best.

He gave you an example to follow. So you should do as he did. 1 Peter 2:21.

In the Bible text today Peter uses a word that is translated into English as "example." Jesus is our example. But the original word he used was actually *"hupogrammos."* This is the Greek word for the writing at the top of the page of a handwriting assignment— the words that the students must try to copy.

Kids have had handwriting assignments for a very long time.

Jesus is like that beautiful handwriting at the top of the page. And our job is to try to live as He did.

Maybe your handwriting assignment for today could be the letters "WWJD." When we see those letters, it reminds us of that saying "What Would Jesus Do?"

It's more than just a saying. That question can keep you out of trouble. When someone is mean to you and you have something mean you'd love to say back to them, ask yourself, "WWJD?" Would Jesus ever say mean things? Of course not.

What did He do to mean people? He loved them. And that is hard to do. Way harder than handwriting. But Jesus will help. He will put His hand over ours and guide us. Our Example is also our Helper.

Inspiring

Have you studied the respiratory system in science class? That's the part of your body that helps you breathe—your lungs, your nose, etc. (Unless you are a fish or a worm. Then there are gills and other things.) *Respire* means "to breathe." *Expire* means "to stop breathing," "to die."

If you look closely you can find the root word *spirit* hidden inside the words *respiratory* and *respire*. So *spirit* is like *breathing*. It is like *life*.

How is the Holy Spirit like breathing? Well, you need to breathe in order to live, and you need the Holy Spirit in order to survive as a Christian.

Is the Holy Spirit like air? Air is everywhere. It surrounds our earth. The people on the other side of the world are breathing air, just as we are. And the Holy Spirit is everywhere. The Spirit can be with you and with a person in China at the same time.

The Holy Spirit is also like a wind. The Bible says that when the Holy Spirit came to the disciples after Jesus went to heaven, "it sounded like a strong wind blowing" (Acts 2:2). That must have been something.

Wait, there's more. Look inside the word *inspire*. Can you find *spirit* hidden inside there as well? When someone is inspired, their spirit is especially strong, their life seems more alive. It's as if they are breathing in ideas and excitement and energy.

Jesus sent the Holy Spirit to inspire us—to breathe Himself into us.

It Spreads

First, a safety message: you must never play with fire. But it is a fascinating thing, isn't it? It's so different from everything else in the world that it's hard to talk about what it is. About the only thing you can do is describe what it does.

He will baptize you with the Holy Spirit and with fire. Luke 3:16.

One of the most interesting things that fire does is spread. If I light a match, then I can use the flame from the match to light a candle or a stove or a campfire. If I light a candle, then I can use the flame to light another candle. And the first candle flame doesn't lose anything. It still has as much fire as it did before.

The Holy Spirit is like fire. It is hard to describe who the Holy Spirit is without talking about what He does.

The Holy Spirit is like fire. The Bible says that when the Holy Spirit came to the disciples after Jesus went to heaven, there was the sound of a strong wind—and there was something else. "They saw something that looked like flames of fire. The flames were separated and stood over each person there" (Acts 2:3). It doesn't say it was fire—it just says it looked like fire. No one had seen anything like it before; that was the best way they could describe it.

The Holy Spirit is like fire. It spreads. It spreads within us— the more we learn about God, the more we want to know. And it spreads among us—when we are filled with the Spirit, the flame spreads to others. And when you share the Spirit with someone else, you don't lose anything. You still have as much fire as you did before.

67

The Gift of Power

The Spirit of the Lord will enter you with power. 1 Samuel 10:6.

Have you ever done a push-up? You push your body away from the floor with your arms. It's not easy, but this kind of exercise will make your muscles stronger.

You need fuel to give you the energy to exercise. Getting fuel is easy—you just have to eat. Fortunately, for most of us that is no problem.

Are you learning your times tables? It's important to know them by memory. All your life you'll need to be able to know what 6 x 7 is, and you won't want to have to stop and figure it out. You'll want to just know, instantly. That's why you learn them now.

Exercise gives you power. Food gives you power. Learning gives you power.

The Holy Spirit gives you power.

The last thing Jesus said before He went back to heaven was "The Holy Spirit will come to you. Then you will receive power" (Acts 1:8). And that's just what happened a few days later, with the sound like wind and the flames like fire. The believers were filled with the power of the Holy Spirit.

The Holy Spirit gave them the power of courage. They were able to face danger and trouble because they knew God would be with them.

The Holy Spirit gave them the power of wisdom. The Holy Spirit helped them make the right decisions. He helped them know whom to talk to and what to say.

The Holy Spirit gave them the power of joy. They were happy to be doing what Jesus wanted them to do. He will give you this power too.

Many People, Many Gifts

Have you played the game Compliments at school? You make a list of everyone in your class, and by each name you write something nice—a compliment. It's not something you can do in 10 minutes. It takes time to think carefully about how each person is special.

Is there a person in your class who can play the piano really well? Probably someone else is good at sports. One student is the math whiz, and another is always nice to the little kids. And in every class there is someone who is always making jokes.

Isn't it wonderful? Everyone has something they're good at. Wouldn't it be boring if everyone was the same? Imagine if everybody was always making jokes. Nothing would ever get done. People would shout so their jokes were heard. The poor teacher.

The Bible says that the Holy Spirit gives different kinds of gifts. Some people have been given the gift to speak with wisdom. Some people have the gift of faith. Some have the gift of healing. Because of these gifts we are able to help others.

In your church some people teach, some people preach, some set up chairs, some give special music, some pick up the offering, some run the sound system, some greet visitors and make them feel welcome. You are special. What can you do?

There are different kinds of gifts; but they are all from the same Spirit. There are different ways to serve; but all these ways are from the same Lord. And there are different ways that God works in people; but all these ways are from the same God.
1 Corinthians 12:4.

One in the Spirit

Do we share together in the Spirit? Philippians 2:1.

Has your school ever held a School Spirit Week? Some schools set aside a special week for fun activities. For instance, Monday might be Clash Day, when you wear plaids, stripes, flowers, and red, orange, and pink all at once. And Friday might be Pajama Party Day, when everybody (even the teachers) wears pajamas and carries around a stuffed animal all day. (Really, there should be popcorn, too, don't you think?)

Does that sound like fun? But it's more than just fun, otherwise it would be called School Fun Week. It's called School Spirit Week because it promotes school spirit. It helps everyone feel as though they are members of the group, an important part of the school. When all the people in your classroom are wearing their clothes backward, it raises school spirit. It's crazy, but it works.

It's important for our church to promote a spirit of unity, too. But, of course, we go about it differently.

Jesus promised that the Father would send the Holy Spirit to make us one in the Spirit. One of the Holy Spirit's jobs is to turn us into a group with the same goals and the same hope and the same love. The Holy Spirit connects us to God and to each other.

So once a week we get together at church to show that we are one in the Spirit. We don't wear silly hats or mismatched socks. In fact, we wear our nicest clothes and are on our best behavior. We come together as a group, and we pray for the Holy Spirit to bring us together.

Peace Be With You

Imagine that life in your family is perfectly peaceful.

May the Lord watch over you and give you peace. Numbers 6:26.

Imagine that the family rules are totally fair. Your parents agree that the rules are fair. You and your brothers and sisters agree that the rules are fair, and everyone wants to obey every rule. No one ever gets in trouble.

Imagine that everyone in your family always gets along. No one ever argues. No one's feelings ever get hurt. Everyone works together, helping each other, encouraging each other, listening carefully.

Imagine that there is always plenty of good food to eat and clothes that fit and are always clean. You have all the books you can read and a piano and a computer and nice furniture and, why not, a pool in the backyard. Can you imagine? It would be perfect.

Before our world was created, there was perfect peace in heaven. God's family worked together in peace. The rules were fair; the angels knew the rules would bring peace and make them happy. They loved God. They wanted to obey the rules.

Some people think that peace means there isn't any war. Peace is more than that. In the Bible, peace is not just the absence of fighting—it is the fullness of living. In the Bible, peace means having everything you need to be happy.

Some people think that peace is boring or that heaven will be boring. Now you know that it's not, it won't be. Peace doesn't just mean that no one will argue with you. It's not emptiness. It means that someone will love you. It is fullness.

The Morning Star

Okay, here's a little quiz. It'll be fun. Name the three brightest objects in the sky.

Yes, of course, the brightest is the sun. If you didn't know that, perhaps you ought to turn off that TV and get out a little more.

And in second place we have the moon. If you didn't know that, maybe you should talk to your mom and dad about making your bedtime a little later.

But what is the third brightest thing in our solar system? I'll give you a hint: it's a planet that's next door to the earth and closer to the sun. It's Venus. Venus is so bright that sometimes you can see it during the day. And on a dark night with no moon, Venus can be bright enough to cast a shadow. Sometimes Venus is called the morning star or son of the morning.

In heaven, before the earth was created, there was an angel whose nickname was son of the morning. Next to the sun and moon, Venus is the brightest thing in the sky. And next to God and His Son, this angel was the best and brightest being in heaven. His name was Lucifer, and he had it good.

Lucifer was the leader of the angels. He was noble and wise and talented. All the other angels admired and respected him. They looked to him for guidance and were eager to do whatever he told them. God had honored him with power and glory.

Lucifer had everything. He had the freedom to do anything he wanted. His life was perfect. Lucifer was happy. How could he be anything but happy?

The Peace is Ruined

Have you ever had to pull weeds? A lot of people like to garden, but not very many like to pull weeds. All the same, it's got to be done. If you don't pull them, they just get bigger. They sink their roots deeper and get harder to pull. Then they go to seed, and there are little weeds everywhere. Before long the weeds have taken over the garden.

Sins can grow like weeds. That's what happened to Lucifer, the head angel.

Lucifer's first mistake was pride. He began to think about how smart and handsome and important he was. He didn't bother to think about the fact that it was God who had made him that way. Lucifer imagined he was responsible for being so wonderful.

Then Lucifer began to be jealous. He compared himself to everybody else. It began to bother him that God and His Son had more honor and power than he did.

Next Lucifer became selfish. He thought that the honor given to God took away from his honor. He wanted all the glory. It didn't matter that he had everything he needed. It mattered only that someone else had something he didn't have.

Lucifer's next sin was rebellion. He began to talk to the other angels. They were losing their freedom, he said. The laws of heaven weren't really fair. His words were clever, sneaky. He made it sound like he was being loyal, and the angels all knew how smart he was, so some angels were fooled by his lies. They also became dissatisfied.

The sins kept growing. One sin led to another. Before long the perfect peace of heaven was ruined—the weeds wanted to take over the garden.

Pride will destroy a person. A proud attitude leads to ruin. Proverbs 16:18.

73

War in Heaven

He and his angels lost their place in heaven. Revelation 12:8.

Don't you hate it when this happens? You are taking your science project to school. There's a poster and a model made out of clay and a two-page report in your best handwriting. And the wind blows them into a puddle. Argh! You could just cry.

Imagine how God must have felt when Lucifer began disturbing the peace.

God was patient with Lucifer. From the start He tried to talk to him. God begged him to give up this revolt. He warned him of the suffering it would bring. But Lucifer wouldn't listen. He was too proud to say he was wrong or ask for forgiveness.

The angels who were loyal to God could hardly believe what was happening. How could Lucifer tell lies about God like this? They begged Lucifer and the rebellious angels to stop, to come back to their perfect life. But Lucifer said there was no turning back. He blamed them for being disloyal to him in his fight for freedom and justice.

God could have killed Lucifer to stop the rebellion. But that's not how God works. If God had done that the angels would chose to serve Him out of fear, not love. Besides, God wanted to show the universe that Lucifer's arguments were wrong—and the best way to do that was to let Lucifer prove it.

God called a big meeting of the angels. Lucifer demanded to be equal with God. God said no. God said only those who wanted to follow the rules of heaven could stay. Then there was war in heaven, where there had been perfect peace. God cast Lucifer and the rebel angels out of heaven. There was peace again—but it felt empty and sad.

In the Beginning

You've probably studied synonyms in school. You remember—that's when two words have nearly the same meaning.

Make and *create* are synonyms. People would get the same idea whether you said "I'm going to make a cake," or "I'm going to create a cake." Almost. No two words are exactly alike. Otherwise we wouldn't need them both.

Make a cake suggests mixing eggs, sugar, and flour; pouring the mixture into a pan; baking it; frosting it; eating it. But *create a cake* suggests drama. Perhaps there won't be a recipe. Or perhaps there will be an unusual flavor or ingredient. And it won't be frosted; it will be decorated!

We are more likely to say *make* than *create* when it comes to cakes. When we say *make,* we usually mean we will make something out of other ingredients. When we say *create,* we usually mean we will make something out of nothing. Something new.

You create a poem. Yes, it's made out of words and ideas, but they can't be measured or handled or seen. They come from your mind, from inside you. New. So we could say God didn't "make" the world. He created the world. God created something where before there had been nothing. He created something new. When God decided to create our world, He started at the beginning. In the beginning our world was empty. There was nothing here—no people, no animals, no plants, nothing. It was dark and empty. Then God spoke, and created.

In the beginning God created the sky and the earth. The earth was empty and had no form. Genesis 1:1, 2.

75

Bara

Then God said, "Let there be light!" And there was light. Genesis 1:3.

If I were to show you an empty paper bag and ask you what was in it, you would probably say, "Nothing." And you would be right.

But then, if I were to shine a flashlight into the empty paper bag and ask you what was in it now, what would you say? It's not the same as it was before. So would it be correct to give the same answer, to say, "Nothing"? Not really. So what's in the bag now? Light.

When our world was created, in the beginning there was nothing. There was the opposite of light. There was darkness.

If you close you eyes, maybe you can imagine it. The Bible says, "The earth was empty and had no form" (Genesis 1:2). That's probably what you are seeing right now, with your eyes closed. But wait. If your eyes are closed, how can you read this? Maybe this isn't going to work. You'll have to imagine with your eyes open, I guess.

OK, imagine the rest of the verse now: "Darkness covered the ocean, and God's Spirit was moving over the water. Then God said, 'Let there be light!' And there was light" (Genesis 1:2, 3).

God spoke. That's all it took.

In the Bible the Hebrew word for "create" is *bara*. In English you can create, I can create, anyone can create. But in the Bible only God can *bara*. Only God can say, "Let there be light," with this result: light.

Out of the Darkness

Are you afraid of the dark? Some people are. Except that for a lot of them, it's not the actual dark they're afraid of. It's the stuff they imagine is lurking in the darkness.

Although darkness all by itself is scary enough.

When it's dark, we can't see. We can't see where we're going or even where we are. We can't see anyone around us or even—if it's really dark—our own hands if we hold them in front of us.

When we think of darkness, we think of being scared, being lost, not knowing what's going on.

We hate being left in the dark.

First, there was light. In the beginning, that was the first thing.

When sin entered the world, it brought another kind of darkness. Sin made things harder to understand. Because of sin, we couldn't see God. The prophet Isaiah promised that it wouldn't be dark always. "They live in a place that is very dark. But a light will shine on them" (Isaiah 9:2). And that Light was Jesus.

Now when it seems dark, when we are afraid of the dark, we can pray for the Light. We need the Light so that we can see each other and see ourselves. We need the Light to see where we are and where we're going.

God won't leave us in the dark. He's given us the light.

God once said, "Let the light shine out of the darkness!" And this is the same God who made his light shine in our hearts. 2 Corinthians 4:6.

Light is Good

God is light, and in him there is no darkness at all. 1 John 1:5.

What's your favorite season? There are a few people who like winter best. They enjoy sledding and other winter sports. And hot cocoa around a cozy fireplace.

Other people get tired of the cold, gray days. They look forward to the mild weather and gorgeous colors of spring—the lovely flowers, budding trees, singing birds.

Other people prefer the blazing colors of autumn—the blue, blue skies and the turning leaves. The crisp weather makes them feel alive.

But lots of people like summer best—glorious summer, when the days are hot and the sprinklers are cold. No school. Lots of time to play. Watermelon. Corn on the cob.

Lots of people like summer best because the first day of summer is the longest day of the year. The sun comes up early and stays up late. There is lots of light.

Light is good. On the first day of Creation, when God saw the light He had made, He saw that it was good. It was exactly what it was supposed to be.

Light is good. The Bible writers valued light; they knew it was good. They sometimes used light to describe God. They said that God actually is bright with light. But they also used light to describe how God helps us, teaches us, takes care of us.

David wrote, "The Lord is my light and the one who saves me. I fear no one" (Psalm 27:1). John wrote, "The true Light gives light to all" (John 1:9). Isaiah promised, "The Lord will be your light forever" (Isaiah 60:19).

God will be your light. Year round. Night and day. All your life. Forever.

Shadows

The dark isn't all bad. We sometimes use the word "darkness" to describe awful things such as evil, sadness, or ignorance. But darkness can be good, too.

You know how we all love having the sun stay up so late in the summer. It's wonderful. Except for one thing—when bedtime comes before the sun goes down. That's horrible! It's so hard to try to get to sleep when it's still light outside. Darkness is good to go to sleep in.

You could say that shade is a form of darkness. And shade is definitely a good thing on a hot day. When the sun is blazing down it's more pleasant to be in the shade.

Shadows are another kind of darkness that can be good. Light doesn't shine through some things. It doesn't shine through you. The light hits you and stops; that's why you have a shadow. A shadow can be fun—do you ever try to make shadow pictures on the wall? And a shadow can be useful. If you don't have a shadow then you know it's either a cloudy day or it's time to eat lunch.

When God created light He also created shadows. On the first day of Creation He "divided the light from the darkness" (Genesis 1:4). God made a place for darkness and shade and shadows.

And sometimes God gives us a place in the darkness to rest. The Bible says, "He hid me in the shadow of his hand" (Isaiah 49:2). In His hands we're safe, cool, and calm.

God saw that the light was good. So he divided the light from the darkness.
Genesis 1:4.

This Little Light of Mine

You should be a light for other people. Matthew 5:16.

You've probably done this a hundred times. You stick your finger in the air and sing, "This little light of mine."

Do you have any idea why? What does that mean, anyway?

When you stick your finger up like that, you are pretending your finger is a candle or lamp.

Why would you want to pretend something like that? Because of what Jesus said in today's Bible text. You are singing about being a light for other people.

What does Jesus mean when He says we should be lights? Look at the next sentence in this text: "Live so that they will see the good things you do." Jesus wants us to be good. He wants us to do the right thing. He wants us to love each other.

Why does Jesus want us to be a light? Look at the next sentence in the text: "Live so that they will praise your Father in heaven." When we treat people right, when we love them, we can help others see and understand God's love. We don't let our light shine so that people will notice how good we are. (That could be embarrassing.) Our lights shine away from us, like flashlights that help people see how good God is.

How can we be lights? Well, on our own we can't. Jesus said, "I am the light of the world" (John 8:12). When we "let it shine," we aren't shining with our own light. We are reflecting Jesus' light. We are sharing Jesus' light.

Now when you sing "This Little Light of Mine," you can really shine.

Rainbows

Here's a trick question: What color is light? You might think it is invisible or clear because, after all, you can see through it. If you needed to color light for some reason, you would probably use your yellow crayon because the sun, if you look at it (which you are not supposed to do), is yellow.

The crazy thing is that light is actually all the colors blended together. You can see the colors "unblend" when you look at a rainbow. Rainbows appear when sunlight shines through raindrops. The drops of water bend the light and sort of break it open so the colors spill out.

We don't get to see rainbows very often. Most people, when they see a rainbow, are a little surprised, and then they holler, "Look! A rainbow!" to whoever is around.

Some people might think that the first day of Creation is a little boring. They'd rather move right along to talking about the third or fourth day. But then they'd skip right over colors, and a world without colors would be a very different sort of a world.

God didn't make everything the same color. Creation is chock-full of all kinds of variety, and it has been since the very first day.

Look at today's text. When we "get up and shine," we all shine in different ways. When the glory of the Lord shines on us, it shows a rainbow of different ways to shine for Him. Our many different lights reflect the rainbow of God's glory.

Get up and shine. Your light has come. The glory of the Lord shines on you. Isaiah 60:1.

Bringing Order

God is not a God of
confusion but a
God of peace.
1 Corinthians 14:33.

Let's pretend you have a bowl of oatmeal for breakfast and you decide you'd like to swirl in some strawberry jam. You put a spoonful of jam in the middle of the oatmeal and stir it in a spiral that gets bigger and bigger until you get to the edge of the bowl.

Then you change your mind. You don't want the jam after all. Can you unswirl the spiral by moving the spoon in reverse? Nope. The jam is in your oatmeal for good.

When you read the Creation story in the Bible, sometimes it sounds as if God spoke and it appeared. But other times it sounds as if the elements of the earth were swirled together, like jam in oatmeal. It sounds as if God had to separate things and organize them and give them a name and a job. This "unswirling," this bringing order, sounds like a lot more work than just speaking.

On the first day God said, "Let there be light!" But He also divided the light from the darkness. He "unswirled" them. Then He gave them names: day and night.

So He spoke, but He also organized.

The same kind of thing happened on the second day. He not only separated the air from the water, it sounds like He pulled the water apart and put the air in the middle. "So God made the air to divide the water in two" (Genesis 1:7). Then He gave it a name: sky.

In the beginning the earth "had no form" (verse 2). We have another word for this: chaos. God brought order to the chaos. He created harmony out of confusion.

Water Above, Water Below

Did you know that you are drinking the same water Adam and Eve drank? It's true. We have the same water now that they had in the beginning. No new water gets made. It just gets recycled.

If clouds are full of rain, they will pour water on the earth. Ecclesiastes 11:3.

Perhaps you have studied the water cycle in science class. Water from an ocean or lake evaporates. It travels, as water vapor, up into the sky where it gathers into clouds. Then rain falls from the clouds to the ground where we use it. Then it evaporates again, and so on and so on, as it has since it was created on the second day.

Here is how the Bible describes the second day of Creation: "God made the air to divide the water in two. Some of the water was above the air, and some of the water was below it" (Genesis 1:7).

When you think about water, you probably think of the water below: the oceans, rivers, ponds, streams, and lakes.

But what is the water above? Clouds. And then there are the forms of water that travel between the water above and the water below: rain, snow, hail, mist, fog.

And what about icebergs and icicles and waterfalls? It sounds like the second day of Creation is more complicated than it seems.

And that water is the same water you will use today. You'd better take good care of it. Keep it clean. Don't waste it. This is all the water we've got. We can't get any more. And we can't survive without it.

The Water of Life

I will pour out water for the thirsty land. . . . My blessing will be like a stream of water flowing over your family. Isaiah 44:3.

Think about the things you do each morning when you first get up—washing, brushing, flushing. Most of them involve water. Now think about getting ready for bed at night. You need water then too. When you're thirsty, what do you want most? Water. Where is the most fun place to play? Water.

We need water from morning to night, for just about everything we do.

Water was very important to the people of the Bible, too. They didn't have plumbing and faucets; they had to go to the well and haul the water home. But what made water even more precious was that they lived in a dry land. Water was scarce.

Water is mentioned a lot in the Bible. It's there from the first chapter ("God's Spirit was moving over the water" [Genesis 1:2]) to the last ("If anyone is thirsty, let him come; whoever wishes it may have the water of life as a free gift" [Revelation 22:17]).

Water is necessary for life; so water was a good symbol for the Bible writers. They compared God to life-giving water. And they often wrote about being thirsty for God. Our souls need God, just as our bodies need water.

Jesus used water as a symbol too. He met a woman at a well once. Jesus told her, "Whoever drinks the water I give will never be thirsty again" (John 4:14). He was talking about the thirst we have for God. Jesus will bring us to God so we can satisfy this thirst. Jesus is the Water of Life—eternal water for eternal life.

Living Water

Jesus sat by the well. Soon a woman came up
To get water for lunch. Jesus asked for a cup.
"I have water that lives," Jesus said, "and I think
If you knew who I was, *you'd* ask Me for a drink.
You'll never get thirsty." It was easy to tell
She was tired of trudging each day to the well.
"Living water sounds lovely. I want it," she said.
Then she found out He meant something different instead.
It was lovelier still. It was good news indeed.
She had found the Messiah, and He filled every need.
She ran to the village and made everyone come
To see the Man whom living water came from.
Women still must fetch water in some far-off lands.
It takes lots of time, and it takes many hands.
Missionaries are helping the people find water
To make life less hard for mother and daughter.
When they don't have to search for clean water all day
There's more time to learn. There's more time to pray.
They can learn about Jesus and make His way first.
Living water flows in and quenches their thirst.

Sir, give me this water.
John 4:15.

Digging Leaky Wells

They have turned away from me. And I am the spring of living water. And they have dug their own wells. But they are broken wells that cannot hold water. Jeremiah 2:13.

Imagine that you get to go camping. Imagine that it is a beautiful place to camp, but it is especially famous for the cold, delicious water that gushes out of a nearby spring. The people in your group can't wait to get there and have a good long drink. Except for one person. He is bringing buckets of his own water from home.

That would be crazy! Why would anyone do that?

But that's what the prophet Jeremiah said the nation of Israel was doing. Look at today's Bible text. God is saying that His people are rejecting His wonderful, refreshing, living water. This text means that the people were rejecting God's agreement to take care of them. They were rejecting God's offer to save them.

They wanted to take care of themselves. They wanted to adopt the pretend gods of other nations. It was as crazy as digging a broken-down, leaky well of stale water when there was a fresh spring already there.

We may not want to worship idols, but we can make the same mistake. We can make the mistake of trying to save ourselves instead of letting God save us. Then we are digging our own pitiful wells and ignoring the living spring.

You don't have to dig your own well. You don't have to try to save yourself from sin. The living water is already here, free and clear. God sent Jesus to take care of it. All we have to do is accept His gift of salvation. We can quit digging—and enjoy the water.

Floating

God made two kinds of water: salt water (the water in the ocean) and fresh water (the water in a river). They are not the same. For one thing, if you get salt water in your mouth, it tastes nasty. And the salt water might sting your eyes or make your skin itchy.

Be kind and loving to each other. Ephesians 4:32.

You might notice something else: It's easier to swim in salt water. Salt water has a lot of salt in it. The salt sort of pushes up against your body and supports it. The more salt there is in the water, the more buoyancy it has, and the easier it is for you to float.

The Dead Sea between Israel and Jordan is very salty—a swimmer can't stay below the surface. People bob along on top of the water as if they were on air mattresses.

People who are unkind and selfish seem to be always struggling against something. They worry that someone's out to get them and that everyone else is getting a bigger cookie and that they can't win unless you lose. Their selfishness is like a weight, dragging them down. They fight to keep their heads above water.

People who are kind seem to be able to float past that kind of thing. They aren't thinking about themselves all the time. They are happy to share. Their attitude is that if they can help you win, they win too. Their kindness pushes them up and supports them so they can see better and not worry so much. Kindness adds buoyancy to their life.

Look at today's Bible text. The words are easy to understand. But it's harder to do. Just as most people have to learn to float, we have to learn how to be kind too. Jesus will help you, and once you get the hang of it, being kind will make your life easier.

Evidence

The sky was made at
the Lord's command.
Psalm 33:6.

If you study the water cycle, you may get this assignment: Draw a picture of the water cycle, using arrows to show how the water travels. It's easy to draw the clouds. It's easy to draw the raindrops. It's easy to draw the ocean. But how do you draw the water vapor? When water evaporates into the air, it becomes invisible. Maybe you could draw wavy lines that are rising like steam. That would work, even though it is showing what it is doing more than what it looks like.

When things are invisible we can't draw a picture of them. They are more difficult to describe. We have to talk about what they do instead of what they look like.

On the second day of Creation God made air. Air is invisible (except in some big cities, and we're trying to fix that). We can't see air, but we can see what it does.

If you blow air out of your mouth, you can't see it. But there is a way to see what it does. If you put your hand in front of your face and blow, you can feel it. If you blow air at a burning candle, the flame will go out. If you blow that air into a balloon, the balloon will get bigger. We can see evidence that shows us what air is like.

We can't see God, but we can see what He does. Creation is a good place to start looking. There is evidence of God everywhere in nature. Some people like to call nature "God's second book" because it shows what God is like—just as the first book, the Bible, shows us what God is like. Creation shows us that God loves us and has given us many wonderful gifts. Just look around. There's evidence.

Breezes

Have you ever wondered why a fan can cool you off? After all, the air the fan is blowing around is the same temperature as the rest of the air. Why does it feel cooler?

He sends the breezes, and the waters flow.
Psalm 147:18.

It is because you are like a little heater. Your body is warm enough to heat up the air surrounding you. So on a hot day, wherever you flop down, you start heating up the air around you, and you just sit there getting hotter and sweatier and stickier.

When a breeze blows by, it pushes away the air that you have been heating up. Cooler air takes it place. The moving air also helps the sweat on your skin evaporate more quickly, which helps you feel cooler too. A breeze feels good because it is moving.

Sometimes people flop down on a certain idea and won't move. They think, *This idea is right,* and they won't listen to any other ideas. It gets stuffy.

John the Baptist could see the people of his time doing that. He told them what Jesus was going to do: "He will come ready to clean the grain. He will separate the good grain from the chaff" (Matthew 3:12). Chaff is the papery cover on the seed; it is worthless.

At harvesttime farmers fanned the grain while it was being tossed in the air. The breeze blew the chaff away from the useful part of the grain, which fell back to the floor.

John was warning that Jesus was coming to shake things up, blow away a lot of bad ideas, find the people who were willing to change. Jesus is still trying to do that. Don't be afraid of change. Keep your mind open. Invite Jesus to breeze into your life.

The Winds of Change

Have you ever seen a weather map? You can find them in the newspaper or on the TV news. They look kind of complicated, with curvy, bumpy lines and H's and L's scattered about. Some of those marks explain what is happening to the air—high pressure, low pressure, which way the wind is blowing, etc.

These maps can be a little hard to understand. However, that air is moving, whether or not we can read the weather map. The wind blows even if we don't understand where it comes from or what makes it blow or why it changes direction.

We can feel the wind. Sometimes we can hear the wind. Often we can see what the wind does—it pushes the kite up into the air, it blows the branches of the trees. But understanding how the wind works is more difficult.

A man named Nicodemus came to see Jesus. He said he didn't understand what Jesus meant by being born again. He said he didn't see how it worked, how it could happen. Jesus told him it meant being born from the Spirit. Then He said, "you don't know where the wind comes from or where it is going" (John 3:8). This was a pun, a joke. In Greek the word for "spirit" and "wind" is the same.

Jesus was telling Nicodemus that even though he didn't understand how and why the wind blows, he could still see what it did. And even though he didn't understand how the Spirit works, he could still see the effect the Spirit had on people when they believed.

How's the Weather?

On the second day of Creation God made air. Now, the Bible doesn't say this exactly, but doesn't it seem logical to say that weather was also created on the second day of Creation?

God divided the water below from the water above by putting air in the middle. The water above refers to clouds, rain, snow, and that kind of thing. Doesn't that sound like weather to you?

Perhaps the Bible doesn't talk about the weather in Genesis 1, but the weather does get mentioned in other places. Look at today's Bible text. It sounds as though people have always liked to talk about the weather.

When you can't think of anything else to talk about, you can talk about the weather. If you talk about politics or sports, your opinions might make someone mad. But you are pretty safe if you talk about the weather. Everyone's affected by the weather, and most people are willing to talk back. So it's no wonder people have always talked about the weather.

Weather is especially interesting when it is unusual—a big storm or snow in the summer or drought or a flood. They talk about all those things in the Bible, too.

We need weather. Weather gives us rain to water the plants, breezes to cool us, thunder to thrill us. And it gives us something to talk about.

He brings the clouds from the ends of the earth. He sends the lightning with the rain. He brings out the wind from his storehouses. Psalm 135:7.

First Things First

Let's say you and a friend decide to play a board game. Can you just instantly start playing? Probably not. You'll have to find the game. Find a place to play it. Make sure no pieces are missing. Pass out the cards or playing pieces or pretend money. You've got to set it up, get everything ready. Then you can play.

Lots of things have to be done in a certain order. First you make a sandwich; then you eat it. First you put your pajamas on; then you get into bed. First you study your spelling words; then you take the test. First we do the things that are supposed to come first. First things first.

It was first things first when the world was made. On the second day of Creation God made air. He made air before He made plants or animals because plants and animals need air to survive. It makes perfect sense.

God put the air between the waters above and the waters below because humans can't live in the water. We need that air to breathe.

God always does first things first. He knows the best time for everything to happen. He knew the best order to create the different parts of the world. He knew the best time to create the nation of Israel. He knew the best time to send Jesus to earth. He knows when it will be best to come back again and take us to heaven. He knows the best time for wonderful things to happen to you.

God has perfect timing.

The Mountains Rose, The Valleys Sank

Promise that if you ever get a chance to see a volcano you will do it. It's a sight worth seeing. It doesn't seem as though something like that could really happen—that mountains could really explode like that, with melted, fiery rock flowing down. But it's true. Volcanoes really happen.

Then God said, "Let the water under the sky be gathered together so the dry land will appear." And it happened. Genesis 1:9.

Volcanoes happen underwater, too. When the fiery lava hits the cold ocean water, it cools quickly and turns to rock. It builds up over years and years, turning into an underwater mountain that pokes up out of the water—then we call it an island.

The Bible says that on the third day God made land. Did volcanoes explode and form islands and mountains and canyons? Maybe. Listen to this poem about it:

"You covered the earth with oceans.
The water was above the mountains.
But at your command, the water rushed away.
When you gave your orders like thunder, it hurried away.
The mountains rose. The valleys sank.
The water went to the places you made for it"
(Psalm 104:6-8).

If you think that seeing a volcano would be exciting, imagine seeing this. And though the water was obedient, it sounds rather rowdy as it rushes to the places God made for it. It sounds as if the third day of Creation started out very wild and noisy.

93

Caves

Do you think God made caves on the third day of Creation? Probably. And He's still making them. Limestone is a rock that dissolves in water. Year after year rain soaks into the ground, making cracks in the limestone, dissolving it little by little. These cracks become hollows, which grow larger and larger; after ages and ages they become caves.

Other interesting things happen with water and limestone inside the caves. As water slowly drips from the roof of the cave, it leaves behind a tiny deposit of limestone. Over the years these deposits add up and start to form a spike hanging down from the top of the cave. These spikes are called stalactites; they look like icicles made of stone.

The same thing happens upside down when water drips onto the floor of the cave. The deposits that build up and poke up in spikes from the floor are called stalagmites. Stalactites and stalagmites grow only a fraction of an inch each year.

Some people think "small" and "unimportant" mean the same thing. But they don't. The caves prove it—the drops of water are small, but they are important.

Some people may think that because you are small you can't make a difference. But you know that's not true. You do make a difference in your family and your school and your church and your world.

It certainly doesn't make any difference to God whether someone is small or big. Look at today's Bible text. God has big plans for you. Right now. You don't have to wait until you're big to make a difference.

Desert

On the third day of Creation God called dry land to appear. That sounds like desert. If you were going to choose only one word to describe desert, it would have to be "dry." More than anything else, dry is what deserts are.

He will be like streams of water in a dry land. Isaiah 32:2.

Deserts are dry because it doesn't rain. Hardly ever. But even though a desert is very dry with very little rain, there is some water there. Otherwise there wouldn't be any life at all in the desert. Even rattlesnakes need water to live.

Where is the water? Deep in the ground. There are underground rivers and streams and ponds all over the world (or rather, all *under* the world). It doesn't rain much in the desert, but it rains in other places. That rain water seeps into the ground and joins the underground streams, which can flow deep under the desert.

Sometimes these underground streams come near the surface of the desert and a pool will form. That's called an oasis. Plants will grow there. Animals come there to get a drink. People who live in the desert often live near an oasis. People, animals, and plants all have to have water.

The people in the Bible knew about deserts. There are a lot of deserts in that part of the world. The Bible sometimes uses the idea of deserts to teach about other ideas. For instance, in today's Bible text Isaiah promises that the Messiah "will be like streams of water in a dry land." Finding Jesus is like finding water in the desert. Jesus is like a life-giving oasis in a dry and burning desert.

The Rock

God named the dry land "earth." He named the water that was gathered together "seas." God saw that this was good.
Genesis 1:10.

Do you have a rock collection? Someone who wasn't very curious might think that rocks are boring, but they aren't. Rocks can be rough or smooth, dull or shiny, so hard you can't break them with a hammer or so soft you can break them with your bare hands. And they come in lots of different colors, shapes, and sizes.

Rocks are more than just interesting things to collect. They are useful. We build with rocks. We make beautiful statues out of rock. We even eat one special rock—salt.

Imagine that a Bible writer was traveling on a hot day through the dry land where there were hardly any trees. Up ahead he saw a huge boulder. Shade! A place to rest, protected from the sun and wind. It's no wonder people from Bible times often compared God to a rock: "The Lord is my rock, my place of safety, my Savior" (2 Samuel 22:2).

The third day of Creation came in two parts. God made rocks in the first half.

On the third day of Creation God called the dry land to appear. He told the water to gather together, and it obeyed. So then there were two things to look at: earth and seas.

That might sound boring. There were valleys and hills and plains, but they were totally bare. There was no grass. There were no trees or bushes or flowers. And yet right now, halfway through day three, God saw that this was good.

God could see that it was exactly right for its purpose. That's what *good* means. This bare, naked earth set the stage perfectly for what was going to happen next.

They're Alive!

We've looked at Creation up to the middle of day three. Let's take stock of what we've got so far: light and darkness, air and water, dry land.

These are all really important things—things we couldn't live without. But the things that were created next are very different in one big way: they're alive.

On the third day, after God created the land, He said, "Let the earth produce plants" (Genesis 1:11). Plants are living things. They grow. They need light and air and water.

What do you suppose it looked like when the plants were created? It could be that one minute there was only dry land and the next minute there were plants everywhere—on the hills and plains, in the mountains and valleys, beside the rivers and even under the seas.

Or it could be that the plants started as little seedlings and quickly grew and grew to full size, spreading over the entire earth? It would be like watching a video on fast forward.

It could be. But we don't know. The Bible doesn't say. It just says, "And it happened" (Genesis 1:11).

It happened. We know that for sure. God created plants. They were alive and growing. It was good.

Let the fields and everything in them show their joy. Then all the trees of the forest will sing for joy. Psalm 96:12.

Growing Happiness

When you see these things, you will be happy. You will grow like the grass. Isaiah 66:14.

There are some things that are just beautiful. They aren't useful in any way; they are just pretty. The pictures that hang on our walls—we can't cook with them or pound nails with them. We just look at them. They make us happy.

There are other things that are just useful. They aren't pretty. The batteries that we put in our flashlights aren't beautiful, but they sure are useful. As long as they do their job, they help us see. And that makes us happy.

Imagine how happy we can be when something is both useful and beautiful. That's the kind of happiness God created on the third day when He made plants.

The dry land God made was good. It was very useful. But when He decided to decorate the land with grass, trees, and flowers, that was even better. Plants are beautiful.

They are especially beautiful this time of year. Just look out the window. If you're lucky, what you'll see most of all is green—green grass, green trees, green bushes. Could there be a more delightful color? Yes—you might also be able to see flowers. Red, yellow, pink, purple—flowers come in every color of the rainbow.

And the beauty goes beyond what you can see. Plants also come with beautiful smells. Flowers smell especially good. But it's hard to beat the smell of newly cut grass. And trees not only smell nice; they keep the air smelling fresh too.

Next chance you get, take a walk. Soak up the beauty and the happiness.

Take Care

Plants are beautiful. Their beauty is useful; it makes us happy. And if we feel stressed and upset, a little time spent with nature can calm us down.

God has trusted you with many things. Keep those things safe. 1 Timothy 6:20.

But their usefulness goes beyond what they do for our emotions. Plants are so useful that we couldn't live without them.

Plants clean the air. Air has two parts: oxygen and carbon dioxide. We breathe in the oxygen and breathe out the carbon dioxide. Plants do the opposite. We need plants to keep the air in balance.

Plants save the soil. Rainstorms would wash all the soil into the rivers if plants didn't hold the soil in place. Plants slow down the falling drops of rain and help the water sink more gently into the ground.

Plants give us shelter. Trees protect us from storms—the wind and the rain. We cut trees down and use the wood to build our houses. We use plants as fuel to keep us warm and to cook our food. Plants even provide us with clothing—many fabrics are made from plants.

Plants give us healing. Many medicines are made from plants. Scientists say that many more ways will be discovered to use plants as medicine. We're still learning.

It's obvious we can't live without plants. It is also obvious that we must take care of them. We must not waste them. When we use them, we must use them carefully and thoughtfully. Plants are a beautiful, useful, precious gift from God's third day of Creation.

Glorious Food

Of course we are all very grateful that plants give us shelter and medicine and fuel. But what we love most about plants, what we find most useful, what makes us happiest, is this: we eat them. Plants are delicious. Plants are food.

On the second day God made air for us to breathe. Air is absolutely necessary, but there isn't a lot of variety. It can be cold or warm, fresh or stale, but that's about it. We don't really pay much attention to breathing. We don't look forward to it or plan parties where we all get together and breathe.

It's different with food.

When God made plants on the third day, He made variety. Food is not boring. There are so many wonderful things to eat, and none of them taste the same. It's a good thing—different people like different foods. And different foods have different vitamins.

Plants are good for us. They give us energy. They help us grow. They make us strong. They keep us healthy. And best of all, they taste good.

You remember that sometimes the Bible writers wrote about being thirsty for God. They also wrote about being hungry for Him. God says, "Listen closely to me, and you will eat what is good. You will enjoy the food that satisfies your soul" (Isaiah 55:2). God gives us food for our bodies and food for our souls.

Don't Worry; Be Happy

It is perhaps understandable that Jesus' followers were a little anxious. They had abandoned their jobs to follow Jesus. They never knew where they were going to sleep or whether they were going to find something to eat. This made them nervous.

Look at the flowers in the field. See how they grow. Matthew 6:28.

And what did Jesus do? The same thing he always did: He told them a story.

He told them to look at a field of wildflowers growing nearby. He asked them to think about why the flowers never worried about stuff.

What would that be like? Imagine a poor little flower who is all upset: "Oh, dear! I simply must have an insect come along to spread my pollen so that I can make seeds. I've got to look colorful and bright and gorgeous or I won't be able to attract anything."

Imagine this worried flower: "I've got to try harder to smell better; otherwise, the bugs won't even know I'm here. I know I can do it if I try. One, two, three: s-m-e-l-l."

Or imagine a flower that is afraid it isn't sweet enough: "Look at how the bees are flocking to that flower over there. It's not fair! What does *it* have that I don't have? My nectar is just as sweet, and I've got plenty of it too. Hey, bees! Get over here!"

It's silly, isn't it? The flowers will be able to make seeds. Their nectar is sweet enough. They smell good enough. They are beautiful. Flowers don't need to worry.

Neither do we. God will take care of us. Jesus says, "The thing you should want most is God's kingdom and doing what God wants. Then all these other things you need will be given to you. So don't worry about tomorrow" (Matthew 6:33, 34).

It Depends

How do you feel about dandelions? They have pretty little flowers, so very yellow and cheerful. But most people think they are weeds. When the dandelion turns into a fluffy ball, you may find one of life's great pleasures in blowing on it. But other people just think about all those seeds growing into more and more and more dandelions.

There are some questions that you can answer with a simple yes or no. For instance: Is a dandelion a plant? Yes. We call this a black-or-white question because the answer is as obvious as the difference between black and white.

But some questions can't be answered with yes or no. For example: Is a dandelion a weed? That depends on your feelings about dandelions. It's a gray question; neither black nor white. It's questions like this that make life so complicated and interesting.

Life is full of gray questions. What do you do about them? First you have to be sure about the black-and-white answers. Then you are able to think about the gray ones.

Look at today's Bible text. That is the black-and-white answer. The next verse explains how to deal with gray questions: "All the law and the writings of the prophets depend on these two commands." You see, all the gray answers depend on love.

Black-and-white question: Should you love your neighbor? Answer: Yes. Gray question: Should you pull the dandelions in your neighbor's yard as a surprise? Answer: That depends. Do you know how to pull dandelions properly? How does your neighbor feel about dandelions? about other people digging in their yard? about surprises?

No one ever said it was going to be easy.

Plants by the Sea

Most plants can't grow at the seashore. The problem with sand, as far as plants are concerned, is that water runs right through it. Since plants need water, they have a hard time growing in the sand. Another trouble with sand is that the wind blows it around. If a plant gets covered by blowing sand, it can't get sunlight, which it also needs.

I have no choice. I must tell the Good News. 1 Corinthians 9:17.

Another problem is the water. It's salty. Salt water kills most plants. And then there's the tide. When the waves come in, they cover up the plants and drown them.

Yet some plants still can grow at the seashore. Some of them have long roots that reach back to the fresh water away from the ocean. If they are buried by the blowing sand, they send new shoots to poke up through the sand. The salt water doesn't seem to hurt them. It's amazing. Their job is to grow, and they do it even if they get buried in sand or covered in salt water or scorched by the sun or blown around in the wind.

These plants are a bit like the apostle Paul. It didn't matter what happened to him—all he wanted to do was preach about Jesus. If they put him in jail, he preached. If he was in a shipwreck, he preached. If they beat him up or ran him out of town or dragged him to court, he still preached. Whenever something terrible happened, he saw it as a great opportunity to preach. It was amazing.

Paul was explaining this behavior when he wrote today's Bible text. No matter what happened, Paul knew that he was doing what Jesus wanted him to do and that Jesus would help him. Jesus helps us grow, no matter where we are planted.

Unchanging Rules

Every seed will produce more of its own kind of plant. Genesis 1:11.

It is reassuring to know that there are some things you can count on, some things that always happen the way you expect them to. When you play the keys at the right end of the piano, they always sound higher than the ones at the left end. When you throw a heavy rock into the water, it always makes a satisfying plop and sinks to the bottom.

Some of these unchanging rules are created by humans (piano keys), and others are rules of nature (rocks in water).

God made an unchanging rule of nature on the third day of Creation when He created plants. Plants have seeds. Each seed grows into the same kind of plant. When you plant a cantaloupe seed, a cantaloupe plant will grow from it. Not a carrot.

Seeds are a wonderful idea. Plants make their own seeds. That's how we get more plants. Because of seeds, we don't need to worry about eating up all the tomatoes. We can plant a tomato seed and another tomato plant will grow.

There are many rules of nature that we can count on. Seeds. Gravity. The temperature at which water freezes. God created these rules, and nature obeys them. We know that they won't change.

It's also reassuring to know that God doesn't change. We can count on Him. When He makes a promise He always keeps it. One of the last things Jesus said before He returned to heaven was "You can be sure that I will be with you always" (Matthew 28:20). God is with us. Always. Unchanging.

Leaves

Do the leaves change color where you live? In some parts of the country the leaves on some of the trees turn yellow or orange or red in the fall. It is a beautiful sight.

Whoever looks for good will find kindness. But whoever looks for evil will find trouble. Proverbs 11:27.

Do you know why the leaves change color? Because it gets cold. The leaves always have yellow or orange in them; you just can't see it in summer because they are full of chlorophyll, which is very green. When the weather gets cold, the chlorophyll in the leaves breaks down and fades away; then you are able to see the yellow and orange.

When the chlorophyll is gone, the leaves quit making food. The leftover food in the leaves turns red, which is darker than yellow or orange. That's why some leaves turn red. Then the leaves fall off, and the trees are bare until spring, when new leaves appear.

It makes some people sad when they see the leaves turning color. But the trees aren't dying. They're just resting until spring. In fact, that cold weather is good for some trees. Cold happens. It can make you sad, or it can make you stronger. You choose.

Life is a mixture of good and bad. If you look for sadness, it's easy to find it. But wouldn't you rather look for the good in life and for the kindness in people? Wouldn't you rather see the colors of fall and, when they're gone, look forward to spring?

We don't have to be sad about the leaves. We know they'll return in the spring. We don't have to get upset when bad things happen to us. "We know that in everything God works for the good of those who love him" (Romans 8:28).

Easter Flowers

*We believe that
Jesus died and that
he rose again.
I Thessalonians 4:14.*

One of the best things about spring is the flowers. People like flowers. The plants don't care; they have colorful flowers to attract insects to spread their pollen.

But people see so much more when they see flowers. The colors are gorgeous. The shapes are beautiful. The smells are splendid. One flower is lovely all by itself—and a whole field of flowers can just about take your breath away.

There are pretend flowers made out of plastic and silk, and some are pretty. But there is something special about a real flower. Part of its specialness might be because it actually grew— it is miraculous to plant a seed and watch it poke up out of the ground and grow into a flower. And part of its specialness might be because we know it will die.

That sounds strange. But when we know the flower will be beautiful for only a little while, somehow that makes its beauty more precious. When we know that the colors will fade and the petals will wilt, we treasure the loveliness more, while we can.

It is Eastertime. At Easter we think about Jesus' death. He died to take the punishment for our sin. We also think about Jesus' life. He taught us how to live. But mostly at Easter we think about Jesus' resurrection. Jesus rose from death. He lives. In the Bible some other names for Jesus are the Rose of Sharon and the Lily of the Valley. You can see that Jesus is like a flower. He is perfectly lovely. Because of His death, His life is ever so precious to us. And now at Eastertime we can rejoice, because Jesus is the Rose that rose from death. Jesus is the Lily that lives forever.

Learning Names

Parents who are normally quite sensible can get a little anxious about picking out a name for their baby. They don't just say, "Bob will do. Or Jane, if it's a girl." They agonize over the choices. They buy books about it. They ask all their friends what they think. They worry about how a name will affect their little darling.

I, the God of Israel, call you by name.
Isaiah 45:3.

That's because a name is important; it does affect you. It's a part of you. If your name were different, you would be different. When someone forgets your name, it's as if you are forgotten. A very mean way to tease someone is to make fun of their name.

In Bible times names were even more carefully chosen. Perhaps you've noticed that God gave names to the things He created—even the things that weren't alive. On the first day of Creation "God named the light 'day' and the darkness 'night'" (Genesis 1:5). On the second day He named the sky. On the third day He named the earth and the seas.

We have names for all the different plants that God created on the third day. We've given them names because it is important. We need to be able to identify them and talk about them. It is good that your parents are able to tell you that you can pick the dandelions but not the tulips. It's very practical.

But learning the names of plants is more than just practical. When you learn the name of a type of plant, it is almost as if you have learned the name of a friend. Once you know its name, you have more respect for it. You have a connection to it. You don't just know more about nature; you are closer to it. It is important to learn names.

Avoiding Names

Dogs don't understand English; however, they do seem to recognize some words. They know their names, and if they've been trained they know a few words like *come* and *sit*. No one has to teach them other words, such as *walk* and *treat*. Some owners can't mention the word *walk* in conversation without their dogs getting all excited. They may even have to spell *"w-a-l-k"* instead of saying the word out loud.

Words have power. Sometimes it is best to stay away from certain words and avoid trouble.

Words are being avoided in today's Bible text. Look at it carefully. What word could have been used instead of *brighter light*? *Sun.* And the *smaller light* is the *moon.*

On the fourth day of Creation God made the sun, moon, and stars. But Genesis 1 doesn't use those exact words. It isn't a mistake. It was written that way on purpose. And it's not poetry—although the Bible uses poetic language in many other places. The author was avoiding the words *sun* and *moon* for a reason.

When Genesis was written, many of the nearby nations worshiped the sun and moon as gods. The author of Genesis wanted to avoid that kind of wickedness. He didn't even want to use the names *sun* and *moon,* so he used these other words that didn't have any ties to heathen gods. He wanted to make it clear that God the Creator is the only God.

The Brighter Light

There is a certain dessert called cookies. Perhaps you've heard of them. There are many different kinds of cookies—chocolate-chip, gingersnap, oatmeal, to name a few. When we discuss cookies, we can talk about cookies in general (I like cookies) or we can talk about a particular kind of cookie (My favorite are chocolate-chip).

You know that language works this way. A word can have more than one job.

That's what is happening with *light* in the Creation story in Genesis 1. It can be confusing. Some people might read that God made light on the first day and think it's talking about the sun, because our light comes from the sun. Then they are confused when they read that the sun was created on the fourth day.

But the light on the first day isn't the sun. It is light. The first day is talking about light in general (I like light) and the fourth day is talking about light in particular (My favorite is the sun).

The Bible says the sun was created "to rule the day" (Genesis 1:16). That's poetry. It means the sun gives us our light during the day. It's in charge of daytime light.

The sun makes things grow. Plants use the light from the sun to make their food.

The sun keeps us warm. It is very, very far away, but the sun burns so hot we can feel its heat on earth.

The sun is placed exactly the right distance from our earth. Just close enough to give us light, make things grow, and keep us warm. Thank God for this brighter light.

He made the sun to rule the day. His love continues forever. Psalm 136:8.

The Moon Seems to Change

It will last forever, like the moon, like a lasting witness in the sky. Psalm 89:37.

Today's Bible text is from a song about God's loyalty. What is it that will last forever? If you look back a few verses you can see that it is God's agreement, God's promise. God's promises will last forever, like the moon.

But is this some kind of joke? Like the moon? Wouldn't it make more sense to say that it will last like the sun? The sun never changes. But the moon is always changing; one night it is round and full; a few nights later it is just a sliver.

No. The song is correct this way. The moon doesn't really change. It just seems to change. The moon is always the same. What changes is the way we see the moon.

The moon is shaped like a ball. Always. It never actually changes shape. Sometimes we see different shapes because of the way the sun shines on the moon.

The sun shines because it is burning. The moon does not burn; it only reflects the light from the sun. Half of the moon reflects the sunlight; the other half is in the dark.

When we see a full moon, a complete circle, we are seeing all of the lighted half of the moon. Because the moon spins, we can't always see the lighted half. Each night we see a bigger or smaller part of the moon.

Yes, the moon looks like it is changing, but it is changing reliably. It always changes the same way. If we see the moon tonight, we know what it will look like tomorrow. We can predict when the next full moon will be. The moon never really changes. It is always shaped like a ball. It is a lasting witness in the sky.

Like Clockwork

Have you ever looked inside a clock? It probably wouldn't be a good idea to take a clock apart, but maybe you could get a library book that shows how a clock works.

These lights will be used for signs, seasons, days and years. Genesis 1:14.

There are gears linking up with other gears, which move still more gears. It's very complicated. Everything has to move at exactly the right speed. It all works together.

On the fourth day God organized our solar system to work like clockwork. In the middle is the sun. Orbiting around the sun are the planets, including our earth. The earth itself is spinning around, while it is orbiting. The moon is spinning while it is orbiting the earth, which is orbiting the sun. Very complicated. Very, very big.

The spinning of the earth makes day and night. Every day our earth makes one turn. In the morning we turn toward the sun. All day we see the sun in the sky. In the evening it gets dark because the spinning earth is turning us away from the sun.

The spinning of the moon makes the months. A month lasts about as long as it takes to get from one full moon to the next.

The orbiting around the sun makes the years. It takes one year for the earth to complete its circle around the sun.

And God tilted the earth a little bit to one side. That's why we have seasons. As we tilt toward the sun, we have summer. We tilt to fall, winter, spring, then back again.

On the fourth day God organized the "signs, seasons, days and years" (Genesis 1:14). It is very complicated, but it all works perfectly. Like clockwork. Only bigger.

Be a Star

Have you ever seen a shooting star? They are rare. When you see a shooting star, you are likely to point and say "Oh!"—even if there is no one else around. Actually, shooting stars aren't really stars at all. The real name is "meteor."

A shooting star looks as if it is the same size as a real star, but actually they could hardly be more different in size. A real star is huge, maybe a million miles around. But a shooting star is tiny, usually no bigger than the head of a pin.

A star is an enormous ball of burning gas. A shooting star is a small particle of rock or metal that burns up when it enters the earth's atmosphere.

How can they possibly look alike when they are so different? A star looks small, even though it is actually gigantic, because it is so very, very far away. A meteor catches your eye, even though it is tiny, because it burns so brightly.

The Bible says you can be a shining star. How? "Do everything without complaining or arguing" (Philippians 2:14). Can you imagine never complaining or arguing? Paul can. In the next verse he writes: "You are living with crooked and mean people all around you. Among them you shine like stars in the dark world."

Someone who never argued or complained would be rare, a joy to be around, and even more important, a good example. Paul says the shining stars have something for those crooked and mean people: "You offer to them the teaching that gives life" (verse 16).

The only way to push away the arguing and complaining is to invite Jesus into your heart. He'll make you a shining star; then others will be drawn to Him by your light.

The Stars Sang

Bad things had been happening to Job. All his children had been killed in a tornado. All his animals had been stolen and his servants had been attacked and left for dead. His wealth was gone. He got a horrible disease with painful sores from head to foot.

Who did all this while the morning stars sang together? Job 38:7.

Then things got even worse. Some friends came to cheer him up. It would have been better if they'd stayed away. They told him that God must be punishing him for some wicked thing he'd done. Job knew he hadn't been sinning, and he told them so.

Pretty soon their conversation was nothing but questions. Why is this happening to me? What did you do to deserve this punishment? Why was I even born? Why won't you repent? Where is God? Why can't I find Him? Why? Why? Why?

Then God interrupted. But instead of answering those questions, He had a few of His own. Basically God asked, "Who do you think you are, anyway?"

The Bible text for today asks one of God's questions. Do you know who created the world? Do you know who made the stars sing and told the sea to behave and ordered the morning to begin? God did. And don't you forget it. Job never forgot it.

Sometimes it is better to answer a question with a question. It helps people think. God didn't tell Job why these bad things had happened to him. But God's questions showed Job what he really needed to know: This is my universe. I created it. I take care of it. Look at creation to see me. See my goodness, my power, my wisdom.

Sometimes just looking at the stars helps us remember this.

The Living Seas

On the fifth day of Creation God made more living things. On the fifth day God began to make animals: fish and birds.

We say "fish," but we mean much more. We actually mean all the creatures that live in the water—fish, whales, octopus, shrimp, dolphin, oysters, crabs. Thousands of different kinds of animals, of all shapes and sizes.

Oceans cover 75 percent of the earth. That's way more water than land. And that water is full of living things.

We humans don't live in the water. So it can be difficult for us to learn about the creatures that do. However, some sea creatures live in the tide pools on the edge of the ocean. Twice a day the ocean surges high onto the beach; that's high tide. When it goes back out, at low tide, we can explore the animals and plants that live among the rocks and pools at the edge of the ocean.

It's not an easy place to live. The creatures are covered and then uncovered by the water twice a day. When the tide is high, the waves constantly pound and slam against the shore. When the tide is low, the sea animals are exposed to the hot sun and hungry birds. How do they survive? Some hide under the rocks. Some have hard shells. Some cling to the rocks with suction or glue. They like it; it's the perfect home for them.

Someday you may get the chance to go to a tidal pool. It's a wonderful way to see up close some of the living things God made to fill the waters.

Fish Facts

If you've ever watched fish in an aquarium, you've probably noticed how they open and close their mouths. It looks like they are gulping water. But actually fish don't drink. They get all the water they need from moisture in the food they eat.

He who guards Israel never rests or sleeps. Psalm 121:4.

When they open their mouths like that, water does go in. But they don't swallow the water. They breathe it. There is oxygen in the water.

Fish were created with gills instead of lungs. The gills look like a slit on each side of a fish's head. The fish takes water into its mouth. The water passes over the gills. The gills take out the oxygen that is in the water. Then the water goes out the gills and back into the ocean or lake.

Fish are very interesting.

You may have heard that fish never sleep. But they do sleep. The idea that fish don't sleep probably got started when someone noticed that fish don't have eyelids. They have these great big eyes and they never close them. If fish can't close their eyes, how can they sleep?

They sleep with their eyes open. They might go down to the bottom of the water to nap or they might sleep while they are floating or swimming. They're still alert enough to wake up if they sense that an enemy is near.

Fish sleep. People sleep. But today's Bible text tells us that God never sleeps. He is always awake to protect us. We can rest in peace knowing that God will keep us safe.

115

Fishers of Men

Jesus said, "Come follow me. I will make you fishermen for men." Matthew 4:19.

Have you ever been fishing? Some people really like it. Other people don't understand why.

There must be something to it, though, because Jesus chose several fishermen to be His followers. A lot of people think that makes sense; they say that if you are good at fishing you already have many of the skills you need to become a follower of Jesus.

If you are going to fish, you must have patience. If you are in a hurry, you will never catch a fish. A follower of Jesus needs to be patient too. Many of the things Jesus asks us to do take time and patience. It is important to learn to wait.

You also must keep trying. You can't get discouraged if the fish aren't biting today. A follower of Jesus must also never give up, even if it seems like nothing is happening. You never know how big a difference you are making.

Someone good at fishing knows the right time to fish. Jesus followers knew that they couldn't catch fish during the daytime, so they didn't even try—unless Jesus told them they should. Someone who is going to share the love of Jesus also looks for the right time. Jesus will help us know when it is a good time to talk and when it is a good time to be quiet.

Jesus told Peter and Andrew, two very good fishermen, that He would make them fishers of men. They seemed to understand. They "left their nets and followed him" (Matthew 4:20). Instead of bringing fish to market, they brought people to Jesus.

The Cleaner Wrasse

I t's a fact of life in the ocean: the little fish is eaten by a bigger fish, who is eaten by an even bigger fish, and so on. In the ocean it seems as if everyone eats everyone else.

But not always. Some sea creatures cooperate with each other. Even in the ocean, some creatures realize that it makes more sense to help each other out.

For instance, look at the cleaner wrasse, which takes care of other fish. The cleaner wrasse cleans away parasites and bacteria that are growing on bigger fish. Using its strong lips and teeth, the wrasse cleans the eyes and skin of the bigger fish. Then, if you can believe it, the big fish opens its mouth wide and the wrasse swims right inside and cleans the big fish's teeth!

If the cleaner wrasse didn't remove the parasites, the big fish would get sick. So the big fish somehow knows better than to eat the little wrasse. The big fish even wait their turn to be treated by the wrasse.

It's what we call a win-win situation. The big fish win because they get rid of the parasites and stay healthy. The wrasse wins because it gets to eat all the yummy parasites.

Sometimes it seems as though we are living in a world where everyone is out to get everyone else. But Jesus offers a better choice, a win-win situation. Jesus wants us to love each other, not tear each other apart with hurtful words or actions. When we help each other, everybody wins. When we cooperate, good things happen. Just ask the cleaner wrasse.

If you go on hurting each other and tearing each other apart, be careful! You will completely destroy each other. Galatians 5:15.

Fish School

Love is what holds you all together in perfect unity. Colossians 3:14.

English has some funny names for groups of animals. We normally call a group of birds a *flock*, unless it's a group of geese. Then it's called a *gaggle*. A group of lions is called a *pride*. And when fish swim in groups, they are called schools.

Why do you suppose a group of fish is called a school? Maybe it's because the fish are paying such good attention. If they see the fish in front of them or beside them turn, they turn too. Yes, that must be it—a group of fish are probably called a school because they always pay attention, just as children in school always pay attention.

Sometimes it seems as if all the children in a classroom are doing the same thing in the same way. They are all listening to a story. They are all working on their math assignment. They are all eating lunch. Or at least they're supposed to be.

Sometimes it is important for everyone in the class to do the same thing. It saves time, and more learning can get done. It's also necessary for safety. It's very important during a fire drill, for instance.

Fish swim in schools for safety. When a small fish travels with a large group, there is less chance that it will get eaten. Because all of them are watching for trouble, a school will notice danger sooner than a single fish will. If a big fish does attack them, they scatter; in the confusion the big fish often can't pick out one fish to attack before they all escape.

It is good we have each other. We can keep each other safe. We can help each other in trouble. We can help each other do the right thing. There is power in a group. Like today's Bible text says, love can hold us together.

Swimming Upstream

Perhaps you've seen a school of fish in a lake or at the aquarium. It almost looks as if they are one fish with one brain, swimming left and right and everywhere, all going the same way at the same time.

We saw yesterday that sometimes it is good to move together like a school of fish. When people work together and cooperate, amazing things can get done. When we stay together and help each other, we are safer and happier.

But other times you have to be careful of the "school of fish" idea. You cannot turn your brain over to the group. You have to think about what they are doing and decide if you want to be a part of it.

If the crowd is doing something wrong, you do not need to be a part of the crowd. If everyone else is being mean or naughty, you do not have to do what everyone else is doing. You don't need to swim left and right and everywhere with the school of fish. You do not need the crowd to be safe. You have better help than that.

Look at today's Bible text. It doesn't matter if you are small. It doesn't matter if you are weak. God is strong. And He promises that "the people who trust the Lord will become strong again. They will be able to rise up as an eagle in the sky" (Isaiah 40:31).

Do you remember what the song says? "Little ones to Him belong. They are weak, but He is strong."

The Lord gives strength to those who are tired. He gives more power to those who are weak. Isaiah 40:29.

Regeneration

Create in me a pure heart, God. Make my spirit right again. Psalm 51:10.

Starfish have the amazing ability to break off their own arms. If a hungry enemy grabs one of their arms, they just break it off and escape—leaving the enemy with an arm appetizer instead of a starfish supper. It doesn't even hurt; the arm has a built-in snap-off point where the tissue pulls apart easily.

That's amazing. But what's even more amazing is that the starfish doesn't have to live out the rest of its life with only four arms. Starfish are able to grow replacement arms. A few other animals can also grow back broken body parts: for example, crabs can grow new claws.

This process of growing back a lost body part is called regeneration. Scientists hope that someday they will be able to help people grow a new finger or toe. But humans can't regenerate body parts yet, so it's a good idea to try to keep the ones you've got.

Regenerate also means to revive spiritually. Fortunately, humans are able to do that. Everybody has bad days, when everything goes wrong. Sometimes all we need is a good night's sleep or a big hug. Other times that's not enough. Our spirits need regeneration. God is our only hope.

The best plan is to take time for regeneration every day. You need to spend time with God. He can restore your soul. When you pray, it calms you down. God can help you think of ways to solve your problems. Reading the Bible helps too.

God made the starfish so it can make itself whole again. God can help you regenerate so that you can be whole each day too.

Flying

Have you ever wished you could fly? Oh sure, we can fly in airplanes, and that can be nice. But we don't have wings. We can't sail through the air. We can't just flap over the trees to a friend's house. We're stuck on the ground.

I wish I had wings like a dove. Then I would fly away and rest. Psalm 55:6.

God created birds on the fourth day of Creation, and we've all been a little jealous ever since.

If we want to be practical, we have to admit that flying probably wouldn't be all that wonderful. It must be exhausting, and you'd have to eat your weight in worms every couple hours just to get the energy to do it. But still, we dream of flying.

Birds can fly because they have wings. If you watch birds carefully you can see that different kinds of birds fly differently.

Most small birds, like sparrows, have wings designed for quick takeoffs and landings. They flap their wings, which causes them to go up; then they pull their wings in and rest, which causes them to drop. Flap, glide. Flap, glide. So they don't fly in a straight line; they sort of swoop up and down in a wavy line.

Some scientists believe that bigger birds, like geese, have a different way of saving energy while flying. Have you seen them fly in a V formation? When a bird flaps, the air behind its wings moves upward. Scientists believe that a group of birds flying together in a V are taking advantage of these updrafts.

The Bible doesn't say that we'll fly in heaven. But it doesn't say we won't, either.

Singing

Another wonderful thing about birds is that they are noisy. If you've ever been near a flock of seagulls or a gaggle of geese, you know that birds can make a lot of noise: honking, hooting, cheeping, peeping, cooing, cawing, trilling, calling, gossiping, quarreling.

But the best thing is that not all of their noise is just noise. Birds also make beautiful music—they sing.

Different types of birds sing different songs. A robin's song is different from a meadowlark's. Some birds sing a single, simple tune; others know many complicated songs. Many birdwatchers can identify a bird just by hearing its song.

Now, we like to think that birds sing because they are happy. And that may be so. But mostly a bird sings to attract a mate and to warn rival birds that they'd better not invade his territory.

When we hear birds sing, we also like to think that they are praising God. That also may be so. Listening to them sing certainly makes us want to praise God.

One of the best ways to praise God is to sing. And human songs have something that bird songs don't have: words. When we sing praises to God, the music gives praise and the words give praise. When you hear a songbird, you can join in with thanks to God for the music He gave us on the fourth day of Creation.

Head in the Sand

You are my hiding place. You protect me from my troubles. Psalm 32:7.

Have you ever heard someone say, "They've got their head in the sand." That saying means that someone isn't facing their problems and just wishes their troubles would go away. It comes from the notion that an ostrich sticks its head in the sand when it is in danger—that the ostrich thinks its enemies can't see it because it can't see them.

Actually, that never happens. In real life, if an ostrich feels threatened it gives its enemy a swift kick that can break its bones.

Ostriches live on flat land where there is no place to hide. An ostrich scratches a nest in the sand, right out in the open. While an ostrich sitting on its eggs spies an enemy, it will scrunch down as flat as it can and lay its long neck along the ground. If the enemy is fairly far away and only about as smart as a hyena, the ostrich will look like a bush. Maybe that's where the idea came from that it hides its head in the sand.

Even though ostriches don't hide their heads in the sand, it is still a useful saying. People do try to hide from their problems. It's not a good idea. It's better to face problems and deal with them—they don't go away just because you wish they would.

Jesus is a good place to hide when you have troubles. Look at today's Bible text. Actually, you aren't hiding from your problems when you take your troubles to Jesus. Look at the next verse: "The Lord says, 'I will make you wise. I will show you where to go. I will guide you and watch over you'" (Psalm 32:8). When you hide in Jesus, it's the opposite of hiding your head in the sand. He guides you as you face your troubles.

Scarecrows

Sometimes people stuff straw into old clothes and hang it on a pole in their garden. This scarecrow is supposed to scare away the birds that like to eat their corn.

Why do you suppose birds are afraid of scarecrows? You might think it's because the scarecrows look like people and birds are afraid of people. But that's not the reason. Or maybe the birds are startled when the wind blows the scarecrows and makes them move. That's not the reason either. You have these ideas because you think like a human. If you were going to be scared of a scarecrow, those would be the reasons why.

If you want to know why a bird keeps away from a scarecrow, you have to think like a bird. Well, *think* isn't exactly the right word. *Smell* is more like it. Birds stay away from scarecrows because the old clothes smell like people. You smell scary!

Sometimes God asks us to do something and we don't know why. We can't understand because we think like humans. We see the way things look to us. But God can see more. God sees how things are going to work out in the end. So when He asks us to do something, He has a good reason—even if we don't understand.

That's why we need faith. When we have faith, we trust that God knows best. We look to the past and see that things worked out when people followed God's plan. We know that God will be with us too, and that He will help us do what He wants us to do.

When you do what God wants, you start to understand. The more you follow His plan, the more sense it makes. With faith you begin, in a small way, to think as God thinks.

Eagle

The bald eagle is famous, but not very many people have actually seen one in the wild. Years ago bald eagles were disappearing—people were hunting them, cutting down their forests, and poisoning them with pesticides. Now there are laws to protect the bald eagles, and they are making a comeback.

Bald eagles aren't actually bald, by the way. Their heads are covered with white feathers. The bald eagle got its name from the English settlers that came to America. In those days *bald* meant "covered with white fur or feathers." The meaning of the word changed, but the name of the bird didn't.

Eagles are good parents. They carefully choose the spot for their nest. Bald eagles eat fish, so they like to build close to water where they can snatch fish from the surface.

The mother and father eagle take turns guarding the nest and searching for food for their hungry babies. When a parent returns to the nest, the babies open their mouths wide and the adult pokes the food down the babies' throats. It keeps them very busy.

Eagles have keen eyesight—eight times better than ours. They fly high into the sky in a spiral pattern, searching for prey. When they see a movement below, they dive quickly with their wings folded back and capture their meal with sharp, strong claws.

The Bible says that God the Father is like an eagle. He takes good care of His children. He protects us and provides what we need. He carries us on His wings.

He was like an eagle building its nest. It flutters over its young. It spreads it wings to catch them. It carries them on its feathers. Deuteronomy 32:11.

Hen

Many times I wanted to help your people. I wanted to gather them together as a hen gathers her chicks under her wings. But you did not let me. Luke 13:34.

Some baby birds, such as blue jays, are born blind and without feathers. You might think they are really funny-looking, but no doubt their parents think they are beautiful. These babies depend entirely on their parents for everything. All they can do is open their mouths and squawk for food.

Other baby birds, such as chickens, are able to learn how to scratch in the dirt and peck for food right after they hatch. If you've ever seen baby chicks, you know what cute little yellow puffballs they are.

But even though baby chicks can scratch and peck for food, they still need their mothers. They need someone to watch over them.

The chicks concentrate hard on learning how to scratch and peck; they aren't able to worry about danger, too. They don't need to. The mother hen is constantly on the alert for snakes or hawks or other enemies that would like a baby chick for dinner.

If she sees trouble, the mother hen calls to her babies, and they come running. They scramble under her wings and hide until the danger is past.

Jesus says that He wants to be like a mother hen for us. He offers us safety under His wings. All we have to do is let Him. In today's Bible text Jesus is sad because the people of Jerusalem wouldn't accept His help. He offered love, and they rejected it.

When you're in trouble, let Jesus help. Let Him gather you under His wings.

Dove

There are two stories in the Bible with doves. They both have happy endings.

In the first story, Noah, his family, and the animals were penned up in the ark. Everything else had been destroyed by the Flood. Noah wanted to find out if the water had dried up enough so they could safely leave the boat. He sent out a dove, but the dove couldn't find a place to land, so it came back.

A week later Noah sent the dove out again. Now, you'd expect the dove just to stay put after it found a place to live. It doesn't seem as though it would go back to the ark. But it did go back. And it brought a fresh olive leaf in its beak, showing that plants were alive.

Can you imagine how much that leaf must have meant to Noah and his family? Surely they must have danced with joy to see this proof that the world would survive, that they could start again. That dove brought hope and the promise of a new beginning.

In the second Bible story, the dove appears at Jesus' baptism. As Jesus came out of the water, God's voice said, "This is my Son and I love him" (Matthew 3:17). And the Holy Spirit came down to Jesus like a dove.

Can you imagine how much that must have meant to Jesus? This was proof that He was God's Son, that He had been sent to teach people about God and to save them from sin. This showed that God's Spirit would be with Him. The dove brought hope. It brought us the promise of a new life, a new beginning.

Noah again sent out the dove from the boat. And that evening it came back to him with a fresh olive leaf in its mouth. Genesis 8:10, 11.

God Blessed Them

God blessed them and said, "Have many young ones and grow in number. Fill the water of the seas, and let the birds grow in number on the earth."
Genesis 1:22.

On the fifth day of Creation God made the sea creatures and birds. He saw this was good. Now, the earth was not only beautiful, with green hills and blue lakes. It was full of beautiful living creatures—splashing, swimming, flying, singing. It was full of life.

God had made living things already; He made plants on the third day, and plants are alive. However, although plants and animals are both alive, they are different in many ways. For instance, plants don't move from place to place. They are rooted to the ground.

Also, plants don't think. At all. They don't have brains. Birds and fish may not do a lot of thinking, but they do have brains, and they do think in a birdy or fishy way. They make choices. A bird chooses the best place to build its nest. A little fish decides on the best way to escape from a big fish.

And so, at the end of the fifth day of Creation, God saw that this was good—just as He had at the end of the other days. But this time He added something more. This time He gave a blessing.

God blessed His new creatures. He blessed the bluebird with happiness. He told the sea creatures to be happy little clams. He told the birds to build nests, to raise families, to "have many young ones." He told the sea creatures to fill the sea with life. He blessed them: "I see that you are good. Keep it up! Be good. Live good lives."

Live in the Land

I f you put the first six days of creation into two columns, it could look like this:

First day—light

Second day—air between the waters

Third day—land

Fourth day—sun, moon, and stars

Fifth day—creatures of the air and water

Sixth day—creatures of the land

Trust the Lord and do good. Live in the land and enjoy its safety. Psalm 37:3.

The left column lists the habitat for the right column. The creatures of the right column live in the places of the left column.

For instance, on the second day God made the air to divide the waters below from the waters above. And on the fifth day He made the creatures that live in the air and the water.

So first God made the places, then He filled the places with creatures. (You have to stretch this idea a little bit to imagine the sun, moon, and stars as being creatures that live in the light.)

We have talked about days one through five. And now we are ready to talk about day six. Days one through five are so amazing, we could study them for the rest of our lives and never come close to learning all about them. And day six would take several more lifetimes.

Day six. That's us. And all the animals that share the land with us. The place was all prepared. There was air to breathe and water to drink. There was the sun in the morning and the moon at night. And there was the land, covered with plants, a place for us to live.

Tame

Then God said, "Let the earth be filled with animals. . . . Let there be tame animals and small crawling animals and wild animals." Genesis 1:24.

The water and air were full of living creatures. Now, on the sixth day of Creation, God filled the land with animals. Now the fun really began.

The Bible text divides the animals into three groups: tame animals, small crawling animals, and wild animals.

The tame animals are our pets and farm animals. Small crawling animals are reptiles, insects, spiders, and those kinds of critters. Wild animals live in the forest or jungle or prairie; they take care of themselves.

The tame animals are the ones we know the best. They are our friends, our companions. You might say we are in the same boat. We travel through life together.

The tame animals depend on us. We take care of them. We give them food, water, a place to live. We try to keep them clean and healthy.

And we depend on them. Pets are our friends. They love us. They comfort us. They are always happy to see us. We need farm animals, too. They give us eggs and milk and wool, among other things.

Tame is something you can do. You can make friends with a lamb or a puppy and treat it gently, and it will love you and follow you around. You have tamed it. And *tame* is something you can be. When something is tame, it is gentle and willing to help. When an animal is tame, it needs you and you need it. You take care of each other.

Learning to Love

This is my command: Love each other. John 15:17.

Have you noticed what dogs do when they're happy? They wag their tails. Some dogs have long tails; when they are happy, their wagging can knock stuff off the coffee table. Some dogs have hardly any tail, but they sure can wiggle those little tails fast.

Dogs wag their tails for lots of reasons, but the best reason is they're happy to see you. It is nice when someone is happy to see you. That's one of the reasons people have dogs for pets.

It is a big responsibility to have a pet. A dog depends on its owner for food and water. You have to make sure it gets enough exercise and gets its shots and learns good manners. And you need to love your dog. Everything a dog understands about love, it learns from its owner.

Humans have to learn about love too. It's the most important thing you can learn how to do. Think about all the people who love you—family, friends, teachers, the people at church, neighbors. Their love teaches you about love. You can also learn about love from hearing stories. You just have to pay attention.

Jesus gave us a rule in today's Bible text. Imagine what this world would be like if people obeyed that one rule. There would be no fighting, no killing, no stealing. No one would be mean. All kids would be happy. All dogs would wag their tails.

You can't make the whole world obey that rule. But you can obey it. Love each other. You can start now—and keep learning how for the rest of your life.

Taking Baths

Take away my sin, and I will be clean. Wash me, and I will be whiter than snow. Psalm 51:7.

Some dogs don't like to take baths. They hide under the bed. They jump out of the tub. Or they sit there forlornly and look at you like, "How could you do this to me?"

Perhaps dogs don't like to take baths because they don't want to smell clean. They want to smell interesting. Dogs smell lots better than humans; that is, their noses work lots better. That's one way they communicate. To make an impression on other dogs, they hope that an interesting smell will attract attention and make a statement.

That may be why a dog, when it sees something you might think is really disgusting, will instead think, *This would be a good thing to roll around in.* Then it can trot down the street and have all the other dogs thinking, *H'mm. What an intriguing smell.*

People are a little like dogs in this way. I don't mean that people don't like to take baths (although I wouldn't be surprised to hear that you used to not like baths). And I don't mean that people like to roll around in smelly things (although I wouldn't be too shocked to learn that you had done that once or twice when you were very young).

I mean that people have a hard time being good. Staying "clean." King David really wanted to be good. He even wrote songs about it. Look at today's Bible text.

But then (just like a dog who goes in the backyard after a bath and sees a nice place to dig in the dirt) David forgot about keeping clean and being good, and he would make a mistake. Then David would pray, "Wash away all my guilt and make me clean *again*" (Psalm 51:2). God answered David's prayers. He'll help you keep clean too.

Purr

It's pleasant to pet a cat. Its fur is soft and warm, and the cat snuggles up to you. But the best thing is the purr. When a cat is happy and contented, it starts to purr. What a wonderful sound! It's sort of a little rumbly noise that comes from deep in their throats.

Cats start purring when they are very young. If you've ever seen tiny little kittens drinking milk from their mother, you might have heard them purring. They purr because they are so hungry and the milk tastes so good and they are so cozy, all cuddled up with their mama and brothers and sisters.

And have you ever seen a mother cat give her babies a bath? She washes them with her tongue! Would you like that? Well, kittens love it! It makes them feel safe and happy. So, guess what they do—they purr!

Some people think cats are pretty smart. Every day a human is there to feed them and give them fresh water and pet them. Every day they get to sleep as much as they want and play whenever they feel like it. A cat doesn't care if the cat next door has more toys or gets more expensive cat food. A cat is content.

And it is very smart to be content. You cannot be happy if you want something you can't have. It doesn't make sense to be worried about what you can't have—you never get time to enjoy the wonderful things you can have.

Look at today's Bible text. God is with you. That's the most important thing. He will give you what you need—and you can be content.

Be satisfied with what you have. God has said, "I will never leave you." Hebrews 13:5.

Turn an Ear

He paid attention to me. So I will call to him for help as long as I live. Psalm 116:2.

Rabbits can make good pets. They're soft and gentle and very, very cute.

But there are wild rabbits, too. And sometimes you might wonder if your pet rabbit is truly tamed, or if it would hop off if it got half a chance.

One cool thing about rabbits, both wild and tame, is that they can move their ears. Do you know how to wiggle your ears? Not many people can. Usually there's one kid in every school who can make their ears move up and down a little bit. For those of us who can't make our ears move even a smidgen, it seems like a pretty impressive talent.

Rabbits can move their ears much better, but their ears don't wiggle—they swivel. Rabbits can turn their ears in any direction. If they hear something to the right, they swivel their ears to the right. If they hear something behind them, they don't have to turn their whole head—they just turn their ears.

Sometimes we ask people to "turn an ear " when we want them to listen to us. We don't expect them to actually turn their ear—it's just an expression. Maybe we want them to turn their eyes. If they are looking at us it makes us feel as though they are paying attention.

The New International Version of today's Bible text says, "Because he turned his ear to me, I will call on him as long as I live." Sometimes we might wonder if God really is listening. We can't see whether or not He is paying attention. But the Bible tells us that He is listening. His ear is turned to you, to catch every prayer.

Discriminating

Goats are great for petting zoos. They are gentle. They don't mind if kids pat them all day long. They are cute and small—just the right size for petting. However, although they're small, they're usually very fat. They like to eat. You've got to be careful—sometimes they even try to nibble on your clothes.

People joke that goats will eat anything—paper, cardboard, tin cans. You might think it's strange for a goat to eat paper or clothing. But paper is made out of wood, and clothing is often made of cotton. Wood and cotton are plants. Plants are good to eat. Goats smell the plant smell in the paper or clothing and think it is something to eat.

Goats are not discriminating eaters. Most people are. It is important for us to learn to discriminate about some things. We learn to discriminate between the things that are good to eat (such as apples) and the things that are not good to eat (such as dirt).

But we have to be careful. Discrimination is wrong when we make our decisions based on the wrong type of things. It is easy to judge other people by the way they look—by what color their skin is or how old they are or what kind of clothes they are wearing. These things don't really tell us much about the person—and if we decide we don't like someone based on how they look, we are discriminating against them.

Look at today's Bible text. God sees our potential. He sees what we can become. God can help you learn to see the way He sees.

God does not see the same way people see. People look at the outside of a person, but the Lord looks at the heart.
1 Samuel 16:7.

Sheep

He saw the crowds of people and felt sorry for them because they were worried and helpless. They were like sheep without a shepherd. Matthew 9:36.

Since the beginning, sheep have been important animals. In Bible times, if you had a lot of sheep you were rich. Sheep were better than money. They gave wool and milk and you could eat them. But best of all (if you didn't eat them), sheep would have babies and then you would have even more wealth. Money doesn't have babies. Too bad.

Since sheep were so valuable, people always took good care of them. The shepherds brought their flocks of sheep to graze in good pasture. They led them to water. They chased away attacking animals. And if a sheep got lost, the shepherd went out looking for it.

The sheep really needed all this careful attention. No one ever said that sheep were smart. Sheep have always needed someone to help them find food and water. They are helpless; they need someone to watch over them and keep them safe.

Even though sheep equaled wealth, most shepherds didn't treat their sheep as things. They treated them well, but not just because they were valuable. They loved their sheep. They gave them names. The sheep were like family.

It didn't take long before someone noticed that people can be a lot like sheep. And that we need God to be our shepherd. Jesus said, "I am the good shepherd. I know my sheep" (John 10:14). It's a comforting idea. Jesus takes care of us.

One Little Lamb

Sometimes a king thinks he can do whatever he wants and take whatever he wants. King David wanted to marry a woman who was already married. So he sent her husband to a war, where he was killed. Then David married her.

I have wandered like a lost sheep. Psalm 119:176.

Nathan the prophet came to see King David, and he told him this story.

"There were two men in a city. One man was rich, but the other was poor. The rich man had very many sheep and cattle. But the poor man had nothing except one little female lamb he had bought. The poor man fed the lamb. It grew up with him and his children. It shared his food and drank from his cup. It slept in his arms. The lamb was like a daughter to him.

"Then a traveler stopped to visit the rich man. The rich man wanted to give food to the traveler. But he didn't want to take one of his own sheep or cattle to feed the traveler. Instead, he took the lamb from the poor man. The rich man killed the lamb and cooked it for his visitor" (2 Samuel 12:1-4).

Doesn't that make you mad? It made David mad too. He said the rich man should die. Then Nathan told David who the rich man was: "It's you. You did this."

Finally David saw the horrible thing he had done. Before this he had been able to pretend nothing was wrong. But the story made him feel sorry for the poor man and his one little lamb. The story made him despise the rich man. The story showed him how awful he really was. And David was sorry for what he had done.

Ruminate

If someone asked you to name a farm animal, chances are the first one you would think of would be a cow. Cows are some of the most valuable animals in the world. They give us milk, which we turn into cheese and yogurt and other treats. They are strong enough to pull plows and carts. Their manure makes great fertilizer for the soil, and you can burn it for fuel. Their hide can be turned into leather, and cows provide a lot of meat.

But cows are more than useful. They are patient and gentle. They are just about the perfect farm animal.

Have you ever seen a cow lying in the grass and chewing? They look so peaceful and thoughtful. It looks like they're chewing gum, but they're actually chewing their cud. They do that because they eat grass and grass is hard to digest.

A cow has a special stomach with four parts. It can bite off and swallow a lot of grass quickly. Then the cow lies down, maybe in a nice shady spot. It brings the grass back up into its mouth and chews it well while it is resting.

There is a word for how a cow chews again—*ruminate*. We also say that people ruminate, but we don't mean that they are chewing food again (yuck). We mean they are thinking something over, carefully and slowly. They are "chewing" an idea over and over in their mind. It's a good habit. The Bible says, "If you act too quickly, you might make a mistake" (Proverbs 19:2). So avoid mistakes. Be like a cow. Ruminate.

Away in a Manger

At Christmastime people often set up Nativity scenes. A Nativity scene shows how things might have looked the night Jesus was born. Inside the stable there are the shepherds and Wise Men (usually three of each), some sheep and a cow and a donkey. Mary and Joseph are beside the manger where dear Baby Jesus is lying, wrapped up tight.

But ask the animals, and they will teach you. Job 12:7.

Sometimes when we unpack our Nativity scenes to decorate the house for Christmas, we remember that Jesus was born in a barn. Of course we've known that all along. But the Nativity scene reminds us.

What is it that reminds us? The animals. The animals—as well as the shepherds and the Wise Men and the angels—were there to welcome Jesus.

It's nice to think about the animals that must have been there. Maybe Mary had ridden a little donkey to Bethlehem; maybe the donkey was there in the stable. Maybe the shepherds had brought some sheep along with them. Maybe the Wise Men had camels. Maybe there was a cow; we like to think there was a cow.

People who don't know anything about Jesus might think that a Nativity scene looks strange. They might think it is weird to be born in a barn with the animals. But for those of us who know the story, it looks comfortable and right. The animals are peaceful and calm. They are supposed to be there; it's their barn. We think it's nice that the animals were invited when Jesus came to our world.

139

New Skin

You have left your old sinful life and the things you did before.
Colossians 3:9.

On the sixth day of Creation God created "small crawling animals" (Genesis 1:24). Reptiles, amphibians, insects, spiders. Some people aren't too fond of these creepy, crawly creatures. But God made them for good reasons. We need them. Our world needs them.

When you think about small crawling animals, snakes might come to mind. Most snakes are small (thankfully), and they crawl. Some people don't like snakes; they have a bad reputation. But many rumors people believe about snakes just aren't true.

For instance, lots of people think snakes are wet and slimy. They aren't. Perhaps people think snakes are slimy because they can see that a snake's body, like that of a fish, is covered with scales. A snake's skin might look like a fish's skin, but it doesn't feel like it. A snake's skin is dry and soft. It feels like leather.

The scales overlap and can stretch apart. This flexibility allows a snake to bend into any position. It's very important for a snake to be flexible—that's how it travels.

A snake sheds it's skin several times a year. The old skin gets worn out, and as the snake grows the old skin gets too tight. The snake just crawls out of the old skin. Perhaps you've seen a papery old skin that a snake has left behind.

Humans can't crawl out of their skin. We lose a few skin cells at a time. But today's Bible text sounds like something a snake could do. When we decide to follow Jesus, we leave our old life behind—like a snake crawling out of its old skin.

Not What It Seems

In India there is an unusual form of entertainment. Men called snake charmers seem to make cobras dance. A king cobra is the largest poisonous snake in the world.

The snake charmer sits in front of a basket and begins to play a flute. A cobra rises up out of the basket. It watches the snake charmer play the flute. The cobra swells out its throat, forming a hood. The hooded snake begins to sway back and forth. Is it really dancing to the music?

No. It can't even hear the music. Snakes don't have ears; they can't hear noises coming through the air the way we do. They have a sort of inner ear, so they can hear vibrations that come through the ground. But they don't hear music and they don't dance.

Whenever a cobra is frightened, it lifts up the front part of its body. That's why it rises out of the basket. Whenever a cobra is angry, it displays its hood. The cobra sways from side to side because the snake charmer is swaying from side to side. The cobra is on guard, tracking the movement of this possible enemy, ready to strike.

Things are not always what they seem to be.

Sometimes it may seem as if it is useless to do the right thing. Sometimes it seems as if it won't do any good, it won't make any difference. But the Bible says it's important to do what is right anyway. We can't always see the good it is doing. We can't always see the whole picture. Things aren't always what they seem. Choose to do right.

It is important that you do what is right, even if it seems that we have failed.
2 Corinthians 13:7.

True Colors

Finally, be strong in the Lord and in his great power.
Ephesians 6:10.

A chameleon is a very odd reptile. Chameleons have really long, sticky tongues—their tongues can be longer than their bodies. They have big pop eyes—they can roll one eye forward and one eye back so they can see behind and ahead at the same time. So when a bug comes along, the chameleon is going to see it. It shoots out its long tongue, the bug sticks to it, and the chameleon reels in the bug for dinner.

But probably the oddest thing about the chameleon is that it can change color. When it is in the sun, sitting among green leaves, it looks green. When it is in the shade, sitting on a log or among brown leaves, the chameleon looks brown.

This is a handy thing to be able to do. When the chameleon is the same color as its surroundings, it is hard for its enemies to see it. It is also hard for flies and other delicious insects to see the chameleon in time to avoid being eaten.

What makes chameleons change color? The light gets brighter or darker. The air gets warmer or colder. The chameleon gets angry or afraid. These things happen to us, too, but we don't change color. We don't have the same color-producing cells in our skin.

But sometimes, if people change how they act depending on whom they are with, we say they are like a chameleon. We can't trust them. We never know what they are really like or what they really think.

It's important to decide what you believe and stick to it. Jesus will help you be strong. He'll help you show your true colors.

MYOB?

Have you ever seen a mother turtle sitting on her nest, keeping her eggs warm? I doubt it. After she lays her eggs, a turtle just covers them with sand and swims away.

Have you ever seen a mother and father frog hunting for food to bring to their precious little tadpoles? Nope. Tadpoles are on their own. They never even meet their parents. Some animals don't take care of their babies at all.

But other animals do. They teach their babies how to find their own food. They protect their babies from enemies. They are involved. They intercede.

Have you ever been told to MYOB? It stands for "mind your own business." Usually that's good advice. We don't want to be tattletales. But we aren't reptiles. We take care of each other. We don't always mind our own business. We intercede.

What does *intercede* mean? It means we try to do something to help someone else. We get involved. We don't leave other people to survive on their own.

When the Bible says "intercede," it often is talking about prayer. When people are sad, you can ask God to comfort them. When people are sick, you can ask God to help them feel better. When people are in trouble, you can ask God what you can do to help.

People are praying for you. They want you to know Jesus and the wonderful life He can give you. They refuse to mind their own business about this. They'll never stop praying for you. They love you.

First, I tell you to pray for all people. Ask God for the things people need, and be thankful to him. 1 Timothy 2:1.

143

Both Lives

If you've ever had the chance to explore a pond, you may have heard a big plop and looked up just in time to see a big bullfrog disappear into the water. Frogs are cool. They won't hurt you (although some brightly colored frogs have poison skin). And they are fun to try to catch—they're fast, but not so fast that it's impossible.

Frogs are amphibians. *Amphibian* means "both lives." It is as if amphibians have two lives—their life in the water and their life on land. Their eggs are laid in the water. When the eggs hatch, the little tadpoles live in the water and breathe with gills, like fish. Tadpoles don't look like their parents—they look like fish.

But as they get older, the tadpoles begin to grow legs and lungs. Their tails begin to disappear. They gradually turn into frogs. Then they live on the land and breathe air—but they usually stay near the water.

If amphibian means "both lives," then we are amphibians too. We will have both lives. There is our life here on earth, now. Now we try to live as Jesus taught us to live. With His help we try to help others and share the good news about Jesus. We are getting ready for our next life.

Our next life will be in heaven. Jesus promised that He would come back. Look at today's Bible text. He will come get us so we can be with Him. Our next life will be with Jesus in heaven.

In our next life everything will be happy. Our next life will last forever.

Payback

Evidently tadpoles are delicious. Lots of animals like to eat them—birds, mammals, reptiles, insects, and even other amphibians. Mother frogs lay thousands and thousands of eggs, but only a few of them survive and actually become adult frogs.

If anyone slaps you on your cheek, let him slap the other cheek too. Luke 6:29.

One of the tadpoles' enemies is the dragonfly nymph. Dragonfly nymphs are baby dragonflies. Their eggs are laid in the water, and after they hatch they live and grow in the water. As the nymphs grow they shed their skin many times; when they reach full size they've turned into dragonflies, and they leave the water and fly away.

And what helps them grow and grow and grow? Eating tadpoles.

Ah, but things change completely when the babies grow up. What is one of a frog's favorite snacks? Dragonflies! They both live out of the water now. And if a dragonfly gets within range of a frog's long, sticky tongue, it's payback time.

Actually dragonflies and frogs don't think about revenge. They just like to eat each other. It's nothing personal.

People do think about revenge, sometimes entirely too much. Thinking about revenge is one of those things that can take over your life, pushing everything else out of the way. Revenge can ruin the life of the person who wants it. Payback doesn't pay.

Jesus knew this. Look at the advice He gave in today's Bible text. That may seem foolish, but it's really very wise. It takes two people to fight. If you won't fight, you can stop it. Turn the other cheek. Let it go. Don't let revenge ruin your life.

Insect Invasion

The army destroys the land like a burning fire. The land in front of them is like the garden of Eden. The land behind them is like an empty desert. Nothing will escape them.

Joel 2:3.

On the sixth day of Creation God created "small crawling animals" (Genesis 1:24). Reptiles and amphibians are small crawling animals, but there are some animals that are even smaller and crawlier. Insects.

Insects are everywhere—on the ground and under the ground, on the water and in the water. They are even in the sky—many insects can fly as well as crawl. They live in burning deserts and icy lakes. Everywhere. Millions and millions of them.

There is a book in the Bible that is about an invasion of an insect army. The book of Joel describes what it is like when a swarm of locusts destroys the land. The army in today's Bible text is an army of locusts.

"What the cutting locusts have not eaten, the swarming locusts have eaten. And what the swarming locusts have left, the hopping locusts have eaten. And what the hopping locusts have left, the destroying locusts have eaten" (Joel 1:4).

The locusts ate it all. There was nothing left. They even ate the bark off the trees. The insects destroyed every growing thing.

Why is this story in the Bible? The prophet Joel is asking the people to repent. "The Lord says, 'Now, come back to me with all your heart'" (Joel 2:12). And Joel reminds the people that God can make the locusts leave and the plants grow again.

Joel is an interesting book—only three chapters long. Take a look.

Metamorphosis

Butterflies have a fascinating life cycle: first an egg, then a caterpillar, then a cocoon, then a butterfly. But the most amazing is the cocoon. Do you know what happens inside that cocoon? The caterpillar changes into a butterfly. Those words make it sound simple, but it's not—it's very complicated. The whole body is reorganized. All the caterpillar muscles, nerves, and other structures dissolve, and new ones form.

But he is not here. He has risen from death as he said he would. Matthew 28:6.

The scientific word for this is *metamorphosis*. It means a change in form and appearance. Butterflies aren't the only creatures who have a life cycle that involves metamorphosis. Many insects do: bees, ants, and beetles, for instance. So do frogs.

Some people think caterpillars are kind of creepy. Their continual munching destroys plants. But after the magic of the cocoon, they turn into butterflies, flitting from flower to flower, sipping nectar and spreading pollen. Many butterflies are so beautiful that when you see them, you stop and watch. What a difference that cocoon makes!

When Jesus died, His friends wrapped His body in cloth. Then they put Him in a tomb that had been cut out of a wall of rock. Look at today's Bible text. That's what an angel told the women who went to the tomb on Easter morning.

The tomb is empty. Jesus is alive. Because Jesus died, we are saved from sin. Because Jesus lives, good triumphs over evil, life triumphs over death, loves conquers all. Because Jesus lives, we can experience metamorphosis. We can leave behind our destructive, hungry selves. We can emerge, useful and lovely, into a new life with Jesus.

147

Moth Holes

Some people have summer clothes and winter clothes. In the spring they get their summer clothes from the attic and pack up their winter clothes. There is one thing you don't want to find next fall when you're getting out your winter clothes—moth holes. Sometimes moths get into woolen clothes and chew holes. Then the clothes are ruined.

Wait a minute. Moths don't have teeth. How can they chew holes in anything? They can't. We call them "moth holes," but we should call them "caterpillar holes."

Sometimes moths lay eggs on woolen clothes; after the eggs hatch, the caterpillars nibble on whatever is nearby. If it is your sweater, then it will be full of holes when you unpack it in the fall. But hey, it's just a sweater. That's what happens to stuff. Bread gets moldy. Cars get rusty. Stock markets crash. Clothes get holes.

Look at today's Bible text. What kind of treasure cannot be stolen from you? Who you are. What kind of treasure can you store in heaven? The things you do.

Your character is a treasure that no one can take away. It is the only thing you can take with you to heaven. The things you do in kindness are another kind of treasure. When you are kind it helps others, but it also enriches you. It builds your character.

"Your heart will be where your treasure is," Jesus says (Matthew 6:21). If you love clothes and cars and money, you're going to be dealing with moth holes and rust and inflation. But if your heart is in heaven, then you will know what's really important, and you will pile up treasures of kindness and love and character.

Busy as a Bee

A bee family can have thousands of bees in it. Every bee has a job to do.

Each bee family has one mother. She is the queen, and all she does is lay eggs. Certain bees take care of her—they feed her and groom her and keep her safe and happy.

Other bees have household chores. Some help build the home or keep it clean. Some work in the nursery, taking care of the eggs and the baby bees. Some bees guard the home (with their stingers!), and others fan with their wings to stir up a breeze.

Many of the bees have the job of gathering food. They fly off in search of flowers, from which they collect nectar and pollen. They bring it home, and other bees turn it into honey. We might think that the bees who make honey are the most important ones (because we really like honey), but in the bee family all the jobs are important.

We have families too (although not nearly so big). In our families we all work together to take care of each other. You are an important part of your family.

We also are part of a bigger family—the family of God. Look at today's Bible text. God is the Father, and all of us are His children. We are brothers and sisters in the family of God.

Each of us is an important member of this family, and each of us has a job to do. When you go to church you can't just expect the people there to take care of you—you've got to help take care of them. You can't just say, "Tell me a story; sing to me." You've got to participate; you've got to sing along. Families take care of each other.

The Father has loved us so much! He loved us so much that we are called children of God. 1 John 3:1.

149

Watch the Ants

Go watch the ants, you lazy person. Watch what they do and be wise. Proverbs 6:6.

Like bees, ants are social insects. That means they live and work together in big colonies. Each ant has a specific job that it performs to find food or build the nest or take care of the baby ants

You may wonder how they run things when they can't talk to each other. Well, they can't make sounds, but they do talk, in their own way. They use their antennae, or feelers, to communicate with each other.

Ants smell with their antennae. They talk to each other with smells, not with sounds. When they go somewhere, they lay down a chemical trail. That way they can always find their way back home. Also, if they find food, they let the other ants know about it so they can follow the trail to help bring the food back to the nest.

It seems as if ants are always busy. When you see them, they are always going somewhere in a great big hurry, often carrying something twice as big as they are.

It's important for people to be busy too. When you're bored, you're likely to do something that will get you into trouble. When you're lazy, you expect other people to do your share of the work. That's what today's Bible text is about.

So next time you're bored, go watch the ants. And next time you're feeling lazy, do whatever it is you're supposed to do, and then go watch the ants.

Mosquito Bites

Have you ever been bitten by a mosquito? Technically, you haven't. Mosquitoes can't bite. They don't have teeth. They can't even open their mouth—no jaws.

But later it bites like a snake. Like a snake, it poisons you. Proverbs 23:32.

So how do you get those red itchy bumps that we call mosquito bites? A female mosquito lands on your skin. Out pop six small, sharp needles, called stylets. They poke through your skin—maybe you feel it, maybe you don't—until they hit a vein.

When you spring a leak like this, your blood automatically begins to clot. However, if it clots, the mosquito can't drink it. So she drips saliva into the wound. Mosquito saliva has a chemical in it that stops the blood from clotting.

Most people are allergic to mosquito saliva. That's why you get that itchy bump. Even though it isn't actually a bite, we call it a bite because it is like a bite.

Today's Bible text talks about something else that isn't actually a bite, but it is like one. Verses 29 and 30 explain: "Some people drink too much wine. They try out all the different kinds of drinks. So they have trouble. They are sad. They fight. They complain. They have unnecessary bruises." Alcohol brings you trouble.

Why do people drink? They think it will make them happy. They hope it will make them brave. They wish it would make them forget. But alcohol can't make their problems disappear. It just adds more problems.

People need Jesus. Jesus can make us happy and brave. Jesus won't help us escape our problems—but He'll help us face our problems.

Camouflage

The Lord says, "Come, we will talk these things over. Your sins are red like deep red cloth. But they can be as white as snow." Isaiah 1:18.

Has this ever happened to you? You're outside—maybe sitting in a tree or lying in the grass or standing by a bush. All of a sudden you are startled to find that right beside you there is a bug. Now, where did this bug come from? Did it just appear out of nowhere? No. It was there all along. You just didn't see it because of its disguise.

The trouble with being a bug is that so many other creatures want to eat you. But if they can't see you, they won't eat you, so lots of insects use camouflage to hide. Their color and markings blend in with their surroundings and make them hard to see.

Satan says that we are sinners and that we deserve to die. He's right.

But Jesus says, "I died for their sins. I paid their penalty." And He's righteous.

Jesus' righteousness covers our sins. Jesus gives us "camouflage" that will protect us from our enemy, Satan. We don't have any righteousness of our own. Try to imagine yourself without Jesus' camouflage. It would be as if you were standing in the middle of the white, white snow in bright-red long underwear. That's what today's Bible text says.

The camouflage works only if you ask for it. When we ask Jesus to forgive our sins, we are also asking for His righteousness. Jesus' righteousness can cover us. Try to imagine yourself in His camouflage. It would be as if you were a polar bear in the middle of the white, white snow.

Jesus can make your sins as white as snow. Jesus can keep you safe.

Caught in a Web

Spiders were created on the sixth day. They are small and crawly, but they are not insects. Insects have six legs; spiders have eight.

Spiders build webs. A spider lives in its web, but mostly the web is a trap to catch insects for food. The back end of a spider has special organs called spinnerets, which produce different kinds of thread.

When a spider spins a web, first it spins several threads that look like spokes on a bicycle tire. Then it starts in the middle and spins bigger and bigger circles.

When an insect gets caught in the web, the more it struggles, the more tangled it gets. The spider hurries over and has the insect for lunch.

Why doesn't the spider get caught in its own web? There are two kinds of thread. The circles are sticky; the spokes are not. The spider walks only on the spokes.

Today's Bible text says that lies can trap you like a spider's web. When you lie you try to make someone believe something that is not true.

The trouble with a lie is that it doesn't match with what people can see. So you often need to tell another lie to try to cover up the first one. This only makes things worse. And the more lies you tell, the more tangled up you get in the lies. And before long you are trapped in your lies, like an insect trapped in a spiderweb.

If you lie to people, they will stop believing you. It will be hard to earn their trust again. Don't get trapped in a web of lies. Tell the truth.

People tell lies as they would spin a spider's web. Isaiah 59:5.

153

Wild

*Even the wild animals
will be thankful to me.
Isaiah 43:20.*

On the sixth day of Creation God said, "Let there be tame animals and small crawling animals and wild animals" (Genesis 1:24). Wild animals!

Wild animals don't need people to take care of them. They find their own food. They have their own homes in the jungle or desert, forest or meadow. They are wild.

Usually when the Bible mentions wild animals, they are very scary. They are ripping or stalking or trampling. Fierce. Wild. But in a few places the wild animals seem wise and at peace.

After Jesus was baptized He went into the desert alone. But He wasn't exactly alone. "He was in the desert 40 days and was there with the wild animals" (Mark 1:13).

Maybe the story mentions the wild animals to show how lonely and dangerous it was in the desert. But maybe the story wants to show that the wild beasts were Jesus' friends.

While the Jews waited for the Messiah, they dreamed of a time when humans and animals would be friends. They remembered prophecies promising that "the wolves will live in peace with lambs. And leopards will lie down to rest with goats" (Isaiah 11:6).

Maybe Mark tells this story to show that their dreams were coming true with Jesus, the Messiah. Maybe the wild animals recognized that Jesus was the Messiah, before most humans did. The tame animals welcomed Jesus when He was born in their stable. And maybe the wild animals welcomed Him when He came to their desert.

A Nose Above the Rest

What can you do with your nose? You can smell with it. You also use your nose to breathe. That's about it. Oh, you can blow your nose. And maybe wiggle it. And some people can sort of hum through their noses. But none of that is very impressive.

"All things are here because I made them," says the Lord. Isaiah 66:2.

Now, an elephant has an impressive nose. It even has a special name: a trunk. The trunk is not just a nose; it is also an upper lip. And a trunk is so very useful.

An elephant can carry its baby with its trunk. A trunk can reach up to pick leaves or reach down to pick grass. The tip of an elephant's trunk is sensitive enough to grasp even little things, the way you use your fingers.

An elephant drinks by sucking up water with its trunk, as if it were a straw. Then it shoots the water into its mouth. That's how it takes a shower, too. Elephants can call to other elephants with their trunks—like a trumpet. And, don't forget, the elephant also uses its trunk to smell with.

It would be hard to be humble if you had a nose that could do all that.

You probably have something you are proud of. Maybe you are a good speller or you know how to do cartwheels. Is it OK to be proud of this? It depends. The trouble starts when people begin thinking they are responsible for whatever they are proud of.

Look at today's Bible text. God gave you all your talents. God is responsible.

It is good that you can spell or do cartwheels. Be happy about it. And be humble about it. Remember who made you so special.

Prickly

But I tell you, love your enemies. Pray for those who hurt you. Matthew 5:44.

A porcupine is covered with long fur that is rough and prickly. About halfway down its back some of the fur turns into long quills that are extremely sharp at the tip.

A porcupine's quills are strong and sharper than needles. When a porcupine is threatened by an enemy, first it rustles its quills in warning. Then the porcupine simply backs up into its enemy. The quills fall out of the porcupine and stick into the enemy.

Quills come out of the porcupine easily, but they don't come out of the enemy easily. They have little barbs that hold tight once they are stuck. And it hurts like crazy. Once an animal has been stuck by a porcupine quill, it never tries that again.

Sometimes we say a person is prickly when we think that that person is unfriendly. People don't have quills; they show prickliness by being rude or selfish or mean.

When people are prickly, they don't want other people to bother them. If someone tries to be friendly, the prickly person might ignore them or say something mean. The friendly person is unlikely to try that again.

What do you do with a prickly person? Jesus says you should love them. Look at today's Bible text. This won't work if you try to love a prickly person the warm and cozy way you love your family. You can't force yourself to get this feeling.

But there is another kind of love; it makes us willing to work for other people's good—even when they don't like us and we don't particularly like them. With this kind of love, we treat everyone with respect and dignity and kindness (even if they don't treat us the same) because that's how Jesus treats them. That's not easy—but Jesus will help.

156

Is It Fair?

You have seven bones in your neck. Guess how many neck bones a giraffe has. Here is a hint: a giraffe's neck is about 11 feet long. A human neck is a few inches long. Surprise! Giraffes have seven neck bones too. They're just longer.

Now, how many neck bones does a whale have? Hint: a whale doesn't even have a neck. (Perhaps you are beginning to suspect that these hints are not very helpful.) Surprise again! Whales have the same seven bones, even though they don't have a neck.

Is it fair that a giraffe, with such a magnificently long neck, is given only as many neck bones as a whale, who has no neck at all? Evidently. Giraffes manage just fine with seven neck bones. And they don't seem to be upset about the whale's neck bones.

Jesus told a story (Matthew 20:1-16) about some vineyard workers. Some of them started working early in the morning. Some were hired at 9:00, others at noon, and others at 3:00. The owner even brought in some workers at 5:00. Here's the surprising part of the story: At the end of the day, each worker was paid the same amount.

The people who worked all day didn't think that was fair. They thought they should get more than the people who worked for only one hour. It's understandable. But Jesus says it was fair, and here's why: The people who worked all day long were promised one silver coin when they came to work. They got what they were promised.

We don't need to worry about whether God will be fair. God is fair—fair in ways we can hardly understand. He keeps His promises. He gives us what we need. If you have only seven neck bones, they'll be long enough. Just ask a giraffe.

Then you will understand what is honest and fair and right. Proverbs 2:9.

Naturally

Serve each other with love. Galatians 5:13.

Sea otters are cute as can be, with their funny whiskers and bright eyes and their wet fur sticking up in little spikes. They'll be calmly floating on their backs, feet poking out of the water. Then in a flash they'll zoom off to play tag or turn a somersault.

Otters know how to play. They know all kinds of swimming, sliding, and chasing games. If you were going to be another animal, it would be fun to be an otter.

Sea otters are more than just fun and games. They are important to the environment. A giant plant called kelp grows on the ocean floor; many creatures depend on the kelp forests to survive. Sea urchins eat kelp—and they would eat it all if they got the chance. If that happened, many plants and animals would lose their food and shelter.

Otters to the rescue! Otters dive down and grab the sea urchins. They bring them to the surface, turn on their backs, and float around while enjoying a sea urchin snack.

By eating sea urchins, sea otters help preserve the kelp forests. They probably don't realize they are helping the other creatures in their neighborhood—they just like to eat sea urchins. It is the natural thing for them to do.

Being helpful is not the natural thing for humans to do. Today's Bible text tells us we should, but serving others doesn't come naturally. Fortunately, it is Jesus' nature. Jesus is good and kind and loving. Jesus will share His nature with us. With His help, it can be as natural for us to serve others as it is for an otter to turn a somersault. It can be as joyful as playing tag. When we ask Jesus to give us His nature, He can help us learn to serve each other with love.

Blind as a Bat

When bats fly, they zigzag all over, darting left and right—they are catching and eating insects. Bats may not be cuddly and cute, but if it weren't for bats, there would be way more bugs. One bat, all by itself, can catch up to 1,000 insects in an hour! Even if it's completely dark, bats still zoom around, catching bugs.

Then I will lead the blind along a way they never knew. Isaiah 42:16.

How can they do that? Radar. Bats make high-pitched squeaking sounds as they fly. They listen for the echoes that bounce back. From the echoes they are able to tell an object's shape, size, and distance. If the echo bounces back quickly, they know something is nearby—and they can tell if it is an insect to eat or a tree to dodge.

Because bats dart around so erratically, and because they can fly in the dark, some people think bats are blind. In fact, there is a saying that someone who has trouble seeing is "blind as a bat." But bats aren't blind. They can see pretty well.

Bats can see—they just act as if they can't. Jesus said that some people have the opposite problem. They can't "see"—they just act as if they can. He wasn't talking about seeing with their eyes. He meant seeing with their hearts—understanding.

Mostly He was talking about some of the Jewish leaders. "They are blind leaders," Jesus said. "And if a blind man leads another blind man, then both men will fall into a ditch" (Matthew 15:14). These leaders were complaining that Jesus didn't wash His hands according to their rules. They taught that the way to God was by following their rules. Jesus said no: "I am the way" (John 14:6). Jesus shows us the way to God.

I'll Scratch Your Back

Have you seen monkeys groom each other? One monkey sits still while the other monkey uses its fingers to comb through its hair. Dirt gets trapped in their hair; fleas and other parasites think it's a great place to live. So monkeys help each other keep clean.

Both monkeys benefit. The grooming monkey cleans the hair of the other monkey. And when it comes across a particularly luscious-looking louse, well, who can blame it for popping it into its mouth? The monkey deserves some reward for all its hard work.

It makes sense for monkeys to help each other this way. It is easier for another monkey to groom those hard-to-reach places. Grooming spreads the group's scent around so it's easier to know who belongs. Also, grooming helps them feel close to the others in their group. And the monkey who is being groomed looks so blissful!

We have a saying about cooperation: You scratch my back; I'll scratch yours. It means if you help me, I'll help you. It is important to learn how to do this.

But Jesus wants us to do more. He wants us to go beyond cooperation. Look at today's Bible text. Jesus is saying that when you have a job to do, don't just do the bare minimum in a grouchy way. Do your best. Do it with a smile. Do it graciously.

We have a saying about this too. We call it "going the second mile." It comes from Jesus' idea. Sometimes we need to cooperate even if the other person won't cooperate. We need to be willing to help even if there's nothing in it for us. We need to be willing to scratch someone else's back, even if they won't scratch ours.

Rest

Have you heard that bears hibernate? Do they sleep all winter long? They don't. Not really. When an animal really hibernates, its heart beats more slowly, it breathes less often, it does not eat. A hibernating animal's body temperature drops very low, and its body is stiff; it cannot be wakened until spring. Bats and hedgehogs hibernate. So do frogs and snakes. But not bears.

When you lie down, your sleep will be peaceful. Proverbs 3:24.

Bears become dormant in the winter. They sleep a lot, through most of the winter, but they will wake up if they are disturbed. Their temperature drops only a little. On a warm winter day a bear might wake up and go out for a snack before going back to bed. A mother bear gives birth to cubs (usually twins) in the winter. She wakes up for that.

Bears don't hibernate. But in the winter they have a really good sleep.

Think about the people of Jesus' time. They had to work so hard just to stay alive. Life was hard. They had many problems. They must have been tired all the time.

Here is what Jesus said to them: "Come to me, all of you who are tired and have heavy loads. I will give you rest" (Matthew 11:28).

Jesus says this to us today, too. There are still people who are tired all the time. They are worried. Life is hard for many people. What they would like, more than anything else, is some rest.

Jesus can give us rest. We can give our problems to Him, and He will help us carry them. He can give us peace of mind, so at night we can have a really good sleep.

Building a Dam

Beavers are very good builders. First of all, they build a dam. They cut down trees with their teeth and drag them to the stream. Then they jam sticks into the bottom of the stream, holding them down with rocks. They keep adding branches until water backs up behind the dam. They coat the dam with mud to make it watertight and strong.

Then they have built not only a dam but a pond. They want to build their lodge in the middle of the pond so the lodge can have an underwater entrance. This hidden entrance keeps them safe from their enemies.

The pond has to be just right. If it isn't deep enough, the entrance won't be hidden under the water. If it is too deep, the water will rise too high in the lodge and cover the shelf where the beavers sleep and eat and raise their babies. The dam is important; the beavers not only build it carefully; they check it often to fix any leaks.

You could think of your feelings as being like a dam. You need to keep them from springing leaks. Look at today's Bible text. If you lose control and start a quarrel with someone, you might say words that you don't really mean. Once your anger has sprung a leak, words can keep pouring out—angry words that can do a lot of damage.

This text is good advice. You can keep your feelings in good repair. It takes two people to fight. You can stop a quarrel before the words ruin a friendship. Don't let a quarrel get started; Jesus can help you repair the leak right away with kind words.

The First People

On the sixth day of Creation God made the wild animals, the tame animals, and all the small crawling animals. He saw that this was good. But He wasn't done yet. Everything was ready for God to make people.

On the first day of Creation, when God made light, He said, "Let there be light" (Genesis 1:3). And there it was. On the fifth day, when God made birds, He said, "Let birds fly in the air above the earth" (verse 20). And it happened. But when God made the first man, it was different.

The Bible says, "Then the Lord God took dust from the ground and formed man from it. The Lord breathed the breath of life into the man's nose. And the man became a living person" (Genesis 2:7). That was Adam.

God gave Adam an assignment. He asked Adam to give names to all the animals. "He brought them to the man so the man could name them" (verse 19). As he was doing this, Adam realized that each animal had a mate. There were two lions and two squirrels and two frogs, but there was only one human. Adam saw that he was alone.

God said, "It is not good for the man to be alone. I will make a helper who is right for him" (verse 18). God put Adam into a deep sleep and took a rib from Adam's body. God used the rib to make a woman; her name was Eve. Now Adam had a wife and Eve had a husband. They weren't alone. They had each other.

Then God said, "Let us make human beings in our image and likeness." Genesis 1:26.

163

Rule Over the Earth

When God created Adam and Eve, He gave them a blessing. But He also gave them a responsibility. He put them in charge. God told Adam and Eve, "Rule over the fish in the sea and over the birds in the sky. Rule over every living thing that moves on the earth" (Genesis 1:28). God told humans to take care of the earth.

God made us light, air, water, plants, sun, animals. He gave us the earth, filled with treasures. The earth takes good care of us.

And we must take good care of it.

We must not waste it. There is only so much water. There are only so many trees. This is all the air we've got. We can't be greedy. There are lots of people; we've got to share.

We must keep it clean. In school your teacher makes you clean up any messes you make. At home you have to clean up after yourself. It's the same with the earth. Don't make a mess. And if you do, clean it up. Want to go the second mile? Clean up litter you didn't throw. Get other people to help you.

We must appreciate it. It's easy to just stay inside. But think of the joys waiting outdoors: playing in the snow, listening to the birds, feeling the sun on your skin, climbing a tree. Don't ignore it or take it for granted. Enjoy it.

We must do our best. The earth God created for us gives us so much. It is our responsibility to rule over it wisely.

Lifeblood

On the sixth day of Creation God made humans. Humans are really interesting. For instance, have you ever put your fingers on top of a bright flashlight? You fingers turn bright red! It looks very weird, especially in the dark. What is going on?

The flashlight is bright enough to shine through your fingers. The light is able to show you the color inside your fingers—the color of your blood. The blood that is flowing through the blood vessels in your fingers is red.

Some people can see their veins showing through the skin on their arms. And those veins are blue. If our blood is red, why are those veins blue? They're full of blood.

That blood is blue. Blood is not always red; it changes color. Your blood is red when it is full of oxygen. When the blood passes through the lungs, it picks up oxygen and is bright red. As the blood travels through the rest of your body, it delivers the oxygen to the cells that need it. As it loses its oxygen, the blood becomes a dark blue, and it travels back to the heart and lungs to pick up more oxygen.

Our blood is like a river traveling through our bodies, delivering food and oxygen to every cell. A river of life.

In the Bible, blood is often used as another word for life. "He shed His blood" is another way of saying "He gave His life." And sometimes blood is used as a symbol for death. So when we say we are saved by Jesus' blood, we mean that He died for us.

He is the One who loves us. And he is the One who made us free from our sins with the blood of his death. Revelation 1:5.

Second Nature

I do not understand the things I do. I do not do the good things I want to do. And I do the bad things I hate to do. Romans 7:15.

Your can think about breathing. You can hold your breath when you jump into the swimming pool. You can take a big breath to blow out the candles on your birthday cake.

You can think about breathing, but you don't have to. There's a part of your brain that lets your breathing be automatic so you don't have to think about it all the time.

Sometimes you think about breathing; sometimes you don't. It's the same with the way you act. Sometimes you think about the things you do; sometimes you don't.

You might think about playing the piano: "Should I practice or not? If I don't, I'll do a terrible job at my piano lesson, but I don't really feel like it now . . . blah, blah, blah." Or you might just be walking by the piano and sit down and start playing for fun.

You can also think about being good, or you can just be good. It is very hard to try to be good—you know that. The apostle Paul knew it too. Look at today's Bible text. It is not our nature to be good. But Jesus will help us. And as we keep trying (and Jesus keeps helping), being good starts to become a part of us so that we don't have to think about it so much. It becomes automatic, like breathing.

When people do something so much that it seems to be automatic, we say that it is second nature to them. Goodness can become second nature to you. As you learn to be like Jesus you can go through your life being kind and loving and thoughtful. That will be the kind of person you are. It will be your second nature.

Sleeping

Your may not like to admit it, but you need to sleep. When you were a baby you slept about 15 hours a day. (Your parents may not remember it being nearly that much, but it's probably true all the same.) As you get older you need less sleep, but even grown-ups need about eight hours of sleep at night.

I go to bed and sleep in peace. Lord, only you keep me safe. Psalm 4:8.

You need to sleep because your body needs to rest. You are so busy all day long. Your muscles get tired from all that running and playing. Your brain gets tired from all that thinking and learning. Your energy gets all used up.

While you are sleeping, your muscles and insides get to relax and take a break. Your body stores up more energy so you can be busy again tomorrow. Your brain gets to sort out all the things you discovered and thought about during the day.

Some people don't like to go to sleep. Some people put off bedtime as long as they can by begging for just one more story or by getting up for another drink of water or by thinking of one more question to ask. Maybe they are afraid they'll miss something while they are sleeping. Maybe they are afraid of the dark.

Here is a good thing to remember when you go to bed: God doesn't sleep. All day and all night He takes care of you. The Bible says, "He who guards you never sleeps. . . . The Lord will guard you as you come and go, both now and forever" (Psalm 121:3-8).

Sleep tight.

Neat and Clean

How do you feel about getting your fingernails cut? Some kids put up quite a fuss. But you have to keep your nails short or else they can break or rip—that can hurt. It doesn't really hurt when you cut your nails. Nails don't have any "feeling" at the tip.

You have to cut your nails because they grow. Nails are formed from skin that has hardened. If you look at your nail, you can see a white curved shape. Just beyond this, under the skin, is the root, where the nail grows. The white part is the new nail, and it is still a little soft. It will get harder as it grows so it can protect the top of your finger.

Besides keeping your nails short, it is also important to keep them clean. Dirty fingernails can make you sick. And they look dreadful.

So are you tired of this topic yet? Fingernails are boring to hear about and boring to take care of, but you've got to keep them under control if you're going to be civilized.

It's the same with your temper. You have to manage it, just as you have to manage your nails. You need a temper. If people never got angry or upset, no one would ever try to fight injustice or make things right. A selfish temper can cause nothing but trouble. But a temper that is used to help others can do a lot of good.

The trick is keeping your temper under control. Jesus can help you do that. He understands about tempers. When Jesus was on earth, He got angry. But it was never a selfish anger. His temper was always under control. You can give Him your temper too, and ask Him to keep it under control.

Your Mind's Eye

Imagine that you are making your bed. (I hope it is not too difficult for you to imagine such a thing.) Can you "picture" your bed in your mind? While you are imagining, can you "see" yourself pulling up the blankets and smoothing the bedspread?

I will put my teachings in their minds. And I will write them on their hearts. I will be their God, and they will be my people. Jeremiah 31:33.

When you think about something so that you can see it in your brain with your imagination, we say that you are seeing with your mind's eye.

You use part of your brain when you see something. You use another part when you do something. And in between those two parts of your brain is the part you use as your mind's eye. You use this part of your brain to make certain kinds of plans.

Let's say you see your neighbor and wave to him. What just happened? You used one part of your brain to see your neighbor. You used another part of your brain to wave. But in the split second between "seeing" and "waving," your mind's eye practiced waving. You rehearsed what you were going to do. You decided that waving your hand after seeing your neighbor was a good thing to do.

This is an important part of your brain. It can help you in many different ways. While you are playing basketball, just before you actually throw the ball, imagine throwing it and making the shot. Your mind's eye can help you focus and do your best.

Look at today's Bible text. We can ask God to put His teachings in our minds. When we invite Jesus into our hearts, it is as if we are inviting Him into our mind's eye. There He can help us make good choices and do our best.

169

Listen

Have you ever heard a recording of your voice? Sometimes when people hear their voice on an answering machine or a home movie, they think, *That doesn't sound like me!* even though everyone tells them that's exactly what they sound like.

When you speak, your vocal cords vibrate, making sound waves. When others hear your voice, they only hear the sound waves traveling in the air. You hear those air-traveling sound waves too, but you also hear sound waves that are traveling through the bones in your head. Because you hear your voice through two pathways instead of just one, your voice sounds slightly different to you than to everyone else.

There's another pathway of hearing. Have you ever heard your conscience? Perhaps you've been tempted to do something and a little voice inside your head tells you that would be the wrong thing to do. Or maybe you've seen someone who looks lonely and you get the feeling that you should go talk to them. This doesn't have anything to do with sound waves. How do we get these feelings?

Jesus sends them. Before Jesus died He told His disciples that He was going away. But He promised to send a Helper so that we would know how to live—the Holy Spirit. Jesus promises that the Spirit "will lead you into all truth" (John 16:13).

The Spirit will help you do the right thing. The Spirit will be your conscience. It takes practice to hear the voice of your conscience. That voice can be very quiet. Listen.

That Smells Good

Let's say you've been playing outside. You aren't particularly hungry because you ate lunch not too long ago. But you are thirsty, so you go inside to get a drink of water. And the minute you walk in the door you know that someone is baking bread. You can smell it. And all of a sudden you are hungry. You want some of that bread.

If the whole body were an ear, the body would not be able to smell anything.
1 Corinthians 12:17.

Smell is an odd thing. It is strangely powerful. Smelling is done inside your nose. When you smell a flower, extremely tiny bits of the flower float through the air into your nose. Sensors in your nose send messages to your brain about the smell, and your brain memorizes that information. So smell can help you remember things—such as that bread is very good to eat. I think the memory for popcorn might be even stronger.

You probably know that it is a good thing for you to read your Bible and learn more about God each day. But sometimes you just might not feel like it.

So what should you do? Remember the power of smell. Remember that you didn't want the bread until you smelled it. If you try to read a little of the Bible, you might remember how wonderful it is, and then you'll want more.

First you smell the bread, then you want to taste it. Smelling is very nice, but when it comes to bread, tasting is what it's all about.

The Bible says, "Taste and see that the Lord is good" (Psalm 34:8, NIV). Isn't that odd? It doesn't say "listen" or "read." It says "taste." We need to experience Jesus. We need to know Him, not just know about Him.

You Can't Believe Your Eyes

Faith means knowing that something is real even if we do not see it. Hebrews 11:1.

Have you ever seen an optical illusion? Maybe on a hot day the road ahead looks like it is wet, but when you get there it is dry. Or maybe you see a stick in the grass and for a split second you think it is a snake.

Your eyes are playing tricks on you. The road surface looks wavy like water because the light is bent by the waves of hot air rising from the road. Or maybe you are scared of snakes, so whenever your eyes see anything that even remotely looks like a snake, your mind goes "Yikes!" Optical illusions fool your eyes.

Faith is sort of the opposite of an optical illusion. An optical illusion is something you see but can't believe. Faith is something you believe but can't see.

After Jesus was raised to life, He went to see the disciples. Thomas wasn't there; when he came back, the other disciples told him they had seen Jesus. Thomas said, "I will not believe it until I see the nail marks in his hands" (John 20:25).

Thomas had trouble with faith. Thomas had seen Jesus heal the sick and feed the 5,000 and still the storm. But he had also seen Jesus die on the cross, and that's all he could remember right then. Thomas's faith wasn't strong enough to remember all the things he knew about Jesus. Later, when Jesus came back, Thomas saw and believed.

We can't believe our eyes. We have never seen Jesus. We need faith to know that Jesus is real, because we cannot see Him. Even though we can't see Jesus, we can learn about Him. And the more we know about Jesus, the stronger our faith will be.

Pass the Salt

People who have been cooking for a long time know how cooking works, so if they read something weird in a recipe, they might decide to do things another way.

When you talk, you should always be kind and wise. Colossians 4:6.

For instance, let's say a good cook is making soup. The recipe calls for two tablespoons of salt. That's a lot of salt! The cook adds one tablespoon of salt, lets it cook for a little while, and then tastes it. If it needs more salt, the cook will add a little more. The cook knows this rule: You can always add more salt, but you can't take it away.

If you have ever eaten a potato chip, you know that salt tastes good. Food that doesn't have salt can be very boring. Would you even bother to eat a potato chip if it didn't have salt on it? Salt makes eating interesting.

Here is another version of today's Bible text: "Let your conversation be always full of grace, seasoned with salt, so that you may know how to answer everyone" (NIV).

What do you think it means to season your conversation with salt? Perhaps it means that you should try not to be boring. When you talk to other people, think about what they are interested in. Perhaps it means that you should be thoughtful and kind—be careful not to hurt their feelings. Perhaps it means you should be pleasant—don't whine.

And remember the cook's rule: You can always add more salt, but you can't take it away. Once you say it, you can't unsay it. Think before you speak.

When Jesus spoke, His words were seasoned with salt. People crowded around to listen. Jesus can help you learn to salt your words until they are just right.

173

Alarm Clocks

I praise you because you made me in an amazing and wonderful way. Psalm 139:14.

Has your leg ever gone to sleep? You might be sitting there with your leg tucked under you when all of a sudden your leg starts tingling and buzzing. It feels like it's being poked by hundreds of tiny pins and needles. Why does that happen? It is so weird.

When you sit on your feet, your nerves get squished between the bones in your foot and the hard floor or chair. To make it worse, you are sitting on your feet, so all that weight is pushing down on your poor nerves. They can't take the pressure. Your squashed nerves begin to go numb. They can no longer get messages from your brain.

So they get your attention by tingling. And you can't ignore it. You get off your knees, you hop around, you rub your leg, you get the circulation going again.

Who knows why they call it "going to sleep." It seems like a better term would be "waking you up." It's more like an alarm clock than a lullaby.

Our bodies are smart. God made them so that they can figure out the right thing to do in order to stay healthy. For instance, if we cut our finger, it hurts. So we bandage it. If we get a cold, we get tired. So we go to bed and get some rest, if we have any sense.

Some of these "alarm clocks" are easy to hear, such as when your foot goes to sleep. Others—getting rest, for instance—are harder to hear. And some are so hard to hear that we sometimes hear the opposite instead, eating brussel sprouts, for example.

You can train yourself to listen to your body. Learn to listen to your "alarm clocks."

Wrinkles

Have you noticed that the skin on your fingers and toes gets wrinkly when you spend a long time in the bathtub or swimming pool? Do you know why? It's the water.

Do not be interested only in your own life, but be interested in the lives of others. Philippians 2:4.

Normally your skin cells just lie side by side in a row, nice and flat. But when you stay in the water a long time, your skin cells soak up water and swell up. The skin on the inside of your hands and the bottom of your feet is thicker than the skin on other parts of your body. There isn't room for those skin cells to lie flat next to each other after they have soaked up so much water, so they bunch up and make wrinkles.

After you get out of the tub, the water gradually dries up and the wrinkles go away. But they look funny for a while. Do you say, "I'm going to quit having fun in the water because I don't want any ugly wrinkles"? Of course not. That would be silly. Someone who worries about something like that is way too worried about how they look.

We say that people who think about themselves all the time are self-conscious. Self-conscious people worry about how they look and what other people might think.

Jesus was not self-conscious. He noticed when people were hungry. He noticed when the children were being shooed away, and He stopped to spend time with them. He noticed, when He was dying, that his mother was sad; He asked John to take care of her.

Jesus was always thinking of others. You can be thoughtful, like Jesus. Before you say something, you can think about how it will make the other person feel. Before you do something, you can think about how it will affect others. Jesus will help.

175

Growwww!!

Have you ever been sitting in church when your stomach starts to growl? Your siblings might find it amusing, but for you it is probably embarrassing. The worst part is that you can't control the noise. There is no way to make your stomach growl softer. Your only option is to act as if the noise is coming from the person sitting next to you.

Or you could do the one thing that will stop your stomach from growling: you could eat. Your stomach is growling because it is empty. Your stomach moves all the time—usually it is busy digesting your food by pushing it and squeezing it. However, when all the food is digested your stomach keeps moving, even though there is nothing left but air. The rumbly, growly noises are made by your stomach pushing air around.

Look at Psalm 136. It's an unusual psalm. Every other line is exactly the same. But there is something else special about this psalm. When you read it carefully, you can see two main ideas: (1) God is the God of creation, and (2) God is the God of history.

Verses 1-9 talk about how God created the heavens and earth. Verses 10-24 talk about how God rescued the Israelites. Then there is something odd. There is one little verse, all by itself—today's Bible text. Why do you suppose that is there?

Because food is important, that's why. The God who created the world, the God who controls history, is the same God who gives us food. God's love is seen in creation and in history—and in the food we eat every day.

That's why this psalm mentions food. And that's why we "say grace" before meals. We thank God for our food. His love continues forever.

Yawn!

Imagine that it is a nice, warm day and you just ate a really good lunch, maybe a little too much lunch. Now you are sitting at your desk. It's time for social studies.

If we love each other, God's love has reached its goal. 1 John 4:12.

You're not really sleepy. You're not really bored—well, maybe just a little. But you can't seem to concentrate. Your brain feels dull. Fortunately, your brain knows what it needs to do. Your mouth opens wide and you gulp in a lot of air. Why did you yawn?

You weren't getting enough oxygen. You were a little tired and a little bored. Your brain was getting sluggish. The respiratory center in your brain made you yawn. Once you send the extra oxygen to your brain, it clears up and you become awake again.

You don't usually yawn on purpose. Your brain does it automatically whenever it feels as if you need it. Sometimes your brain wants you to yawn when it is not an appropriate time. Then you either have to try to stop it or try to hide it. Good luck.

An odd thing about yawns is that they're contagious. When you see someone yawn, it usually makes you want to yawn. Even stranger, sometimes just talking about yawning makes you want to yawn.

Today's Bible text says God's love is contagious. Because He loves us, we are able to share that love with others. We share without having to stop and think about it—it's automatic, the way we automatically yawn when we need to wake up. When someone needs help, we automatically offer to help. God's love can help us become kind and loving and thoughtful—and that will help others want to be kind and loving, too.

Belly Buttons

The next time you catch a frog, carefully turn it over and look for its belly button. You won't find it. Frogs don't have belly buttons. Neither do birds or spiders or snakes. That's because they hatch out of eggs.

You have a belly button because you grew inside your mother, not inside an eggshell. While you were there you got your food and oxygen through a cord. When you were born, the cord was cut because you didn't need it any more. But it left behind a little mark—your belly button. Your belly button proves that you were born.

A man named Nicodemus came to see Jesus one night. Jesus told him, "Unless one is born again, he cannot be in God's kingdom" (John 3:3). Nicodemus said, "That's impossible!" And he was right—a person can be born only once.

But that's not what Jesus meant, is it? Jesus often taught ideas by saying that something was like something else. When Jesus said that we must be born again, He was talking about new beginnings. When we choose to follow Jesus, we leave our old sinful, selfish life behind and start over. That's like being born and becoming a new person.

It is impossible for you to go back to being a tiny baby, to be born again. And it is impossible for you to change by yourself, to stop being selfish on your own, to quit sinning through your own power. You need Jesus to help you.

When you are born again, you don't get another belly button. But there is another mark. Look at today's text. When you love others, it shows that you've been born again.

Keep Growing

So you must be perfect, just as your Father in heaven is perfect. Matthew 5:48.

Have you ever been playing in a swimming pool when your mom or dad says you have to get out now? Don't you just wish you could stay in there forever?

Well, you probably wish it, but you don't really mean it. After a while you'd get hungry and you'd want to get out and eat. Or you'd get sleepy (yes, you would) and you'd want to get out and go to bed. Or you'd have to go to the bathroom, and you know you have to get out of the pool for that.

It is good to enjoy what you are doing. But you've got to also be willing to move on to the next thing. You don't want to get stuck doing one thing all the time. There's so much more to do and learn and see. You need to keep growing.

It is best to keep growing as a Christian. One time the apostle Paul scolded his friends in a letter. He told them, "I had to talk to you as I would to . . . babies in Christ. The teaching I gave you was like milk, not solid food" (1 Corinthians 3:1, 2). Paul wanted his friends to keep learning about Jesus, to keep studying the Scripture, to keep becoming more and more perfect.

Yes, perfect. Look what Jesus said in today's Bible text. He meant perfect, all right, but He didn't so much mean "perfect right now" as "on the way to perfect." Right now you're pretty good. But, to be honest, you know you could be better. Each day you can ask Jesus to help you be more thoughtful and loving, to be kinder and better. Each day you can get a little closer to perfect. But you've got to be willing to keep growing.

It Was Very Good

So the sky, the earth and all that filled them were finished. Genesis 2:1.

On the sixth day of Creation God made animals and humans. And then, today's Bible text says, Creation was finished. The sky was finished. The earth was finished. Everything that filled them—finished.

"God looked at everything he had made, and it was very good" (Genesis 1:31). The sky was good. The earth was good. Everything that filled them—very good.

Very good indeed. Perfect, actually. Everything was perfectly beautiful. Everything worked perfectly. Everything was perfect.

Even the humans. Adam and Eve were perfect. They had been made in God's image. Their character was like God's character. None of the other animals on earth had been created in God's image. Humans were put in charge of the new world and all its creatures. They were given a special relationship with God.

Adam and Eve were given the ability to think and understand and make choices. They were able to choose whether or not they would follow God's plan.

"God blessed them and said, 'Have many children and grow in number. Fill the earth and be its master'" (verse 28).

That was God's plan. Adam and Eve would talk with the angels and walk with God. They would take care of the world and be friends with the animals. They would have lots of children, and everyone would be very happy.

That was God's plan. At the end of the sixth day God saw that it was very good.

The Seventh Day

Everything was finished on the sixth day of Creation. But there is one more day in creation week—the seventh day. "On the seventh day he rested from all his work. God blessed the seventh day and made it a holy day" Genesis 2:2, 3.

On the seventh day of Creation God created the Sabbath. He gave us another present, another blessing. He gave us a holy day.

At the end of the sixth day Adam and Eve watched the sunset for the first time. And that was the beginning of the first Sabbath.

The Sabbath is a day of rest. On the seventh day God quit working. He took the time to enjoy His marvelous new world.

He spent time with Adam and Eve. Perhaps they walked around, making friends with the new animals, trying out delicious things to eat. They probably did a lot of talking; no doubt Adam and Eve had questions, lots of questions.

That first Sabbath was perfect, just like the rest of creation. God decided that we should have a Sabbath every week. We work hard all week; we need the break. But that's not the only reason God gave us the Sabbath.

The Sabbath helps us remember Creation. On Sabbath we remember who created us and gave us our world. And we celebrate.

In six days the Lord made everything. He made the sky, earth, sea and everything in them. And on the seventh day, he rested. So the Lord blessed the Sabbath day and made it holy. Exodus 20:11.

Rechargeable

Now God has left us that promise that we may enter and have his rest. Hebrews 4:1.

How does a battery make a flashlight light up? The battery creates electricity.

Everything is made of tiny particles called atoms. Atoms have even tinier electrons flying around them. The electrons of some metals are able to move around between atoms.

A battery has a special mixture of chemicals inside it. When you flip the switch on your flashlight, a wire connects the plus sign at the top of the battery with the minus sign at the bottom. Because of the chemicals, the free-flowing electrons are able to travel through the wire. This flow of electrons is called an electrical current. That electricity lights up the bulb in your flashlight.

What would happen if you forgot to turn your flashlight off? The light would get dimmer and dimmer and eventually go out. The battery would go dead. All the electrons would be used up. The power would be exhausted.

Sometimes we say we need to get our batteries recharged, and we don't mean our flashlight batteries. We mean that we are tired. Our bodies are tired. Our brains are tired. We need to rest. We need to get our energy back.

That's why God created the Sabbath. We can't work all the time. We need to rest. Sabbath gives us a break from our work. It gives us a chance to sit back and enjoy life. We are refreshed, energized. Sabbath takes us from exhausted back to exhilarated.

Special

Probably the most special day of the year is your birthday, don't you think? Your birthday is special in so many ways.

Special means that something is uncommon, it's not everyday. Your birthday is not everyday—it comes only once a year.

And *special* means that it's important. You birthday is certainly important.

But Christmas is special too. Christmas comes only once a year. And Christmas is important to lots and lots of people. Is Christmas more special than your birthday?

Well, *special* also means that something is unique. Lots and lots of people celebrate Christmas. But your birthday belongs to you. (Oh sure, a few other people have the same birth date as you. But even that is special; when you find out that you share a birthday, you have a special connection with that person.)

Your birthday is special, all right. We sing you a special song. We bake you a special cake. We decorate it with a special number of candles. We give you presents and throw parties. We celebrate the fact that you were born. It's a special day.

Special days are uncommon, important, unique. Sabbath is definitely a special day. We get to do special things. We wear special clothes. We eat special food. We get to be with our favorite people. We get to spend the day with God. Sabbath is a special day full of special blessings.

You should call the Sabbath a joyful day. You should honor the Lord's holy day. Isaiah 58:13.

Together

It's nice when your teacher hands out a worksheet and it turns out to be a crossword puzzle. But it's even nicer when she says you can do the puzzle with a partner.

It's good to eat an ice-cream sundae. But it's even better when you get hot fudge and your dad gets butterscotch and your dad asks if you want a taste.

It's wonderful when your mom takes you to the pool, but it's even more wonderful when she says you can bring a friend.

Some really great things are even greater when you can do them with someone else. Like Sabbath.

Sabbath is a great idea. But one of the best things about Sabbath is the chance to be together.

God created Sabbath because He wants to spend time with us. Sabbath is a wonderful chance to get together with God.

On Sabbath we get the chance to worship God with other people. At church we get to be with other people who believe in the same things.

Sabbath is also a good time to be together with our families. During the week our lives get so busy. On Sabbath it's awfully nice to just spend time together.

On Sabbath we spend time with God, with our families, and with other believers. Sabbath is even better because we can be together.

It's the Law

Let's say a friend tells you that she likes your shirt, especially the color. She thinks you should always wear blue, because it really looks nice on you.

Remember to keep the Sabbath as a holy day. Exodus 20:8.

Are you required to wear blue from now on? Is that the law? No, of course not. It's just a suggestion, just good advice. You don't have to wear blue if you don't want to.

Now, you don't have to wear blue clothes. But you do have to wear clothes. That's not just good advice. That's the law.

It's important to know the difference between advice and the law. If you didn't know the difference, you could make two kinds of mistakes.

You could always do everything everybody suggested—even if it was just advice. Then you would always wear blue, except for when you were with someone who thought you looked better in green or stripes. And you'd never get to wear your favorite color.

Or you could treat everything like a suggestion, and ignore some laws that shouldn't be ignored—like running in the halls or wearing a seat belt or wearing clothes.

Advice is not the law. And the law is not advice.

What about the Sabbath? Is it the law, or is it just good advice? Well, it is a very good thing to keep the Sabbath. But it is not just good advice. God does not just make the suggestion that we keep the Sabbath.

The Bible says that it is the law. It is one of the Ten Commandments, one of God's important laws. God wants us to keep the Sabbath holy.

The Sabbath Is a Gift

When Jesus was here on earth, He kept the Sabbath. However, many of the Pharisees and other Jewish leaders didn't think He kept it properly. They didn't like what Jesus did on Sabbath. They were upset because He broke their rules.

The Sabbath commandment says that no one should do any work on the Sabbath. But that wasn't specific enough for the Jewish leaders—they had made up lots of rules that explained exactly what was meant by *work*.

For instance, there was a list of 39 different types of work that were forbidden on Sabbath. One of the types of work was carrying a burden. They also decided what a burden was. A burden was anything that weighed as much as two dried figs.

People were not allowed to carry things or cook or walk more than a few steps. According to these rules, if you even thought about work you were breaking the Sabbath.

One Sabbath, while Jesus and His disciples were walking by some fields, the disciples picked some grain and ate it while they were walking along. Some Pharisees saw this and accused Jesus of letting His disciples break the Sabbath.

Jesus told them that the Sabbath was created for people to enjoy. People were not created to be ruled by the Sabbath. The rules were destroying the Sabbath blessings. People were so worried about breaking the rules—the Sabbath was a day of worry, not a day of joy and peace. God gave the Sabbath to us as a gift, not a burden.

Revenge

Do you remember what we were talking about way back in March, before we got carried away with talking about Creation? The war in heaven. Lucifer.

So, everything was perfect in this new world, Earth. The world was perfect; its creatures were perfect. It was very good, and everyone was very happy.

Except for Lucifer. He wasn't happy.

He had a new name: Satan. He couldn't very well be called Lucifer now; he was no longer a light bearer. He wasn't light; he was darkness.

Satan hated this new world and everything in it. He hated that everyone was happy. He hated that everything was perfect.

Satan wanted to prove that he had been right—that God was a tyrant and that God's law was impossible. But this new world was proving the opposite. It was proving that Satan was wrong. Adam and Eve were happy. They loved to obey God.

Also, Satan was jealous. He saw the beautiful Garden of Eden and he wanted it. He wanted control of Earth. He wanted to set up his kingdom there, a kingdom against God, a kingdom that would prove that God was wrong.

Satan decided to find a way to trick Adam and Eve, the way he had tricked some of the angels in heaven. He vowed to get Adam and Eve to disobey God.

Satan wanted revenge.

Be careful! The devil is your enemy. And he goes around like a roaring lion looking for someone to eat. 1 Peter 5:8.

187

Deceit

But the snake said to the woman, "You will not die." Genesis 3:4.

Adam and Eve had a test to show that they chose to follow God's rules. God put a tree in the middle of the Garden, and He told them, "You may eat the fruit from any tree in the garden. But you must not eat the fruit from the tree which gives the knowledge of good and evil. If you ever eat fruit from that tree, you will die!" (Genesis 2:16, 17).

Naturally, that is the way Satan decided to trick them.

Adam and Eve had been warned about Satan. The angels had told them about the war in heaven. Adam and Eve were on the alert for Satan.

But they weren't on the alert for a snake. So when Eve was walking by the tree one day and a snake began talking to her, she was probably startled and curious, but she wasn't afraid. She liked snakes—she loved all the animals—so she was no doubt thrilled to discover an animal that could talk.

And this snake had such fascinating ideas. The snake told Eve that he was able to talk because he had been eating the fruit from the tree he was in, the tree of knowledge of good and evil. This should have been a clue who the snake really was, but she missed it.

The snake told Eve that if she ate some fruit, she would receive extra powers, too. And that the reason God didn't want them to eat the fruit was that He didn't want them to be as smart as He was. And of course they wouldn't die.

The snake was so charming. His words were so beautiful. Eve didn't see that Satan was actually saying that God was a liar. Eve picked some fruit and ate it.

The Fall

After Eve ate the fruit from the forbidden tree, she picked some more and ran to find Adam. She began chattering about how she'd found a talking snake and how clever he was, while Adam just stood there, staring aghast at the fruit in her hands. When she noticed, she said, no, no, it's all right, the snake told me all about the tree. And she kept explaining, but Adam wasn't fooled by the snake's arguments.

Trust the Lord with all your heart. Don't depend on your own understanding. Proverbs 3:5.

But what was Adam going to do? He knew that Eve had been tricked. She had failed their test. Now Eve was going to die, and Adam couldn't imagine living without her. He took the fruit and ate it, knowing that this meant he would die too.

When Eve took her first bite of fruit, she didn't fall over and die. The fruit wasn't like poison. When Adam ate the fruit, God didn't send lightning to strike him dead. Adam and Eve didn't die instantly. But that is when they began to die.

When Adam and Eve chose to eat the fruit, they chose to disobey God. They chose not to follow God's plan. They sinned. We call this "The Fall."

When they sinned, things were no longer perfect. Things began to go wrong. Adam and Eve were no longer happy. They argued with each other; they blamed each other. They were worried and embarrassed.

Look at today's Bible verse. How different things would be if Adam and Eve had trusted in God instead of in their own understanding!

The Wages of Sin

*When someone sins,
he earns what sin
pays—death.
Romans 6:23.*

After Adam and Eve sinned, God sorrowfully went down to earth to explain what they had done and what would happen next. Usually when God came to visit, Adam and Eve came running to meet Him. But this time they hid, while God walked among the trees and called, "Where are you?"

Finally they crept out of their hiding place. God asked, "Did you eat fruit from that tree?" (Genesis 3:11). And right away they began making excuses and blaming someone else. Eve said, "The snake tricked me" (verse 13). Adam blamed Eve, his beloved wife whom he couldn't bear to live without just a little while ago. And Adam even tried to blame God by saying, "You gave this woman to me" (verse 12).

Sin was already changing everything. Things were beginning to go wrong.

God told Adam and Eve that they'd have to leave the garden. Adam and Eve were so sorry. They promised they would never disobey again. They had learned their lesson. Couldn't they please have another chance?

But it was too late. Sin was already there, changing things. They couldn't take it back. Things could no longer be perfect. They had broken their connection with God.

Now life would be difficult. They would have to work hard to grow food to eat. The animals would be afraid of them—some would even become fierce and begin to eat other animals. And saddest of all, Adam and Eve couldn't be with God face to face anymore. No more walks together. No more talks. Sin separated them from God.

The Plan to Save

Ood was heartbroken. His people, His best creation, had chosen to disobey Him. He couldn't bear to let them go, to lose them forever. God the Father and God the Son began to work on a plan to save the earth.

Christ Jesus came into the world to save sinners. 1 Timothy 1:15.

Angels went to comfort poor Adam and Eve, who were miserable, scared, and lonely. The angels told them that God had a plan; it was going to be all right.

God had a plan to save those who broke the law. The law does not change. The law had been broken, and a penalty had to be paid. God couldn't just ignore this—even if they said they were sorry and promised never to do it again. That would be chaos. That would not be a good plan.

The penalty had to be paid. God the Son volunteered to pay it. He offered to take the punishment for their sin. That meant He would have to die for our sins.

It was a difficult plan, but it would work. The angels were troubled when they first heard about it, but God explained that the plan could save Adam and Eve and all the people who would live on this earth. And the plan would also destroy sin—it would bring peace back to heaven and earth. It was a wonderful plan.

Angels explained the plan to Adam and Eve—the plan of redemption. Redemption means to rescue, to buy back. Adam and Eve would be redeemed. They would be rescued from sin. God the Son would be the Redeemer. He would pay for their sins by taking their place—He would buy them back.

The Lamb

You were bought with the precious blood of the death of Christ, who was like a pure and perfect lamb.

1 Peter 1:19.

Adam and Eve struggled to understand the mysteries of the plan of redemption. How could the Son give up His life? How could God give up His Son? They couldn't comprehend such love, but they grabbed that hope, that promise, and they didn't let it go.

And in order that they would not let it go, God told Adam and Eve to do something to help them remember. They were to sacrifice a lamb—they would kill a lamb as an offering to God.

It was difficult to do this. Every time the lamb died, they remembered that the penalty for sin was death. Every time they sacrificed a lamb, they thought about the horrible results of sin.

The sacrifice made them think. It helped them understand.

The sacrifice of the lamb represented the sacrifice that God the Son was going to make. The lamb represented Jesus—innocent, gentle, perfect. When they offered their sacrifice, they showed that they believed in God's plan, that their Redeemer would come.

Jesus did come to earth, many years later. John the Baptist was a prophet who preached that the Messiah was coming to redeem His people. John recognized that Jesus was the Redeemer he had been preaching about. When he saw Jesus, John called out, "Look, the Lamb of God. He takes away the sins of the world!" (John 1:29). John saw that the Lamb of God had come to fulfill the plan of redemption.

Spinning Tops

Your can make a top. Cut a circle out of a piece of cardboard. Poke a short, sharp pencil through the center of the circle. Set the point of the pencil on the table, hold the eraser end with your thumb and finger, and set your new top spinning.

If it doesn't spin well, try sliding the circle to different positions along the pencil, and make sure the circle isn't lopsided. You'll probably need to experiment a bit before you can get it to spin. You need to figure out why the top keeps falling.

Sometimes we use the word *fall* to describe when a person sins. When Adam and Eve sinned the first time, we call that the Fall. In today's Bible text, Paul is not actually talking about falling. He's talking about sinning.

Imagine a top when you read this text. A top, spinning strong and fast, hits a bump and starts to wobble, loses its balance and falls. That describes what happens to us sometimes. We think we can be good; we think we can obey the rules. And then down we go.

What should you do when that happens? Get up and try again, of course. But you can do more. You can learn from your mistakes. Figure out what went wrong.

When you make a homemade top, you try to figure out how to make it better. You can think about your life the same way. But in your life you have help. When you *fall* and sin, you don't have to get back up on your own. Jesus will help you get going again. He'll help you figure it out. Keep close to Jesus. Together you can stand strong.

So anyone who thinks he is standing strong should be careful not to fall.
1 Corinthians 10:12.

Symbols of Freedom

The Statue of Liberty has been standing in New York Harbor for more than 100 years. It was a gift to the United States from the people of France. It honors the friendship that grew between the two countries during the War of Independence.

The Statue of Liberty is more than just a statue—it's a symbol. It's a symbol of friendship between countries. And its name tells you that it's a symbol of liberty or freedom. For many people who came to the United States in a boat, the Statue of Liberty was the first thing they saw of their new country. It promised them freedom.

Symbols can be as complicated as you want them to be. You can see the statue and think, *That's a symbol of the United States.* Or you can think about freedom and friendship, the Revolutionary War and independence, liberty and justice for all, and so on.

God often uses symbols to teach us. Sacrifices were a symbol. When the people offered a lamb as a sacrifice to God, it was supposed to help them learn. It was a horrible thing to have to kill a lamb. It made them stop and think how horrible sin was.

But the sacrifice was also a symbol of hope. The lamb was a symbol of the Redeemer. The people could look forward to the day when God would send His Son to take the punishment for sin. Jesus was the Lamb of God.

We don't need to offer sacrifices anymore. Jesus has already died for our sins. But we still have symbols. The cross is a symbol of freedom. Whenever we see a cross, we remember that Jesus has saved us.

The Happiest Thing

Adam and Eve were so lonely. The animals were afraid of them. The angels didn't visit anymore. And most of all, they missed being with God.

Children are a gift from the Lord. Babies are a reward. Psalm 127:3.

Then came the happiest thing, the best possible way to get rid of the loneliness—a baby. Cain.

When you were born, your parents realized that you were the most exceptionally wonderful baby ever born. If you were their first baby, they were probably even more thrilled. And if you were the first grandchild, it's possible your grandparents were even more excited than your parents.

Now, imagine what it must have been like when the first-ever baby was born. Adam and Eve must have been so happy. They probably spent a great deal of time staring at him and marveling that he could open his eyes! And smile! And holler!

Baby Cain was the happiest thing, just what Adam and Eve needed. Now they had someone who needed them. Someone to play with and talk to and make plans for. They didn't think about the past all the time because now they had a future that they could see and touch and love.

Adam and Eve had lots more babies. They named their next baby boy Abel. Cain and Abel grew up together, as brothers and friends. Cain liked to plant things and watch them grow. He grew up to be a farmer. Abel liked to work with animals, especially sheep. Abel became a shepherd.

195

The Saddest Thing

It is better to
obey God than
to offer a sacrifice.
1 Samuel 15:22.

Many times Cain and Abel had heard the story of how they had lost their home in the Garden of Eden. They had been taught the reason they sacrificed a lamb.

It was hard to sacrifice a lamb. It was also hard to think about why it was being done. Cain didn't like to think about the fact that he needed redemption. He began to do just the sacrificing part—and skip over the thinking part.

His first mistake was not understanding that it was the thinking part that was the important part. That was the reason for the sacrifice. His next mistake was imagining that as long as he offered a sacrifice, it didn't matter what it was. He told himself that his vegetables would be a more meaningful offering because he had grown them himself.

However, God had asked them to sacrifice a lamb for a reason. The Lamb of God has to save you; you can't save yourself with things you make or do.

One day Abel sacrificed a lamb, but Cain brought fruit to the altar. God did not accept Cain's offering. Instead of being sorry, Cain became angry. He thought God wasn't being fair. He was jealous of Abel. He tried to pick a fight with his brother. Abel tried to calm him down, but Cain just got angrier—so angry that he killed his brother.

When God asked where Abel was, Cain rudely lied, "I don't know. Is it my job to take care of my brother?" (Genesis 4:9). God knew; He told Cain he would have to go away.

Poor Adam and Eve. This wasn't anything like the future they had planned for their boys. They had never imagined that sin could destroy happiness so completely.

God's Plan for Noah

God's plan to save the world didn't happen quickly. It took thousands of years. Through all those years God told people in many different ways about His plans to save them.

But Noah pleased the Lord. Genesis 6:8.

God's plan to save Noah and his family was very unusual. By the time Noah was born, the sin that had begun with Adam and Eve had just about taken over the world. Most people were wicked, and they kept getting more wicked, more selfish, more cruel. The world was an evil place. This was not what God had planned. "The Lord was sorry he had made human beings on the earth. His heart was filled with pain" (Genesis 6:6).

This was exactly what Satan had hoped would happen.

God decided to send a flood to wash away the wickedness of the world. He chose Noah to help Him because "Noah was a good man. He was the most innocent man of his time. He walked with God" (verse 9).

God talked to Noah. He pointed out that the earth was full of violence. Noah had to agree. He explained that He had decided to destroy all the people. What a difficult thing that must have been for both of them to talk about.

God told Noah that He had a plan—a plan to save the world. God made an agreement with Noah. He promised to save Noah and his family if they followed His plan.

Then God told Noah to build a boat.

Noah Follows God's Plan

Noah did everything that the Lord commanded him. Genesis 7:5.

Noah had a lot to do to get ready for the Flood. First, of course, there was that boat, the ark. It was going to be huge—it had to be because it was going to hold "two of every kind of bird, animal and crawling thing" (Genesis 6:20). Noah and his family had a lot of cypress trees to chop down and cut into boards.

But Noah had a job that was even more important than building the ark. He had to warn the people about the Flood—he wanted as many people as possible to be saved. If anyone came near, Noah seized that opportunity to talk about how wicked the world was and how God wasn't going to let it continue.

Most people thought he was crazy. He was wasting all his time and money building an enormous boat, miles away from any water. They laughed at him. They were especially amused by his preaching; they enjoyed provoking him and insulting him.

It distressed Noah when people teased, but not because it hurt his feelings. He was worried; he knew the people would die if they wouldn't listen. So he kept preaching.

When the animals started coming to the ark, people must have at least considered that Noah might be right about the Flood. But they got over their surprise and just made more jokes. Noah begged them to come inside and be safe, but they just laughed. The only people who went into the boat were Noah and his family. No one else would go.

"Then the Lord closed the door behind them" (Genesis 7:16). For seven days nothing happened. They could hear the people outside, laughing at them.

Then it began to rain.

Safely Through the Storm

The rain that created the Flood was not just a really fierce storm. "That day the underground springs split open. And the clouds in the sky poured out rain" (Genesis 7:11). The water poured from above and gushed from below.

But God remembered Noah and all the wild animals and tame animals with him in the boat. Genesis 8:1.

The people outside the ark panicked—and not just because water was blasting out of the ground. They realized Noah was right. They were going to die.

"Everything on dry land died. . . . All that was left was Noah and what was with him in the boat" (verses 22, 23). It rained for 40 days and 40 nights. The water kept rising; it lifted the ark, and the boat floated away on the sea that the world had become.

The storm must have been frightening, with the boat pitching and tossing and the wind howling. But when the rain stopped, the quiet must have been scary too. Then they had to wonder what would happen next, what their world was like now.

Several months later the ark came to rest in the mountains, but they couldn't tell how far the waters had gone down. Noah sent out birds to scout around; finally a dove brought back an olive leaf. Never has a leaf meant more.

When God finally told Noah they could leave, He didn't have to say it twice. When the angel opened that door, the animals were lined up and ready to run down the ramp, kick up their heels, and get out of there.

God had kept the ark and its precious cargo safe through the Flood.

The Smell Within

Love each other
deeply. Love has
a way of not looking
at others' sins.
1 Peter 4:8.

Some people say the church is like the ark. They have a saying: "If it wasn't for the storm without, we couldn't stand the smell within."

What does it mean? They are imagining what it must have been like on the ark. With all those animals cooped up like that, the ark must have smelled pretty bad. But even though it smelled terrible, it was better to be safe inside than to be caught in the Flood.

These people are also saying that it is like that in the church sometimes. (They usually say it when they get annoyed at other people in the church.) Sometimes other church members can drive us crazy. However, even though other church members aren't perfect, it's better to be together in the church than to be alone in the world.

When we say "the church" we can mean several things. We can mean the building: "My church is built of stone." We can mean the program that we attend on Sabbath morning: "My friend is going to sing for church today." We can mean the organization: "The Seventh-day Adventist Church sends out missionaries."

We can also mean the people of the church. We need this church for support, encouragement, comfort, friendship. We help each other. We forgive each other. And because we believe what it says in today's Bible text, because we love each other deeply, we try to live with the "smell."

God's Plan for Abraham

After the Flood the earth began to fill up with people and animals again. God wanted the people to know about His plan to save them. God chose Abram to help him.

Abram believed the Lord. And the Lord accepted Abram's faith. Genesis 15:6.

Abram worshiped God. When God told him to move to a new country, Abram did it. Then God told Abram He was going to bless him. People would see that Abram was blessed because he worshiped God. Then they would want to learn about God.

God also promised Abram, "I will make you a great nation, and I will bless you. . . . I will give this land to your descendants" (Genesis 12:2, 7). Abram was happy about this; the only problem was that Abram didn't have any descendants. What he and his wife, Sarah, wanted more than anything else was children. But they didn't have any.

God kept promising that he would. God said Abram would have descendants like the stars—more than he could count. And Abram believed the Lord, as today's text says.

When Abram was 99 years old, God promised it again. He said He was going to change Abram's name to Abraham, which means "father of many." Abraham had to laugh—he was 99 years old already! But he still believed.

Then one day the Lord and two angels came by in disguise. While they were eating lunch, the Lord said that Sarah would have a baby by the next year. Inside the tent Sarah overheard, and she had to laugh—she was 90 years old!

But the Lord asked, "Is anything too hard for the Lord?" (Genesis 18:14). The answer to that is no. Abraham and Sarah did have a baby, and they named him Isaac. It means laughter.

God Always Keeps His Promise

God made the promises to Abraham. Hebrews 11:17.

God kept blessing Abraham; he got richer and richer, with servants, sheep and cattle, silver and gold. And Isaac was everything Abraham had ever wanted.

Then God spoke again. He told Abraham to kill Isaac as an offering.

What? That didn't make sense. Isaac was God's promise. If he was killed, how could the promise come true?

Did Abraham hear wrong? No. Abraham had heard God many times. He knew it was God speaking. He didn't know *how* God could keep His promise if Isaac was killed. But he did know that God *would* keep His promise. God had always kept His promises, even when it seemed impossible. Abraham knew that nothing was impossible for God.

So Abraham saddled his donkey and cut wood for the sacrifice. He woke up Isaac and told him they were going to offer a sacrifice on a distant mountain.

When they got to the mountain, they built the altar. They put the wood on the altar. Then Abraham had to tell Isaac what God had commanded him to do.

Isaac could have run away, but he didn't. He knew his father talked with God. He knew about God's promise. Isaac let Abraham tie him up. Abraham raised the knife.

Then an angel called, "Abraham, don't kill your son." Abraham put down the knife. He untied Isaac. They saw a sheep whose horns were caught in a bush, and they offered it as a sacrifice. Then they went home.

Abraham trusted that God would keep His promise. And God did.

Descendants

*G*od promised that Abraham would have as many descendants as the stars. And Abraham had Isaac. There are a lot more stars than that. But "descendants" doesn't just mean children; it also means grandchildren and great-grandchildren and great-great-grandchildren and so on.

Isaac got married to Rebekah (now, there's a great story), and they had twins, Jacob and Esau, who never really got along (another great story). Jacob had 12 sons, and that really got the ball rolling—after that the descendants really started to add up.

Along the way God decided to change Jacob's name to Israel. After that the Bible sometimes calls him Jacob and sometimes calls him Israel. But his descendants are called the children of Israel. And they really did become a great nation, as many as the stars.

Jacob's son Joseph ended up going to Egypt (one of the most remarkable stories ever) and becoming an important ruler. So when there was a terrible famine back in Canaan, Joseph was able to bring Jacob and the rest of his family to Egypt. And they survived. And kept growing and growing and growing.

Today's Bible text is from the promise God gave to Jacob. And guess what the blessing was, the blessing for "all the families of the earth"? The Redeemer. Jesus was a descendant of Abraham. God blessed everyone through Abraham's descendant.

All the families of the earth will be blessed through you and your descendants. I am with you, and I will protect you everywhere you go. Genesis 28:14, 15.

God's Plan for Moses

The children of Israel ended up staying in Egypt longer than they had planned. They had many children, and after a while there were lots and lots of Israelites. This made the new king of Egypt nervous—he was worried they'd take over. So he forced them to become slaves and work hard. He ordered that all baby boys were to be thrown into the river. God made a plan to rescue His people. God made a plan for Moses.

Baby Moses' family hid him in a basket; the king's daughter found him and thought he was cute. Then she paid his family to take care of him. This was a great plan.

Moses' family taught him that God had saved him for something special. When he was old enough, he went to the palace and learned about the way things worked there.

Moses made a mistake and tried to rescue the people on his own. He ended up in the desert as a shepherd. There he learned to be patient; he learned that God was in charge.

Then God talked to him from a burning bush. God told Moses it was time to go lead the Israelites out of Egypt. Moses didn't want to do it. He had all kinds of excuses.

Moses told God that he wasn't a great man; God said, "I will be with you" (Exodus 3:12). Moses said he didn't know what to say; God replied that He'd tell him what to say. Moses said that nobody would believe him; God gave him some signs that he could use to prove that God had sent him. Moses said, "Please send someone else." God said, "Go!" Moses obeyed. And the more he obeyed, the more he realized that nothing is impossible with God.

Working together, Moses and God rescued the Israelites from slavery.

God's Plan for the Israelites

The Israelites had been slaves for so long that they had mostly forgotten about God and His agreement with His people. About His promise to Adam and Eve that He would send a Redeemer. About His promise that Abraham would be the father of a great nation.

Obey me, and I will be your God and you will be my people. Do all that I command, and good things will happen to you.
Jeremiah 7:23.

God wanted to remind this great nation of His promises and their responsibilities. The Israelites were camped in the desert by Mount Sinai. God called Moses to the top of the mountain for a talk.

God told Moses to tell the people that He wanted to make a covenant, an agreement, with the Israelites. He was choosing them to be His people.

God promised to give the Israelites the land of Canaan. He promised to take care of them and bless them.

The Israelites had a part in the agreement as well. God asked the Israelites to obey Him. And they had the responsibility of telling the people of the world about God and His plan to redeem them all.

Moses came down the mountain and told the people what God had said. "And all the people answered together, 'We will do everything he has said'" (Exodus 19:8).

The Israelites agreed to this covenant. They chose God as their ruler. They promised to obey Him. They agreed to be God's people.

God's People

Look at this list of words: Hebrews, Israelites, Jews, God's people. They are all different names for the same group of people.

Abraham was the first person in the Bible to be called a Hebrew (Genesis 14:13). God told Abraham that He had special plans for his descendants.

Abraham's grandson's name was Jacob, until God changed it to Israel. All of his descendants were known as the children of Israel or the Israelites.

At first a Jew was someone from the tribe of Judah (one of Israel's sons). But later it meant any person in any of the 12 tribes—any descendant of Israel.

And what did God call them? His people. When God made an agreement with them at Mt. Sinai, He promised that they would be His special, chosen people.

But for an agreement to work, both sides must keep their promises. Satan did all he could to make the agreement fail. God's people did not always obey. Sometimes they chose to worship an idol or a heathen god—that broke the agreement. But God didn't give up on them, even when they forgot Him. He begged them to come back to Him.

Eventually God sent His Son, Jesus, who showed us that all people are God's people. "Now, in Christ, there is no difference between Jew and Greek. . . . You are all the same in Christ Jesus. You belong to Christ. So you are Abraham's descendants" (Galatians 3:28, 29). You are God's people.

Following Directions

Have you ever made popcorn in the microwave? It tastes good, it's quick, and it's easy—but you've got to follow the directions. They aren't hard, but they're important.

Happy are the people who keep his rules. They ask him for help with their whole heart. Psalm 119:2.

For instance, the directions say that you should remove the plastic wrapper before you put the package in the microwave. If you don't take that plastic off, it won't work properly. It might melt, it might explode, it might burn—who knows. Just do it.

There are several other directions about placing it "this side up," listening while the popcorn is popping, opening the bag carefully, having adult supervision, and stuff like that. There are lots of directions, and they are all there for a good reason.

The person who wrote today's Bible text understood how important it is to follow directions—God's directions. The Israelites needed to learn that too.

Part of the agreement was that the Israelites promised to obey God. So God told Moses to tell the people to get ready—He was going to tell them the rules they needed to obey. God was going to come to Mount Sinai and speak to the people.

This is what it was like: "There was thunder and lightning with a thick cloud on the mountain. And there was a very loud blast from a trumpet. . . . The smoke rose from the mountain like smoke from a furnace. And the whole mountain shook wildly" (Exodus 19:16-18). That got the people's attention. They were listening very carefully.

Then God spoke to the people directly. He told them the rules.

The One and Only God

First of all God introduced Himself: "I am the Lord your God. I brought you out of the land of Egypt where you were slaves" (Exodus 20:2).

It was important for the people to know exactly who was talking, especially because of what He was going to say next: the first commandment. "You must not have any other gods except me."

To you, this commandment probably seems so obvious. Of course there is only one God. But to the people of that time it was an unusual idea. All the other nations had many gods. God was asking the Israelites to do something very different.

And God wanted them to understand more. He was the God of the Israelites, and He was their only God. But there was more.

He wasn't just their local God. It wasn't that the Philistines had their gods and the Egyptians had their gods and the Israelites had their God.

This God, the God who had created the world, the God who had chosen the Israelites as His special people, was the only God in existence. There were no other gods.

That idea was not only unusual; it was revolutionary for the people of that time. And it took the Israelites a long, long time to understand it and believe it completely.

In order for the Israelites to be able to tell the world about the one true God, they needed to believe it themselves. This was an important part of the agreement.

Useless Idols

When you change the batteries in a flashlight, you have to be careful. There is a little "+" near one end and a little "−" near the other. If you put the batteries in backwards or with the two "+" signs together or any way except for the exact right way, the flashlight won't work. Even if the batteries are good and the light bulb is good and the flashlight is good, it is all totally useless unless the batteries are in the right way.

You must not worship or serve any idol. Exodus 20:5.

When God told the Israelites His rules, the second one commanded, "You must not make for yourselves any idols" (Exodus 20:4). He is our God. He made us. It doesn't make sense for humans to worship something they have made themselves.

You may not be even a little bit tempted to make or worship an idol. But the Israelites wanted to do it because everybody else was doing it. For hundreds of years God kept pleading with His people to stop worshiping idols and let Him be their God. But the people didn't get it. The Bible says, "They worshiped useless idols and became useless themselves" (2 Kings 17:15).

God wanted His people to tell the other nations about Him, but instead they worshiped the false gods of other nations. They were useless, just as their idols were useless, just as a flashlight is useless if the batteries aren't put in the right way.

God's people had everything they needed to let their light shine, but it was as if they wouldn't put the batteries in the right way. They couldn't get any power from their useless idols. It was a hard rule for them to follow, a hard lesson for them to learn.

A Jealous God

*Love the Lord
your God with all
your heart, soul
and strength.
Deuteronomy 6:5.*

Your may think that you'll never have any trouble keeping the first two commandments. After all, you totally agree that there is only one God. Also you have never had the slightest desire to make any idols or bow down and worship them.

So you don't need to worry about it, right? Wrong. It's Satan's goal to separate us from God. That's what these commandments hope to prevent. They ask us to put God first in our lives. These two commandments are very basic and very important, now and always.

If Satan can't tempt you with an idol of clay or stone, there are many more idols he can use to try to separate you from God. Satan can suggest that money is the answer to all your needs. He can try to trick you into depending on knowledge instead of depending on God. He can make you think that having power over people is better than trusting in the power of God. He can distract you with entertainment and deceive you with pride.

God wasn't asking the Israelites merely to believe that He existed. They could hear His voice. They could see the mountain smoking and shaking. They believed He existed, all right. God was asking them to believe in His plan. He wanted them to join His team. It's the same for us. It's not enough just to admit that He is the only God. We must join Him.

Look at today's Bible text. If the first two commandments tell you what not to do, this verse tells you what you should do instead. If you love God with all your heart, soul, and strength, you will be obeying the first two commandments.

A Holy Name

Take a word—how about an important word, like "solemn"—and say it over and over. Solemn, solemn, solemn, solemn.

You must not use the name of the Lord your God thoughtlessly. Exodus 20:7.

It doesn't take long before that word just becomes a noise. It loses its meaning—it doesn't mean "solemn" anymore. It just sounds dopey.

There are some words that are too important to play around with like this. Their meaning is too precious. We say these words are holy. We must never let these holy words become a meaningless noise.

Words have power. In Bible times people took words very seriously. In the Hebrew language the word *dabar* means both "word" and "deed." So for the Israelites, saying something was the same as doing it. They knew that once a word is said, it can't be unsaid or taken back. The consequences of that word just keep growing and spreading, the way the rings of water spread when you throw a rock into a lake.

If we say God's name in a thoughtless way when we are startled, God's name becomes a little less holy to us. If we curse or swear and say God's name when we are angry, we are misusing God's name. When we don't treat God's name with respect, we lose some of the respect we have for God.

God the Father's name is Jehovah. It's a very holy word, a holy name. We don't say it very often, because we want to be respectful and because we want the word to keep its power. Angels cover their faces when they say God's name. We must be careful too.

Remember

Remember to keep the Sabbath as a holy day. You may work and get everything done during six days each week. But the seventh day is a day of rest to honor the Lord your God.
Exodus 20:8-10.

Look at the first word in today's Bible text, which is the fourth commandment: "Remember." That word means so much.

The children of Israel needed to remember the Sabbath. They had been slaves for so long—and slaves don't get Sabbath off. They had forgotten about the Sabbath. Now they were free. Now they were God's chosen people. Now they needed to remember the Sabbath.

When God gave this commandment, He explained why we should remember the Sabbath and what we are remembering. "The reason is that in six days the Lord made everything. He made the sky, earth, sea and everything in them. And on the seventh day, he rested. So the Lord blessed the Sabbath day and made it holy" (Exodus 20:11).

When we remember the Sabbath, we remember that God created the Sabbath and that God created us. The Sabbath helps us remember a time when everything was perfect.

The Sabbath can also help us remember that everything will be perfect again someday, that God has a plan to redeem us. We can remember our future.

During the week, the six days when we are getting everything done, we can get so busy. We can forget. It's good to have Sabbath. Sabbath is an excellent time to remember things.

Happy, Happy Home

The first four commandments God gave His people at Mount Sinai taught them how to love God. When Jesus was here on earth, someone asked Him what the most important law was. He answered, " 'Love the Lord your God with all your heart, soul and mind.' This is the first and most important command" (Matthew 22:37, 38). That sums up what the first four commandments are about.

Honor your father and your mother. Exodus 20:12.

Then Jesus added, "And the second command is like the first: 'Love your neighbor as you love yourself' " (verse 39). The last six commandments cover this topic. God gave these six commandments to help His people learn to love others. They show us how we should treat each other.

First there needs to be love at home. The fifth commandment is about families. God told His people that they needed to honor their parents. He wants us to obey our parents. He wants us to show them respect. He wants us to love them.

Being a parent is a hard job. It's a huge responsibility. When you honor your parents, you make their job easier. When you honor your parents, everyone is happier. Instead of punishment, there is reward. Instead of worry, there is trust. Instead of scolding, there is laughing.

The things you do every day can make your home a happier place. You can be kind. You can be helpful. You can be thoughtful.

God wants you to be happy at home. He wants you to honor your parents.

Life Is Precious

The sixth commandment is another one that shows us how we can learn to love others. It's really pretty basic. It says we shouldn't kill each other. This is a very important rule about how we should treat each other.

You may think it's obvious—if we love each other, of course we shouldn't kill each other. God gave us the gift of life. Life is precious and sacred. We must not take it away from anyone.

But when Jesus was on earth, He explained that this commandment means more than that. He taught that this also means that we must not get angry at each other or even say bad things to each other (Matthew 5:21, 22). Later, the apostle John added hatred: "Everyone who hates his brother is a murderer" (1 John 3:15).

When someone gets angry at you, it probably makes you feel terrible. When someone says bad things to you, it hurts your feelings. When someone is hateful, it can take away the happiness in your life. Life is precious and sacred. We must not take its happiness from anyone.

This commandment doesn't just forbid us from killing; it also asks us never even to wish someone were dead. Our thoughts are just as important as our deeds.

So you see, something that at first glance seems so simple and basic is actually quite complicated. We must not kill. We must not even think about it. Even more difficult, we must not get angry or say mean things or hate each other.

Love at Home

The seventh commandment is another one about learning to love others, and it's another one about families, too. In the fifth commandment God tells us that children should honor their parents. In the seventh, God tells us that husbands and wives should honor each other.

When God spoke to the children of Israel from Mount Sinai, He told them the rules for living a happy life—and that includes having a happy family.

If a family is going to be happy and strong, the husband and wife must honor each other. That means they are loyal to each other. They stick up for each other and believe in each other. They depend on each other. They are nice to each other.

Our Bible text today could be about a husband and wife. Two people together can be more successful when they work toward the same goal. They are stronger because they can help each other.

When two people get married, they promise to love and be true to each other. They promise to support each other and honor each other. They promise that they will stick together and take care of each other, in the good times and the bad times.

If you've ever been to a wedding, you've heard the bride and groom make these promises. The seventh commandment tells us that it's very important to keep them.

Two people are better than one. They get more done by working together. If one person falls, the other can help him up. But it is bad for the person who is alone when he falls. No one is there to help him. Ecclesiastes 4:9, 10.

Honesty Is the Best Policy

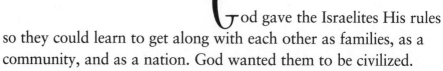

God gave the Israelites His rules so they could learn to get along with each other as families, as a community, and as a nation. God wanted them to be civilized.

An important part of civilization is to respect other people's property. No stealing. You must not take over someone's land or take away their possessions or steal their money. You must not rob a bank or hijack a car or shoplift a candy bar.

All of society suffers when something is stolen. The victim loses their property and is anxious and upset. Other community members worry because they don't feel safe. They end up paying higher prices for insurance and at the store. And people who steal lose their connection to God and to their community. They think only of themselves.

You may feel confident that you will never rob a bank. But there are many other ways to steal. At lunchtime there's a kid who doesn't have many friends but does have a delicious-looking cupcake. You have a cookie that's broken because you dropped it on the floor. And you talk the lonely kid into trading. That's not fair. That's stealing. Or you tell your sister you'll give her a quarter if she'll take out the trash for you; then after she does it you say you were kidding or keep forgetting to pay her. That's cheating. Or you tell your neighbor you'll rake his leaves and then do a lousy job. That's dishonest.

God wants us to be honest with each other. For our own good and for the good of our community, our country, and our world.

Nothing but the Truth

The ninth commandment says, "You must not tell lies about your neighbor in court" (Exodus 20:16). A court is a place where people come for justice. A court can be just and fair only if everybody tells the truth. So this is an important rule.

So you must stop telling lies. Tell each other the truth because we all belong to each other. Ephesians 4:25.

However, most of us will never have to speak in court. Does that mean we don't have to worry about this commandment? No. This rule is important for all of us, all the time. God wants us to tell the truth. Lies cause trouble. Lies make people unhappy.

What is a lie? It seems as though that should be an easy question. But it's not.

Let's say you tell your friend to stay away from those bushes because a monster might jump out and tickle her. Are you lying? No. You're joking, and your friend knows it's pretend. It's not a lie if you both know you're just making it up for fun.

What if you tell your mom that the party is on Wednesday, but then you find out that it's really on Tuesday? Were you lying? No. You just made a mistake.

A lie is trying to make someone believe something that is not true. A lie is deceiving someone on purpose. You can lie with your words by saying something you know is not true. You can lie with your actions by doing something to make people believe something that's not true. You can lie with your silence by being quiet when someone asks for the truth.

Telling the truth is important. Every day. In every way.

Satisfied

The tenth commandment is different. Some of the commandments God gave are about things we should not do. Some of them are about things we should not say. But this last commandment is about things we should not even think!

The tenth commandment says, "You must not want to take anything that belongs to your neighbor" (Exodus 20:17). God already told us in the eighth commandment that we should not take it. Now He tells us that we should not even want to take it.

The tenth commandment tells us that it is important to be satisfied with what we have. God wants us to realize that we can't be happy if we want things we can't have.

People who are not satisfied with what they have see the world as a pie. If someone else gets a piece of pie, they think that means there isn't enough for them. People who are not content think that if someone else wins, that means they lose. People who are eaten by envy think that if someone else succeeds, that means they fail.

And if they allow the envy to keep eating away at their happiness, after a while they don't just think, *I want what you have.* They think, *I wish you didn't have what you have.* Very sad. Very dangerous.

Paul writes in today's Bible text that he has discovered the secret of happiness. Live your life—don't compare it to anyone else's. Look at what you have—God is with you. His gifts never run out. There is more than enough of His love to go around.

The Rules of the Game

What if you were trying to play miniature golf and sometimes you would barely tap the ball and it would sail off into space, while other times you would whack it with all your might and it would barely roll an inch? What if you tried to play baseball, but every once in a while (for no good reason), when you hit the ball with the bat, the ball would shatter like glass? What if, when you kicked the soccer ball, sometimes your foot went right through it as if it were made of water?

Help me obey your commands because that makes me happy. Psalm 119:35.

Playing with a ball would be a lot different if the ball didn't obey the law.

When you're playing ball, it works better if people follow the rules too. The basketball has to remember to bounce, and people have to remember to bounce it whenever they are running. Baseball works best when everyone runs around the bases in the same direction every time. Games work best if people take turns and are good sports.

Life works better with laws—laws about gravity and laws about taking turns and all kinds of laws. That's why God made laws and tries to help us understand them and use them.

People don't follow laws as well as balls do—that's because we are free to make choices. A ball would never dream of trying to defy the law of gravity, but people try to do stuff like that all the time. We have brains with which we make choices. But we've got to use them to think about those choices—or else it could be like trying to play catch with a ball that might explode or melt or simply float away at any moment.

The Way Things Are

This is how God showed his love to us: He sent his only Son into the world to give us life through him. 1 John 4:9.

What happens if you drop a ball? It falls down. Every time. It will never float off into the sky. It will never zoom around, bouncing off walls. When you let go, it falls.

A scientific law explains this: gravity. The earth is so big that gravity pulls all things down to it. That's why you don't float off into space. That's why balls fall down.

Let's say there are two kinds of laws. Gravity belongs to one group. The laws in this group help explain the way things are. There are laws of energy, motion, and light. Scientists use these laws to help understand the world and how things work.

There is another kind of law. Remember the ball that falls when you drop it? Well, you are not supposed to drop that ball on your sister's head. You are not supposed to use a ball to hurt someone on purpose. The laws in this group help explain the way things ought to be. They are family rules, playground rules, rules of fair play. These laws help us get along with each other.

In the Bible there are both kinds of laws. The Ten Commandments are an example of the way things ought to be. They teach the difference between right and wrong. They show us how God wants us to live. They show us how much we need His help.

There are also laws in the Bible that show the way things are. Today's Bible text is an example of this kind of law. God loves us. That's the way things are. He sent Jesus to save us. That's the way things are.

Living Among Us

The Israelites were shaken after God gave them the commandments, what with all the thunder and lightning and the smoke rising from the mountain. "Then all of the people answered out loud together. They said, 'We will do all the things that the Lord has said'" (Exodus 24:3). So the agreement was made. He was their God. They were His people.

The people must build a holy place for me. Then I can live among them. Exodus 25:8.

Then Moses went up on Mount Sinai and talked to God some more. God told Moses that the people should build a sanctuary, a tabernacle—a holy place where the people could worship.

Ever since Adam and Eve, God's people had worshiped Him by building an altar and offering a sacrifice. Now God wanted to show them a way to worship together as a group. Now God provided a way to bring His people close to Him so they could learn more about Him. Now, as a sign that He would always be with His people, God gave instructions for building a special tent where He could live among them.

Even though they were traveling through the desert to their Promised Land, they could take this sanctuary with them. And God would travel with them and guide them.

The people brought gifts of gold, silver, fine cloth, wood, and gems to build a sanctuary for their God. And God was with them. Thousands of years later we still come together to meet in our church, our sanctuary. And God is with us.

God's Plan for Joshua

Moses didn't quite make it to the Promised Land. God chose Joshua, Moses' assistant, to take over after Moses died. Joshua was understandably nervous. After all, Moses was a hard act to follow. Moses had been the leader since they'd left Egypt. Would the people listen to Joshua?

God had a talk with Joshua. He said, "Just as I was with Moses, so I will be with you. . . . I will never leave you alone. Joshua, be strong and brave!" (Joshua 1:5, 6).

Moses was dead, but God was still in charge. The agreement had not changed. God had promised His people a land of their own. Now it was time for that to happen. It started with Jericho.

God gave Joshua the instructions on how to conquer Jericho. They were strange.

The Israelites were to march around Jericho once a day for six days, without saying a word. On the seventh day they were to march around seven times. Then the priests were to give one long blast on the trumpets and the people were to give a loud shout. The walls of Jericho would fall down, and the Israelites would take over.

Joshua was a soldier. He knew these plans didn't make sense. Shouting does not make walls fall down. But Joshua knew that with God nothing is impossible. He knew the only way they could capture Jericho was with God's help. If God wanted them to blow trumpets and march, that's what they would do. Joshua and the Israelites followed God's plan exactly. And the walls came tumbling down.

Taking Risks

Have you ever looked at a book of world records? You can find out about the world's largest grapefruit (six pounds, 12 ounces) or the world's shortest alphabet (11 letters—from a language in Papua New Guinea). People do crazy things to get into this book. They risk their lives by jumping canyons on a motorcycle or by diving out of helicopters.

There's a difference between being reckless and taking risks. When you take a risk, you are brave but careful. It's much smarter to take risks than to be reckless.

Sometimes God asks people to take risks. Gideon started out to fight the enemy with an army of 32,000. But God said that was too many, and Gideon ended up with 300 men. God asked Gideon to trust Him on this, and Gideon did. Things worked out just fine. Did Gideon act recklessly? Well, it would have been reckless except for one thing: God told him to do it. God told Gideon, "I will be with you" (Judges 6:16).

Balaam was reckless. God told him not to go with King Balak to curse Israel. But Balaam went anyway; he wanted the money. When an angel came to stop him, his donkey tried to get out of the way. Balaam beat his donkey, and after the third time the donkey complained. Balaam was so mad, he yelled back at the donkey. Then he saw the angel, who asked, "Why have you beaten your donkey these three times? I have come here to oppose you because your path is a reckless one before me" (Numbers 22:32, NIV).

There is nothing more reckless than disobeying God. There is nothing braver than taking risks for God.

Be careful. Continue strong in the faith. Have courage, and be strong.
1 Corinthians 16:13.

The Promised Land

Joshua led God's people into the Promised Land—Canaan. The problem was that there were already a lot of people there, and they didn't want to leave. That's why the books of Joshua and Judges have so many wars in them.

The battles weren't always as easy as the one at Jericho—because the Israelites didn't always follow God's instructions. But gradually God's people began to spread out and settle by tribes into different areas.

Because the Israelites didn't always obey God's instructions, there were still plenty of original Canaanites around—Philistines, Midianites, Moabites and so on. And they caused no end of trouble.

It seems as if the Israelites were always under attack by someone. But the fighting wasn't the worst problem. It was the heathen gods. It happened over and over.

Here was the cycle: God's people deserted Him and began worshiping Baal or praying to one of the local gods for a rich harvest. Because they weren't following God's instructions, the Israelites didn't have the power to fend off attacks by the Canaanites. So the Israelites cried to God for help. Then God sent a deliverer—a leader, often called a judge. However, after the crisis was past or after the judge died, the Israelites would begin worshiping false gods again. This happened again and again.

Because they didn't keep their half of the agreement, God's people only half received the Promised Land.

Samson Rejects God's Plan

The judges of Israel didn't just sit around a courtroom and make legal decisions. They were people of action—heroes who delivered the Israelites from their enemies. The judges were leaders, chosen by God. God wanted the people to learn that loyalty to Him brought strength, but turning to other gods brought weakness.

Samson was a judge, chosen by God before he was even born. He was different from other judges. He didn't lead the Israelite army into battle; he fought the Philistines personally. By himself.

That was the trouble. He forgot God. Samson didn't need other men to help him fight against the Philistines. But he did need God. God gave him his strength.

God's plan was that through the leadership of Samson, the Israelites would defeat the Philistines. God gave Samson incredible physical strength—He wanted to show people how incredibly strong they could be as a nation if they would follow Him.

Unfortunately, Samson didn't follow God's plan any better than the Israelites did. His character was weak even though his muscles were strong. He mostly wasted his amazing strength playing practical jokes or getting revenge on his enemies.

Because Samson didn't follow God's plan, this story has a very sad ending. Samson did not lead the Israelites to defeat the Philistines. He was not a good example of how strong they could be if they followed God. Samson died, still trying to get revenge.

Depend on the Lord and his strength. Always go to him for help. Remember the wonderful things he has done. Remember his miracles and his decisions. Psalm 105:4, 5.

God's Plan for Ruth

God's plan was that the Israelites would teach the people of other nations about Him. Sometimes it worked very well.

Naomi had gone to Moab with her husband and two sons because there was a famine in Israel. While they were in Moab, her husband died. Her two sons married women from Moab, and then the sons died.

Poor Naomi decided to go home to Israel. She was able to convince one daughter-in-law to stay in Moab, but the other one, Ruth, wouldn't leave her. When Ruth had become a part of Naomi's family, she had learned about the true God. She did not want to go back to her old life.

So Naomi and Ruth walked to Bethlehem. When they got there they needed food, so Ruth went into the fields and gathered leftover grain. The Bible says, "It just so happened that the field belonged to Boaz" (Ruth 2:3).

When Boaz came by to see how the harvest was going, he noticed Ruth. He asked who she was and then went over to welcome her to town. He told her to help herself to the water the harvesters were drinking. On the way out he told his workers to leave extra grain for her to pick up. Before long he started giving her presents, like a half bushel of barley. Boaz was really being very nice to Ruth.

Naomi noticed. She worked things out for Ruth and Boaz to get married. It's such a beautiful story it almost makes you want to cry. It's so nice when things work out.

Messengers

God did not just hand the Israelites the Ten Commandments, get them to sign the agreement, and then leave. He was involved. He wanted this agreement to work. God wanted the people to know about Him, and He wanted them to tell others about Him.

One very important way that He kept in touch was by sending messages to the people through a prophet. God chose a prophet. He told the prophet what to say. Then the prophet gave the people God's message.

Moses was a prophet. The Bible says, "There has never been another prophet like Moses" (Deuteronomy 34:10). Moses hadn't really wanted the job, but once he agreed, he really got into it. Moses and God made a good team.

Sometimes the prophets told God's messages by speaking or preaching. Sometimes the message was for just one person—the prophet showed up, gave the message, and left. Other times the messages were for the entire nation, and the prophet had to go from place to place, preaching to whoever would listen.

Sometimes the prophets were instructed to write down God's messages. Many parts of the Bible were written by prophets— we're still reading these messages.

God has sent many different messages in many different ways through many different prophets, but they all have one main idea: God loves us. He wants us to know Him. He wants us to share His love with others.

You must go everywhere that I send you. You must say everything I tell you to say. Don't be afraid of anyone, because I am with you. I will protect you. Jeremiah 1:7, 8.

God's Plan for Samuel

Samuel started out young. God called him to deliver a message when he was a boy. Samuel wasn't expecting it—it was dark, he was half asleep, he thought it was Eli the priest who was calling him. But once that was straightened out, he became God's messenger from that time on, and everybody knew it.

Samuel was a prophet—the greatest since Moses. Samuel decided early on to do whatever God asked him to do, and they were a powerful team. It was a time when "everyone did what he thought was right" (Judges 21:25), and Samuel made it clear that they had better start doing what the Lord said was right.

Samuel was also a judge—the last and best of the judges. He let the Israelites know in no uncertain terms that if they wanted to be saved from the Philistines, they'd have to quit worshiping the Philistine gods. It worked. Samuel led them to victory.

Samuel was tough and powerful. He worked hard at whipping those Israelites into shape. And once he had done it, when he was old and gray they nearly broke his heart. The people told him they wanted a king.

He told them they were crazy. "A king will take your sons for his army," he warned. "He'll take the best of your crops and your flocks. And besides," Samuel said, "you've already got the only king worth having, and that's God."

But the people insisted. When Samuel talked it over with God, God comforted him. "They have not rejected you. They have rejected me from being their king. They are doing as they have always done" (1 Samuel 8:7, 8). So the people got their king.

Saul Rejects God's Plan

It's easy to feel sorry for Saul. He never asked for the job. He was just out looking for some lost donkeys when Samuel came up and told him that Israel wanted him to be their new king. So Saul set about the job of uniting the tribes into a single nation.

Of course, Samuel never wanted Israel to have a king in the first place, and he made sure Saul knew that. It couldn't have been easy, trying to be king when God's messenger resented you and your job and had told everybody it wasn't going to work out.

Saul made a lot of mistakes. One time Saul panicked when he was surrounded by Philistines and his army was deserting him. He offered a sacrifice to God instead of waiting for Samuel. Just as he finished Samuel arrived and asked, "What have you done?" (1 Samuel 13:11). It seemed as though Samuel was always saying that.

It seemed as though whenever Saul had a choice he made the wrong one. And with each bad choice he turned further away from God and became less effective as a leader.

Finally, after a really big mistake when Saul didn't obey and then lied about it, Samuel told Saul that God had rejected him as king. Then Samuel went and anointed David as the next king.

After that, Saul began to fall apart. He was very upset that God had rejected him. He was jealous of David. The Philistines began causing trouble again. Saul got more and more desperate. And when he died in battle it was a very sad ending to a very sad story.

If you had obeyed him, God would make your kingdom continue in Israel forever.
1 Samuel 13:13.

The Optimist

Have you ever seen somebody do this? They take a glass and fill it halfway with water. Then they ask, "Is this glass half full or half empty?" If you say it is half full, they say you're an optimist. If you say it is half empty, they say you're a pessimist.

An optimist is someone who looks on the bright side of things and thinks everything is going to work out fine. A pessimist is someone who expects the worst. Eeyore, the donkey in the Winnie the Pooh stories, is a pessimist. His friend Tigger is an optimist. You probably know both kinds of people.

David was an optimist. When he was just a boy, he thought he could kill a giant (with God's help). And he did it. As he got older he just got more optimistic. If there was a war, he thought they could win it (with God's help). If he was in trouble, he knew things would work out in the end (with God's help).

Perhaps he was most optimistic the day he brought the ark to Jerusalem. The ark was the holy box that had the Ten Commandments in it. What a celebration there was as the ark was carried to the city! David was so happy that he "danced with all his might before the Lord" (2 Samuel 6:14). And as the people watched their king, they caught his enthusiasm. They felt as though they could do anything. They felt as though God was on their side.

God was on their side. And David knew it. That's why he was an optimist. David didn't see the glass as being either half empty or half full. The way David saw it, "my cup overflows" (Psalm 23:5, NIV).

The Wisdom of Solomon

For a while it looked as if David was going to prove Samuel wrong—that maybe kings weren't such a terrible idea after all. David wasn't perfect—not even close. He made lots of mistakes, some of them pretty awful. But every time he messed up, he was truly sorry. And instead of turning away from God, he turned closer to Him. And the people of Israel adored him. David was a good king, a godly king, a successful king.

Don't depend on your own wisdom.
Proverbs 3:7.

When David died, his son Solomon became king. Solomon started out strong. One night God talked to him in a dream. God said, "Ask for anything you want. I will give it to you" (1 Kings 3:5).

Solomon talked to God about how his father had been such a great king, and how he wanted to do a good job too. He said, "I ask that you give me wisdom. Then I can rule the people in the right way" (verse 9). Wisdom. That was a really good choice.

God was pleased. He gave Solomon wisdom—he was the wisest man who ever lived. The Bible tells many stories of the wise things he did. And many of the wise things he said were written down—you can read some of them in the book of Proverbs.

But sometimes people who are very wise can make foolish mistakes. Solomon began to think he was responsible for his wisdom. Solomon was very, very rich—but he got that money by taxing his people way too much. They didn't like it. Solomon also made the mistake of having too many wives—and the foreign wives brought their gods with them, and dragged Solomon into it. In the end Solomon's wisdom failed him.

Civil War

The country was weak after Solomon died. It had never been easy to hold the 12 tribes together as one nation. Now it proved to be impossible for Solomon's son.

The secret to the Israelites' strength had always been the agreement with God. They were unified because they worshiped the same God, not because they had the same king. Samuel had warned them, "Both you and the king ruling over you must follow the Lord your God. If you do, it will be well with you" (1 Samuel 12:14).

But they didn't. And it wasn't.

The tribes in the north declared their independence. The kingdom split in two. The tribes in the north called their new nation Israel. The southern kingdom was called Judah. They never got along after that.

The city of Jerusalem was in the south, so the people of the northern kingdom didn't go to the Temple to worship anymore. The northern kingdom of Israel moved further and further from worshiping God and obeying His law. All of their kings were bad, although some were more wicked than others.

Once in a while the people in the southern kingdom of Judah had a good king who obeyed God and led the people well. But for the most part things weren't much better there.

However, God didn't just sit back and watch His people slip away from Him. Oh, no. He sent prophets. Good ones. And they meant business.

God's Plan for Elijah

Israel's King Ahab was a bad apple, and his wife, Jezebel, was rotten to the core. When they got married she brought her god, Baal, along with her, and soon there were altars for Baal worship all over the place. Things were at an all-time low.

I have always served you the best I could.
1 Kings 19:14.

So God sent Elijah, a mighty prophet who was thoroughly committed to God and His law. First Elijah got Ahab's attention. Baal was a god of the weather. To prove that God alone has power over the weather, Elijah told Ahab that God had decided that it wasn't going to rain for a few years. Then he left.

Elijah hid out by a brook, where birds brought him food, until the brook dried up. Then God sent him to live with a widow and her son, where God made sure the flour and oil never ran out. After three years God sent Elijah back to Ahab, and Elijah arranged for a showdown on Mount Carmel.

Here was the contest: Elijah and Baal's prophets would each build an altar and prepare a sacrifice. Whichever altar caught on fire would be the altar of the true God. Baal's prophets went first and, after carrying on all day, got no results. Then Elijah took his turn, and after his simple prayer, God vaporized the altar. The people were impressed.

Unfortunately, it didn't last long; Elijah had to keep calling the people to turn back to the true God. Elijah was fearless in calling evil by its right name, except for one crisis. Then God came and spoke in a still small voice, and got him back on track. In the end, when it came time for Elijah to die, God decided to take him to heaven instead.

A Pain in the Neck

When he saw Elijah, he said, "Is it you— the biggest troublemaker in Israel?" I Kings 18:17.

We have the sense of touch in our skin. Just under our skin there are special nerve endings called receptors. When we touch something or something touches us, the receptors send a message to the brain. There are different kinds of receptors. Some feel temperature, some feel pressure, and some feel pain.

The sense of touch is important. It helps keep us safe. If the bathwater feels too hot to your toes, you cool the water down before you climb in. That way you don't get burned. If you fall down and skin your knee, your sense of touch helps you feel pain, so you wash the scrape and put on a band aid. Pain is a warning signal that your body is hurt and you need to take care of it. Pain hurts. But it keeps you safe. If you couldn't feel pain, your body could get into real trouble before you even knew it.

The prophets were special people God chose to, well, be a pain. It wasn't a fun job, because most of the time the people didn't like to hear what the prophets were told to say. In today's Bible text King Ahab tells Elijah that he's a pain.

Elijah and many other prophets did what God told them to do and said what God told them to say. They told the truth. They gave the warning. They were the sense of touch for the body of the nation. They were a pain.

Because He loves us, God gave us a sense of touch to keep us safe. Because He loves us, God sent the prophets to keep us close to Him.

Israel Rejects God's Plan

Once the northern kingdom of Israel split away, they never came back to God and the agreement. Their wicked kings never seemed to last very long—some of them died in battle; many of them were killed by someone else who wanted to be king. The people fought among themselves and with all of their neighbors. They worshiped foreign gods—and they broke all the other commandments, too. This kind of behavior does not make a nation strong; Israel got weaker and weaker.

My people have made up their minds to turn away from me. The prophets call them to turn to me. But none of them honors me at all. Hosea 11:7.

You've played hide-and-seek. It's as if the Israelites were always hiding and God was always seeking. God would send prophet after prophet to seek the people and bring them home, but they wouldn't come, or if they did they'd soon run off to hide again.

It's as if God's prophets would call, over and over, "Ally, ally, in come free. Remember the agreement. If you want to be God's people, He must be your God. If you want His blessings, you must follow His plan." But the people wouldn't come.

In today's Bible text God talks to Hosea about how He keeps calling His people. In the next verse God speaks of His love for His people: "Israel, I don't want to give you up. I don't want to go away and leave you" (Hosea 11:8). It's so sad, it just about breaks your heart. It sounds as if His heart is broken.

The people of Israel abandoned God. The Assyrians attacked, took over the land, and took the people captive. The kingdom of Israel was swept away forever.

235

God's Plan for Isaiah

Then I heard the
Lord's voice. He said,
"Whom can I send?
Who will go for us?"
So I said, "Here I am.
Send me!" Isaiah 6:8.

God sent prophets to the southern kingdom of Judah, too. One of the greatest was Isaiah, who prophesied for more than 40 years.

God chose Isaiah to be a prophet by giving him a vision. Isaiah saw God sitting on a high throne surrounded by angels. The room filled with smoke and began to shake. Isaiah could hardly believe that he was being allowed to see such a holy place. Because he was not worthy he was afraid, until an angel showed him that his sins were forgiven.

Then God asked, "Whom can I send?" And Isaiah said, "Here I am. Send me!"

God warned him, "The people won't listen to you, they won't learn, and they won't understand. But tell them anyway." And Isaiah asked, "How long should I try?" And God answered, "Until there are no people left" (see Isaiah 6:9-11).

So that's what Isaiah did. He told the people whatever God told him to tell them, even when it wasn't what they wanted to hear—which was most of the time. He told them that they were disobedient and faithless, greedy and selfish, phony and mean.

But mostly Isaiah called the people to turn back to God. God told Isaiah to tell the people to "stop doing wrong! Learn to do good" (Isaiah 1:16, 17). So Isaiah told the people how they should behave. Sometimes they listened, but mostly they didn't.

When Isaiah got discouraged, he remembered that he had seen God on His throne, that he had been forgiven, that God had called him—and that he had replied, "Send me!"

Fat Cats

In the Bible, sometimes the word *fat* means rich or powerful or strong. That's why you might find a promise like this: "And the Lord shall guide thee continually, and satisfy thy soul in drought, and make fat thy bones" (Isaiah 58:11, KJV). We still have this idea today. Sometimes we call someone who is rich or powerful a "fat cat."

There is danger in being a fat cat. You can start to think that you made yourself so rich and powerful. That happened to the Israelites. God told the prophet Jeremiah that the people of Judah "have become rich and powerful. They have grown big and fat. There is no end to the evil things they do" (Jeremiah 5:27, 28). God saw injustice everywhere. The kings were evil, the priests were phony, the rich stole from the poor.

God was especially upset that the leaders had turned into fat cats. He said, "How terrible it will be for the shepherds of Israel who feed only themselves! Why don't the shepherds feed the flock?" (Ezekiel 34:2). The kings should be good examples. The priests should lead the people to follow God. The rich should take care of the poor.

Is it good to be a fat cat? It depends. If you walk with God, riches and power can do a lot of good. But then, if you walk with God, you can do amazing things even if you are poor and weak. The important thing to remember is that He is strong. Even if you aren't a fat cat, God can keep you warm and help you share warmth with others. God can "make fat thy bones."

Israel grew fat and kicked. They were fat and full and firm. They left the God who made them. They rejected the Rock who saved them. Deuteronomy 32:15.

237

God's Plan for Jeremiah

I will cry night and day, without stopping. I will cry for my people. Jeremiah 14:17.

Judah was a small country located right on the main road. All the powerful nations trooped by it on their way to conquer other nations or trade spices and stuff. They all wanted to capture Judah; only God's power kept the enemies away. But God's people didn't seem to understand or care. They didn't keep their part of the agreement.

God sent Jeremiah to warn the people of Judah that what had happened to Israel could happen to them too. Jeremiah was shy; he didn't want to be a prophet. But God told him not to be afraid—He would be with him and would tell him what to say.

So Jeremiah said what God told him to say. And it usually got him into trouble.

Sometimes Jeremiah just preached; other times God had him do something to get people's attention first. One time God told Jeremiah to watch a potter make a clay pot. Something went wrong with the shape, so the potter started over, reshaping the clay to make a new pot with it. Jeremiah told the people that that's what God would do to them. They weren't working out. God was going to have to start over and reshape them.

The people didn't like hearing this kind of thing. They wouldn't repent. Instead, they got mad at Jeremiah. They kept trying to make him be quiet. They arrested him and put him in prison. They put him in stocks. They banned him from teaching in the Temple. The king tore up and burned a scroll with his messages on it. They threw him down a well. They blamed him when enemies attacked. Over and over Jeremiah was mistreated, but God kept rescuing him and giving him more messages to deliver.

God's Plan for Exile

Jeremiah was right. Before finally destroying Jerusalem completely, the Babylonian armies invaded Judah several times, taking captives back with them. The people of Judah were taken away from their Promised Land. Exile.

I will put a new way to think inside you. Ezekiel 36:26.

It looked as if the agreement between God and His people had failed. It looked as if Satan had destroyed God's plan. But that's not the way it was. God had told Isaiah, "When I plan something, it happens" (Isaiah 46:10). God still had a plan. God had shown Jeremiah that He was going to reshape the clay. God was going to make a new agreement with His people.

Jeremiah was still alive. God gave him this message about a new agreement: "I will put my teachings in their minds. And I will write them on their hearts" (Jeremiah 31:33). God wanted the people to see that it wasn't enough just to obey the law, to follow the rules, to offer sacrifices. He wanted them to understand. He wanted them to love. He wanted them to be His people with all their heart, mind, and soul.

God promised Jeremiah He'd bring His people back to Jerusalem, to the Promised Land. He promised that He would never leave them, even while they were in exile.

God had reminded Isaiah of His promise to send a Redeemer. God's promise to send a Messiah had not changed and would never change. God would redeem His world. "A child will be born to us. God will give a son to us" (Isaiah 9:6).

Through His prophets God sent messages of hope to His people in exile.

God's Plan for Daniel

He makes known secrets that are deep and hidden. Daniel 2:22.

Daniel was the right man in the right place at the right time. Daniel was taken as a captive to Babylon by King Nebuchadnezzar's army, and God chose him to help with His plan. Daniel was chosen to work in Nebuchadnezzar's court; through Daniel, God made sure that His people were kept together and treated fairly and allowed to worship.

Daniel had many adventures, serving several foreign kings and giving them advice. More than once he had to choose whether to obey the king or God. He knew it was always better to obey God, and God always took care of him.

Nebuchadnezzar saw that Daniel always did the right thing and gave wise advice. He saw that Daniel's God was all-knowing and all-powerful, and the king cooperated with God's plan while God's people were in exile in Babylon.

Daniel was a statesman, but he was also a prophet. Most of the time God gives His prophets messages about how His people should behave—how they should follow Him and treat each other. But sometimes God wants to tell us about the future. The captives in Babylon wanted to know what would happen; they needed hope. The messages Daniel wrote down were mostly about what would happen in the future.

God gave Daniel dreams that showed that His people would go back to the Promised Land. Other dreams showed how many years it would be before the Redeemer would come. God used Daniel to help watch over the chosen people and to give them hope for the future.

God's Plan to Rebuild

Work, because I am with you. Haggai 2:4.

While God's people were captives in Babylon, God was with them. He sent messages through His prophets to help explain what had happened to them. And He sent messages of hope that they would return to their own land. God's people began to turn to Him. They saw how important it was to follow God's laws.

The people had been captives for about 70 years when the new king of Persia, Cyrus, decided to allow them to return to their land. Cyrus chose Zerubbabel to lead the people home and be their governor.

It wasn't easy. Jerusalem had been completely destroyed; the people began rebuilding the Temple. Other people had moved into the area while the Jews were gone; they began to cause trouble. A new king gave orders and forced them to stop building. Everything started to go wrong; crops wouldn't grow; everyone was discouraged.

God sent the prophets Haggai and Zechariah to get things moving again. Haggai told the people that they needed to get busy and finish the Temple. He told them they needed to get their priorities straight: "You are busy working on your own houses. But my house is still in ruins!" (Haggai 1:9).

Zechariah told them that all their problems were no problem for God—they would have success if they would just get to work. God told them, "You will not succeed by your own strength or power. The power will come from my Spirit" (Zechariah 4:6).

The people listened to these prophets. The Temple and the city were rebuilt.

241

Prepare the Way

Every valley should be raised up. Every mountain and hill should be made flat. The rough ground should be made level. Isaiah 40:4.

God's people seemed to have learned their lesson by being exiled in Babylon. They no longer wanted to worship other gods. They became very careful about obeying God's laws; they even made up more laws about keeping the laws. Unfortunately, they saw the laws as a sort of magic formula—if we do these things, then God will make our nation great. God wanted to show them how much better it is to follow Him out of love.

It was time to send the Messiah.

But first God was going to send a prophet to help the people get ready. More than 400 years earlier God had told the prophet Malachi, "I will send my messenger. He will prepare the way for me to come" (Malachi 3:1). Now God chose John to prepare the way. John was chosen to be a prophet before he was even born. An angel told his father that their son would "make people ready for the coming of the Lord" (Luke 1:17).

The prophet Isaiah had also written about someone coming to prepare the way. His description of John's job is in today's Bible text. It sounds as if he'd be more like a construction worker than a prophet—and John did come on strong, flattening and leveling and smoothing. He called the leaders a bunch of snakes, and he told the people that just because they were Jews didn't mean they were saved. He preached, "Change your hearts and lives because the kingdom of heaven is coming soon" (Matthew 3:2).

The time had come. The Messiah was coming to redeem His people.

Angels Tell God's Plan

The angel Gabriel had told John's father that his son would prepare the way. Now Gabriel was sent to talk to Mary. It was the most important, glorious, solemn news he had ever delivered. All the angels were watching to see what would happen.

I am bringing you some good news. It will be a joy to all the people. Luke 2:10.

The angel told Mary that she was going to have a baby, that His name would be Jesus, that He would be the Messiah. As you can imagine, she was startled and confused. She knew about the Messiah—every day she prayed for God to send the Messiah. But she'd never expected anything like this.

Mary was engaged to Joseph. She told him what the angel had said. Joseph was a good man, but he didn't know what to do—Mary's story was hard to believe. That night an angel explained it to him in a dream. Joseph agreed to take care of Mary and the baby.

Just before the baby was born, Joseph and Mary had to travel to Bethlehem. All the inns were full, so the only place there was to sleep was in a stable. Jesus, the Son of God, the Savior of the world, was born in that stable.

The angels were so excited that they had to tell someone. Some unsuspecting shepherds were in a nearby field. Suddenly an angel appeared and told them, "Good news! Your Savior has been born!" Then a large group of angels joined him and started singing, "Glory to God in heaven" (Luke 2:14). What an exciting night for the angels! And the shepherds.

The angels watched as the shepherds found the new baby, the little Light of the World, wrapped up tight and lying in a manger. The angels saw that in the world all was calm, all was bright.

Simeon and Anna See the Light

Now those people live in darkness. But they will see a great light. Isaiah 9:2.

Although the Jews were living in their homeland, the Romans were in charge. Some of the Jews were patriotic—they wanted only Jewish leaders and laws; they were upset that they had to pay taxes and that there were Roman soldiers everywhere.

Other groups—like the Pharisees—were very concerned about the law. They studied it in great detail and demanded that people follow it to the letter. It was as if they were worshiping the law rather than God.

Most people didn't know much about politics or the law. They went to the local synagogue on the Sabbath, and tried to travel to Jerusalem to visit the Temple on feast days.

All of the Jews—the patriots, the Pharisees, the common people—longed for the Messiah to come. They wanted the Messiah to deliver them from the Romans. They seemed to have forgotten that the Messiah was coming to deliver them from their sins.

But some people remembered. Simeon was waiting for the Messiah. The Holy Spirit had told him that he would see the Messiah before he died. Simeon was at the temple when Mary and Joseph went in to dedicate their son to God, as was the custom. And Simeon recognized that Jesus was the Messiah, the one he had been waiting for all his life. "Simeon took the baby in his arms and thanked God" (Luke 2:28). An old prophet named Anna was at the Temple too. She also recognized who Jesus was.

Most of the people at the Temple ignored them. They had important things to do. But Anna and Simeon saw the Light—it was there for everyone, but only they saw it.

Wise Men Follow the Light

Satan has been trying to ruin God's plan from the beginning, so it shouldn't surprise us to find out what he tried to do when the Redeemer came to earth as a helpless little baby. Satan tried to get rid of Him.

Some Wise Men from the East noticed a new star in the sky, so they searched for an answer in their scrolls. They saw a prophecy that made them think the Messiah had arrived. They decided to go and honor this ruler who had been announced by the stars.

And when they got to Jerusalem, the first thing they did was pay a visit to King Herod. That seemed like a good place to start. But it wasn't. Herod was more like a puppet for the Romans than a king. He was as wicked as they come, and he wasn't at all pleased to hear about any new king.

He was no fool. He asked the Wise Men to be sure to let him know when they found the new baby king so he could pay his respects—which was a big fat lie.

The Wise Men followed the star until it stopped above the house where Mary and Joseph were staying. Mary and Joseph were no doubt astonished to see their exotic visitors and the costly gifts they had brought as a sign of honor when visiting royalty.

God warned the Wise Men about Herod in a dream, so they went home another way. But Herod found out anyway, and he gave an order to kill all the baby boys in Bethlehem. Satan doesn't like to lose.

Joseph was warned by an angel, and the family escaped to Egypt.

I see someone who will come some day. I see someone who will come, but not soon. A star will come from Jacob. A ruler will rise from Israel. Numbers 24:17.

245

Jesus Learns About God's Plan

Jesus continued to learn more and more and to grow physically. People liked him, and he pleased God. Luke 2:52.

After Herod died, Joseph brought his family back from Egypt, and they settled down in Nazareth. Mary taught Jesus to read. Joseph taught Him to be a carpenter. They taught Him to be thoughtful and kind. They studied the Scriptures together. God helped them prepare Jesus for the time He would become the Messiah.

When Jesus was 12 years old, the family went to Jerusalem for Passover. During the Passover holiday the Jews thought about how God had saved His people from slavery in Egypt and about God's promise to send a Messiah to deliver them again.

In the courtyard of the Temple Jesus saw lambs being sacrificed, people bowing in prayer, smoke from incense rising to heaven. He began to understand that He was the Lamb of God— the Redeemer for whom these Passover lambs were the symbol.

Then Jesus found a classroom where boys were being taught about God. He slipped in and listened. Then He asked a question. The teachers were amazed—it was a very good question. He asked more. Soon the teachers began asking Him questions.

Meanwhile, Mary and Joseph started for home. They assumed He was with their group of travelers. When they realized He wasn't, they raced back to Jerusalem and searched everywhere. When they finally found him three days later, still talking to the teachers, they were upset. Jesus was puzzled. "Why did you have to look for me?" He asked. "You should have known that I must be where my Father's work is!" (Luke 2:49). Jesus now realized He was God's Son. He knew what His Father wanted Him to do.

Jesus Accepts God's Plan

John was preparing the way, just as the angel had said he would. He lived out in the desert, wearing clothes made of camel's hair (which couldn't have been comfortable) and eating wild honey and locusts (which couldn't have been appetizing). He told everyone who would listen that they were sinners and they needed to repent. And he told them so forcefully that lots of people were lining up to be baptized in the Jordan River.

John baptized them to show that they were sorry for their sins. People began calling him John the Baptist.

When Jesus heard what John was doing He knew it was time to begin God's plan to save the world. He went to the Jordan River and got in line to be baptized. When John saw Jesus, he knew this was the Messiah for whom he had been preparing the way. "Why do you come to me to be baptized?" John asked. "I should be baptized by you!" (Matthew 3:14). Why would John baptize Someone who had never sinned?

But baptism means more than being sorry for sins. It also shows that you are choosing God. Jesus wanted to show that He was accepting God's plan. As John baptized Jesus, the Holy Spirit came down from heaven like a dove. And God's voice said, "This is my Son and I love him. I am very pleased with him" (verse 17).

Jesus was baptized to show that He would follow God's plan. God spoke to show that Jesus had His support and approval. Now Jesus was ready to begin His work.

But the world must know that I love the Father. So I do exactly what the Father told me to do. John 14:31.

Temptations

So give yourselves to God. Stand against the devil, and the devil will run away from you. James 4:7.

After He was baptized, Jesus went to the desert so He could be alone with His Father to talk about His plan. Jesus wanted to be the kind of Messiah God wanted Him to be. For 40 days the only thing Jesus did was pray. He was weak and hungry. That's when Satan decided to attack.

Satan said, "If you are the Son of God, tell these rocks to become bread" (Matthew 4:3). Jesus could go around turning rocks into bread; then people would follow Him just so they could eat. But that was not the kind of Messiah Jesus was going to be.

Then Satan took Jesus to the top of the temple. He told Jesus to jump off—to claim a Bible promise and prove that He had faith. The angels surely would save Jesus if He jumped. Then a big crowd would gather and follow Him anywhere. But Jesus didn't have to prove anything. And that was not the kind of Messiah Jesus was going to be.

Then Satan took Jesus to a high mountain. He offered to give Jesus the world if Jesus would only bow and worship Satan; then Jesus would not have to die. But the world did not belong to Satan; it belonged to God. And the Messiah must die in order to redeem the people from sin. Satan's plan would not work. Jesus wouldn't try to take the easy way out. That was not the kind of Messiah Jesus was going to be.

Jesus told Satan to go away. Jesus was going to follow God's plan. Jesus chose to say no, just as you can choose to say no when Satan tempts you.

Jesus Calls His Disciples

Jesus began His work in Galilee. He began to preach, and crowds of people began to listen to Him. Word spread that He was a great teacher.

They left everything and followed Jesus. Luke 5:11.

It was common in those days for teachers to have disciples who would follow their masters to learn from them. Jesus was ready to choose His disciples.

He was walking by Lake Galilee when He saw two fishermen, Simon Peter and Andrew. They were throwing a net into the lake to catch fish. They were using a casting net, which was shaped like a circle and had weights around the edge. As it sank, it would surround the fish, and the one fishing would draw it back in.

The Bible says, "Jesus said, 'Come follow me. I will make you fishermen for men.' At once Simon and Andrew left their nets and followed him" (Matthew 4:19, 20).

A little further on, Jesus saw two other brothers, James and John. When He told them to come with Him, they also left their boat and their nets and followed Jesus.

Jesus called a group of 12 disciples. They weren't all fishermen; for instance, Matthew was a tax collector. They were all average, ordinary people. They weren't religious leaders or political leaders or leaders of any kind. None of them were rich. None of them were well educated.

Jesus asked them to leave everything behind and follow Him, and they did it. He asked them to give up their old life and take a chance on a new life, and they did it.

Jesus asked them to help Him change the world, and they did it.

249

Totally Happy

I am very happy. And I praise him with my song. Psalm 28:7.

When God made His agreement with His people, the children of Israel, He met them on a mountain called Mount Sinai. He gave them His law.

Hundreds of years later God came to earth again—as Jesus. One day Jesus sat on a different mountainside, a hill in Galilee, and spoke about God's law.

Jesus began to teach. "Those people who know they have great spiritual needs are happy," He said. "The kingdom of heaven belongs to them" (Matthew 5:3).

This is a difficult idea. What did Jesus mean? Who are the people who know they have great spiritual needs? And why are they happy?

Some people don't think they have spiritual needs. They are proud of how good they are. They think they don't need God's help. They think they can earn salvation by keeping God's law.

Other people know they have great spiritual needs; they know they need God. They know they cannot save themselves.

People who know they need God are happy because they know that God has a plan to save them. They trust God to give them help and strength and everything they need.

We have given a name to these sayings Jesus gave on the mountainside: the Beatitudes. The word *beatitude* means that a person is totally happy. In Jesus' talk He describes the ways to be happy and the things that bring joy.

Joy in Forgiveness

On the mountainside Jesus continued teaching, "Those who are sad now are happy. God will comfort them" (Matthew 5:4). This sounds really confusing. How can a person be sad and happy?

Here is what it means. If you are going to be saved, first you have to realize that you need to be saved. You have to realize that you are a sinner and you must be sorry for your sins. You are sorry, and that is why you are sad.

And why are you happy? God will forgive your sins. Because you are sorry for your sins, you are forgiven. Because you are sad about your sins, you can be happy.

Let's say a boy is getting into a bad habit of being mean to his little sister. His mother tries to talk to him; she explains how important it is for him to be kind and to be a good example. It doesn't help; he doesn't listen; he doesn't treat her any better.

There is no happiness in this situation.

Now let's say that one day the boy says something really horrid to his sister. Then he happens to glance up and see the stricken look on his mother's face. All of a sudden he realizes how awful he has been. He can see the pain he has been causing everyone.

Then let's say this boy sincerely apologizes to his sister. He promises his mother that he will change.

He is sad. He is sorry for the way he has been acting. Now things will get better. Now there will be happiness in his family. There is joy in forgiveness.

More Totally Happy

But those who do
right should be glad.
Psalm 68:3.

Jesus taught the people on the mountainside, "Those who are humble are happy. The earth will belong to them" (Matthew 5:5).

Jesus knew the importance of being humble. People who are proud think they know everything already. But a person who is humble can be taught.

People who are proud do not believe that they really need God. A person who is humble is willing to do whatever God asks. When people are willing to work with God, anything is possible. They will be happy.

Just look at Moses, the greatest leader the children of Israel ever had. The Bible says that Moses, this great man, "was very humble. He was the least proud person on earth" (Numbers 12:3). Obviously, it's great to be humble.

Next Jesus told the people, "Those who want to do right more than anything else are happy. God will fully satisfy them" (Matthew 5:6).

Do you want to be good? Of course.

Do you want to be good more than anything else? That's a harder question.

Another version of the Bible says that these people are hungry and thirsty for goodness. They want to be good the same way someone who is starving wants food. If you want goodness this much, you will be happy—even if you make mistakes sometimes.

People who want to do right more than anything else are happy because that's what God wants too. God wants to help them be good.

The Golden Rule

Jesus continued teaching the people on the mountainside, "Those who give mercy to others are happy. Mercy will be given to them" (Matthew 5:7). Many times people will follow your example. If you are kind to others, they will be kind to you. If you forgive others, you will be forgiven. The way you treat others affects the way they treat you. You can see how this leads to happiness.

This doesn't always work. There are some people to whom you can be nice, and they won't be nice back. But still, it is a good idea to be kind—even if they aren't kind in return. It can still lead to happiness. God says that He will be as merciful to us as we are to others. Does this beatitude remind you of the golden rule? That's the nickname for today's Bible text.

Then Jesus told the people, "Those who are pure in their thinking are happy. They will be with God" (verse 8). When God told us from Mount Sinai "Do not steal" or "Do not lie," it seemed so simple. These teachings of Jesus seem more complicated. Jesus asks us to think about why we are doing something. Jesus even asks us to think about why we are thinking something. Jesus asks us to think—and that's hard work.

Have you ever asked yourself, "Why am I giving an offering? Is it because I want everyone to see how holy I am? Is it because my parents put it in my hand and told me to give? Is it because it's a habit? Is it because I really want to give?" It's hard to think, because sometimes that forces us to change. Sometimes that's what we need to do.

> Do for other people the same things you want them to do for you. This is the meaning of the law of Moses and the teaching of the prophets.
> Matthew 7:12.

253

Even More Totally Happy

Jesus talked about two more ways to be happy. He said, "Those who work to bring peace are happy. God will call them his sons" (Matthew 5:9).

There are some people who like to cause trouble. They pick fights and say things to get people mad at each other. And then there are other people who do just the opposite. They help people get along. They help people forgive each other and be friends again. They look for the best in others, and help people do their best. They are working to bring peace. They are happy.

Jesus ends with another difficult idea: "Those who are treated badly for doing good are happy. The kingdom of heaven belongs to them" (verse 10). How can people be happy about being treated badly? They can, if they think about the "doing good" part, not the "treated badly" part. People who are doing good, for all the right reasons, are happy no matter what. They have thought about why they are doing it, and they want to do it with all their hearts because they love Jesus.

They know it's all going to work out for good in the end. They know that God has a plan and that if they are willing to follow that plan, they can live in the kingdom of heaven.

This list of ways to be happy was not what the people who were listening to Jesus expected to hear. It was not a list of do's and don'ts, like the Ten Commandments. This list doesn't include any of the things you'd expect to see on a happiness list—such as a beautiful house or nice clothes. This list makes us think very hard. Jesus offers a happiness that anyone can have and no one can take away.

Salt of the Earth

Perhaps you have been listening to some grown-ups talk and heard one of them say something like "Oh, yes, Tom and Edith are the salt of the earth." What in the world does that mean? Is it a good thing?

You are the salt of the earth. But if the salt loses its salty taste, it cannot be made salty again. It is good for nothing. Matthew 5:13.

Yes, it is a very good thing. It's a nice thing to say about someone. When we say people are the salt of the earth we mean that they are helpful and hardworking and trustworthy. It means that we admire them very much.

The saying comes from something Jesus said when He was teaching the people. It's today's Bible text. You may think it's strange to say someone is like salt, because salt is so common and everyday to us. But in those days salt was precious and valuable. Roman soldiers were paid in salt at one time (that's where the word *salary* comes from).

So when Jesus says that we are like salt, He is giving us a compliment. He is saying that we are valuable and useful.

You can buy potato chips either salted or unsalted. If you've ever eaten an unsalted potato chip, you probably won't have any trouble eating just one. Why bother? We eat potato chips because we like the salty taste.

Salt may be good for preserving things and purifying things and it may even make a good salary, but the best thing about salt is that it makes food taste better. When Jesus says that we are like salt, He means that we can make life better for others.

Jesus and the Law

Don't think that I have come to destroy the law of Moses or the teaching of the prophets. I have not come to destroy their teachings but to do what they said.

Matthew 5:17.

The Jewish leaders were not happy about the things Jesus was saying when He taught the people. They complained that He did not keep the law.

Over the years the law had gotten bigger and bigger. The scribes were Jews whose job was to study the Ten Commandments and turn them into thousands of rules and regulations. The scribes wanted to make sure there was a rule for every possible situation in life.

For instance, the fourth commandment says that we shouldn't work on Sabbath. So the scribes made hundreds of laws about what kinds of things were work. They decided that it was work to write. Then they made law after law about what that meant. If you wrote two letters of the alphabet with your right or left hand, even if they were with different inks or from different languages, you were guilty of breaking the Sabbath. But it was OK if you wrote one letter on the wall and another in the dust.

That was the Jewish leaders' idea of keeping the law and serving God. This was not what God had in mind. Jesus wanted to show the people what the law really meant.

Instead of making more laws, Jesus condensed the law into two great laws. He taught people to "love the Lord your God with all your heart, soul and mind" and "love your neighbor as you love yourself" (Matthew 22:37, 39). Jesus didn't make the law bigger; He made it deeper.

Love Your Enemies

Jesus taught, "Love God and love your neighbor." It may seem that having only these two simple laws would be easier than trying to follow the thousands of laws that the Jewish leaders required. But actually, obeying the many laws might be simpler.

With the Jewish laws, no matter what situation the people were in, there was a law to tell them what to do. Can we move this lamp from here to there without breaking the Sabbath? No. OK, that's settled.

But with these two laws about love, we have to think. Whenever we have a problem, we have to try to figure out the right thing to do. That's difficult.

Having two laws is not simpler than having 10, either. Listen to what Jesus taught about the sixth commandment: "You have heard that it was said to our people long ago, 'You must not murder anyone'" (Matthew 5:21). Of course, everyone who was listening remembered that law very well. Then Jesus told them that this was not enough. He said that if we are going to follow the "love your neighbor" law, we must also not get angry with our neighbors or say bad things to them or call them fools.

Then Jesus took the sixth commandment even further. He told the people, "You have heard that it was said, 'Love your neighbor and hate your enemies.' But I tell you, love your enemies. Pray for those who hurt you" (Matthew 5:43, 44).

Love your enemies? These two laws are not simple at all.

If you love only those who love you, should you get some special praise for doing that? No! Even sinners love the people who love them! Luke 6:32.

Teach Us to Pray

Jesus' disciples knew how to pray. They had prayed all their lives. The Jews took praying very seriously. There were prayers they had to pray at sunrise and at sunset. There were prayers to be said at 9:00 in the morning, at noon, and at 3:00 in the afternoon. There were prayers before and after meals, prayers for when it rained, prayers for getting good news, prayers for leaving a city. Praying was important.

Jesus prayed a lot. But the disciples noticed that He didn't pray the way everyone else did. At 3:00 many people would just pause and mumble their memorized prayer, then hurry on. Others would make sure they were on the steps of the Temple; then they would pray loud and long, impressing everyone around with how holy they were.

Jesus didn't pray like that. After Jesus prayed, He seemed so peaceful and strong. One time, after He had finished praying, His disciples asked Him, "Lord, please teach us how to pray, too" (Luke 11:1). So Jesus taught them a prayer. We still pray it today.

The prayer starts, "Our Father in heaven" (Matthew 6:9). Jesus teaches us to call God "our Father." We can talk to God as we would talk to a loving father.

Notice that Jesus does not teach us to say "my Father." He says "our Father." God doesn't belong to only you or only me. In this entire prayer, you cannot find "I," "me," or "mine." We are not alone. We are God's children. We are brothers and sisters of Christ. We often pray this prayer with our Christian brothers and sisters in church.

Always Holy

We call this prayer the Lord's Prayer because our Lord taught it to us. You should learn by memory the King James Bible version—that's the one we say together in church. But we will study the International Children's Bible version because the words are so easy to understand.

Our Father in heaven, we pray that your name will always be kept holy.
Matthew 6:9.

Jesus taught us to pray to our Father in heaven. We must remember that God is in heaven and we are on earth. He is holy and we must be reverent.

God created us. He deserves our worship and honor. He is special—we must not treat Him as if He were one of us. He is our Father, but He is also our God.

In Bible times a name was more than just a word. Your name stood for everything you were. Your name was your character. So when Jesus teaches us to pray that God's name will be kept holy, He is asking us to respect God's character. We must honor God's holiness and love. We must be reverent. Always. Not just in church.

It's easy to be like the Jews who mumbled their 3:00 prayers and then hurried on their way. It's easy to be reverent during church and then after church put our reverence back in its box on the shelf and go back to our regular lives.

But Jesus wants us to learn to make that reverence a part of our regular lives—so that whatever we do, we do it to honor God. He asks us to live so that we are always aware of God. He asks us to live so that we honor God's name.

The Kingdom of God

We pray that your kingdom will come. We pray that what you want will be done here on earth as it is in heaven. Matthew 6:10.

The Lord's Prayer teaches us to say, "We pray that your kingdom will come." Jesus often spoke of the kingdom of God. He was always telling little stories that started out, "The kingdom of God is like . . ." And He would compare the kingdom to a farmer planting seeds or a great treasure or yeast in bread dough. Jesus really wanted us to know about the kingdom of God.

It's not a place. It's not overthrowing the Romans, as the Jews hoped. The kingdom of God is a way of life. It's the way God rules in the lives of His people when they love and obey Him.

When you say the Lord's Prayer out loud in the King James Version, this part sounds almost like a rhyme: "Thy kingdom come. Thy will be done." Their rhythm goes together.

And their ideas go together. These two ideas belong side by side. The kingdom of God exists when God's will is done.

In this prayer Jesus teaches us to ask God to do what is best. When we pray this, we are saying that we trust in God's wisdom. We are admitting that God knows best. We are also saying that we are sure of God's love. We know that God will do what is best for us if we ask Him to, because He loves us. We are saying that we will do what He wants us to do, because we love Him. We want to live in the kingdom of God.

Our Daily Bread

The first half of the Lord's Prayer is about honoring God. In the second half, Jesus teaches us to ask God for what we need.

Give us the food we need for each day.
Matthew 6:11.

First He teaches us to talk about the present—to ask for what we need right now to keep us alive. God the Father is the Creator of life; He will give us what we need.

We need food. God will help us get the food we need today.

When God rescued the children of Israel from slavery in Egypt, they wandered around in the desert for 40 years before they finally made it to the Promised Land. There was not much food in the desert, certainly not enough for all those people. But God gave them the food they needed for each day. He sent them manna—bread from heaven. God told Moses, "I will cause food to fall like rain from the sky. This food will be for all of you" (Exodus 16:4). God fed the children of Israel.

When Elijah was delivering messages from God, God sent birds to bring him food. Then God sent Elijah to stay at a place where the "jar of flour will never become empty. The jug will always have oil in it" (1 Kings 17:14). God fed Elijah.

Jesus turned water into wine and a little boy's lunch into enough for 5,000 people.

God has no problem giving us the food we need each day. And we don't need to worry about the future. We can live one day at a time, knowing God will take care of us.

Also, notice that we pray, "Give us food," not "Give me food." We ask for others as well as for ourselves. We ask God to help us share His gifts.

Forgiveness

Forgive the sins we have done, just as we have forgiven those who did wrong to us. Matthew 6:12.

Next Jesus teaches us to talk to God about the past—He teaches us to ask for forgiveness. God the Son redeemed us from sin; He died so we could be forgiven.

We make mistakes. We mess up. Sometimes we even sin on purpose. We need forgiveness. We need to admit that we have sinned, and we need to ask for forgiveness.

Then we need to accept that we are forgiven.

And then we need to forgive others. If we aren't willing to forgive others, God will not forgive us (Matthew 6:15). We need to learn how to forgive others. It's important.

Jesus told a story about this. A servant owed the king several million dollars and couldn't pay it back. The king ordered that everything the servant owned should be sold to pay the debt. The servant begged for time, and the king felt sorry for him. So the king told the servant he didn't have to pay any of the money back.

"Later, that same servant found another servant who owed him a few dollars. The servant grabbed the other servant around the neck and said, 'Pay me the money you owe me!'" (Matthew 18:28). The other servant begged for time, but the first servant had him thrown into prison. The king heard about it and angrily called the first servant in. He gave him a huge lecture and threw him in prison until he could pay everything he owed.

Then Jesus says, "This king did what my heavenly Father will do to you if you do not forgive your brother from your heart" (Matthew 18:35). Forgiveness is important.

Full Armor

Finally Jesus teaches us to talk to God about the future—He teaches us to ask for help in resisting sin. God the Holy Spirit will guide us; He will give us strength to say no to temptation.

Do not cause us to be tested; but save us from the Evil One. Matthew 6:13.

In this prayer Jesus is not saying that we should ask God to keep all temptations away from us. We are going to be tempted. Satan is going to try to get us to sin. But God will help us. We don't have to face the evil one alone. God will give us His "armor" to wear. God will give us His power.

The apostle Paul knew about temptation. He wrote, "Finally, be strong in the Lord and in his great power. Wear the full armor of God. Wear God's armor so that you can fight against the devil's evil tricks" (Ephesians 6:10, 11).

How can you put on this armor? What can you do to avoid temptation? Ask the Holy Spirit to help you make good choices.

You can choose your friends carefully. With some people it's easy to be good. But there are others who are a bad influence; they encourage you to do the wrong thing. The friends you choose can make a big difference in the choices you make.

You can choose how you spend your time. In school you can do your best, or you can goof off and keep others from doing their work. And think about your free time. What do you watch on TV? What video games do you play? What books do you read?

God will help you make good choices. God will help you resist temptation.

Making Wishes

Now, any cake is a wonderful thing, but a birthday cake is especially wonderful. Birthday cakes almost always have candles—the same number as your age. Some people say you should make a wish and then blow out the candles; if you blow them all out at once your wish may come true. That's a fun game, but of course the candles don't have any power to make wishes come true. It's just for fun.

Sometimes people get mixed up about prayer. They think prayer is the same thing as making wishes. They think that folding their hands and closing their eyes is sort of like blowing out all the candles. But prayer isn't a game. Prayer isn't making wishes.

Prayer is power. When we ask God for something, He doesn't just deliver it. (Can you imagine how selfish we'd become?) When we ask God to do something, He doesn't just do it. (We would become so lazy!) He gives us the power to do it ourselves.

Prayer is power. When we are having a hard time and we pray for help, God doesn't just make the bad things go away. (We would turn into a bunch of fraidy cats.) He gives us the power to deal with them or accept them.

Some things God simply gives us if we ask—salvation, forgiveness, eternal life. These are things we can't do for ourselves, things only God can give, things He wants to give. But there are other things God doesn't just hand out. He knows a better way. He wants us to become unselfish, brave workers for Him. And when we pray, He gives us the power to deal with our problems and get what we need and do what we have to do.

The House on the Rock

Jesus often had crowds of people around him, listening to what He was teaching. He was a great teacher. He told great stories. People loved to listen to His stories. But Jesus knew that listening wasn't enough. If people only listened, and the stories didn't change their lives, the teaching wouldn't do any good.

The foundation that has already been laid is Jesus Christ. 1 Corinthians 3:11.

So He told a story about it: "Everyone who hears these things I say and obeys them is like a wise man" (Matthew 7:24). Did you notice the words *hears* and *obeys?*

"The wise man built his house on rock," Jesus said (verse 24). If you've ever tried to dig a hole in rock, you know how hard it must have been to dig that foundation. But it paid off. "It rained hard and the water rose. The winds blew and hit that house," Jesus said. "But the house did not fall, because the house was built on rock" (verse 25).

"But the person who hears the things I teach and does not obey them is like a foolish man," Jesus continued (verse 26). Did you notice that this person hears? But it's not enough. The foolish man built his house on sand, and during the storm the house fell.

In Jesus' stories things often stand for something else. Jesus tells us the wise man stands for people who hear and obey, and the foolish man stands for people who only hear. The rock stands for following Jesus; the sand is ignoring what He says. The house is your life. The storm stands for temptation and the bad things that happen to you. People who hear and obey Jesus build their lives on something strong. When something bad happens, Jesus helps them get through it. People who don't follow Jesus are not strong enough by themselves to say no to temptation. It's important to hear and obey.

265

Planting Seeds

Have you ever planted a garden? Before you plant the seeds, you must dig up the dirt. Seeds need air in order to grow. How do they get air under the ground? You put it there. When you dig up the dirt, you mix air into it so that the little sprouts will have air to breathe. Digging up the dirt also lets water soak in better and kills weeds and helps you find rocks. When you dig up the dirt, you make it nice and soft so the little plant can easily push its leaves up toward the sun and push its roots down into the ground.

Jesus told a story once about planting seeds (Matthew 13:1-23). He said the dirt made all the difference. If the dirt was too hard, the seeds couldn't settle into it. If the dirt was rocky, the roots wouldn't be able to grow deep enough and before long the plants would die. If there were weeds growing in the dirt, they would choke the good plants. But if the seeds were planted in good dirt, they would grow and give us food.

Why would Jesus tell a story about seeds? Well, it wasn't really about seeds. The people understood seeds, so Jesus used that idea to teach about a different idea.

In Jesus' story the seed is like His plan for saving us from sin. The different kinds of dirt are the different ways people can react to hearing about that plan. People can choose to ignore it. Or people can hear and obey and let Jesus into their lives.

So what kind of dirt are you going to be? Are you ready to get dug up? Are you ready to throw out the rocks and the weeds and the hardness? Do you want God's plan to be able to grow in you? Hear and obey.

The Rich Young Ruler

Not everyone who listened to Jesus' teaching was willing to hear and obey. Some people heard what Jesus said and chose to ignore it.

It will be very hard for rich people to enter the kingdom of God! Luke 18:24.

Once a rich Jewish leader asked Jesus what he needed to do to get eternal life. This man thought what a lot of people think: that eternal life is something you could earn.

Jesus' answer was what the man expected. "You know the commands: . . . 'You must not murder anyone. You must not steal. You must not tell lies'" (Luke 18:20).

"The man said, 'Teacher, I have obeyed all these commands since I was a boy.' Jesus looked straight at the man and loved him" (Mark 10:20, 21). He wanted to show this man that the commands are not a list to be checked off, with eternal life as the prize. The man was thinking, *I haven't murdered anyone. I do not lie. I haven't done anyone any harm.* Yes, but he hadn't done anyone any good, either. He was selfish.

If this man wanted to live in the kingdom of God, he would have to start thinking about others. He would have to learn to love. He kept the law, but he didn't understand what it meant. He knew that he must not steal. Now he needed to learn to give.

"Jesus said, 'There is still one more thing you need to do. Go and sell everything you have, and give the money to the poor. You will have a reward in heaven. Then come and follow me'" (verse 21). But the man didn't. He wouldn't give up his money and his things and his comfort. He chose to have his reward here rather than in heaven.

"He was very sad to hear Jesus say this, and he left" (verse 22).

267

Asking Questions

Many 2-year-olds have discovered a special word: why. An older person might say, "Drink your milk." The 2-year-old says, "Why?" "Because it will make you big and strong." "Why?" "It has calcium in it." "Why?" "Calcium makes your bones strong." "Why?" And on and on, until the older person gets tired of it or doesn't know the answer and says one special word that stops the questions: because.

Who knows if 2-year-olds actually understand the answers or even listen to them, but it's a step they take on the way to learning to ask better questions. It's important to learn to ask questions. If you want to know the answer, you have to ask the right question in the right way. Questions are a good way to learn.

They are also a good way to teach. Jesus asked a lot of questions.

The first thing we hear Him say is a question. After spending three days amazing the teachers at the Temple with His questions, He asked His mother and father, "Why did you have to look for me?" (Luke 2:49). One of the last things He said before He went back to heaven was to Peter on the shore: "Do you love me?" (John 21:17). And in between He asked lots of questions. He asked the disciples in the storm, "Why are you so afraid?" (Mark 4:40). He asked Martha, "Do you believe?" (John 11:26).

To all of them, to all of us, over and over: Do you hear? Will you obey? Can you see? Do you understand? Do you believe? Do you love Me? He asks questions to help us learn, to help us think, to help us believe. Because.

Prophecy Come True

One Sabbath Jesus went to the synagogue in his hometown of Nazareth. He read to the people from the book of Isaiah, today's Bible text. Then Jesus told the people that the prophecy they had just heard was coming true.

What did He mean? He was saying that He was the Messiah, the one God had promised to send. He had come to "tell the captives they are free." We are the captives. God sent Him to set us free from the power of sin. Jesus came to redeem.

He was saying that He had come to tell us about God and His plan to save us. God had sent Him to "tell the good news to the poor." Jesus came to teach.

He was saying that He had come to make people whole and help those who were hurting. He had come to "comfort those whose hearts are broken." Jesus came to heal.

The people of Nazareth were amazed. They had known this guy since He was a little kid. "They asked, 'Isn't this Joseph's son?'" (Luke 4:22). Who did He think He was?

He had told them. And they didn't like it. So Jesus went on His way.

"Jesus traveled through all the towns and villages. He taught in their synagogues and told people the Good News about the kingdom. And he healed all kinds of diseases and sicknesses. He saw the crowds of people and felt sorry for them because they were worried and helpless. They were like sheep without a shepherd" (Matthew 9:35, 36).

The Lord God has put his Spirit in me. This is because he has appointed me to tell the good news to the poor. He has sent me to comfort those whose hearts are broken. He has sent me to tell the captives they are free.
Isaiah 61:1.

269

Body and Soul

*He bowed before Jesus
and begged him,
"Lord, heal me. I know
you can if you want
to." Jesus said,
"I want to. Be healed!"
Luke 5:12, 13.*

If you open your Bible to the stories about Jesus (Matthew, Mark, Luke, John) and you read the headings above the various stories, you will discover that Jesus spent an amazing amount of His time healing people.

In story after story Jesus is healing people: Jesus Heals a Sick Man, Jesus Heals a Soldier's Servant, Jesus Heals Many People, Jesus Heals Two Men with Demons, Jesus Heals a Paralyzed Man, Jesus Gives Life to a Dead Girl and Heals a Sick Woman, Jesus Heals More People. And that's just two chapters (Matthew 8 and 9)!

In those days people who were sick were usually treated badly. There were laws that said that sick people were "unclean" and that they had to stay away from everybody else. Most people thought that if someone was sick it was because they had sinned. They believed that sickness was one way God got even with sinners.

Jesus knew that that was not true. But He saw the connection between body and soul—if one is having trouble, the other can suffer. He wanted to make people whole.

It's not surprising that great crowds of people followed Jesus wherever He went. People who were blind wanted to see. People who were paralyzed wanted to walk. People who were sick wanted to be healed.

And Jesus wanted to heal them. Not just in body, but also in soul. Jesus wanted to make them whole.

Your Sins are Forgiven

One day word got around that Jesus was teaching in a certain house. So many people crowded in to hear that there was no room to stand, not even outside the door.

Lord, be kind to me. Heal me because I have sinned against you. Psalm 41:4.

On the edges of the crowd were four men, carrying a friend of theirs on a mat. They had heard that Jesus was here. They had heard that Jesus healed people. They wanted their friend to be healed by Jesus. But they couldn't get through the crowd.

Then they got an idea. The house had a flat roof. There were outside stairs they could climb to get on the roof. The roof was made of wooden beams—the space between the beams was filled with brush, then packed with clay. It would be easy to dig out the stuff between two beams and make a hole—and it would be easy to repair the hole later.

So they made the hole and they lowered their paralyzed friend on his mat through the hole, right down in front of Jesus. Everyone noticed. Jesus stopped teaching.

"Jesus saw that these men had great faith. So he said to the paralyzed man, 'Young man, your sins are forgiven'" (Mark 2:5).

There were some Jewish leaders there who got upset when Jesus said this—after all, only God could forgive sins. Jesus wanted to show them that He had the power to forgive sins. So Jesus told the man to stand up. The Jewish leaders believed that if the man was sick it was because he had sinned—he couldn't get well until his sins were forgiven. So by their way of thinking, when the man stood up it proved that he'd been forgiven. By their logic, when the man was healed it proved that Jesus could forgive.

The Jealous Older Brother

He was lost,
but now he is found.
Luke 15:32.

Jesus traveled from village to village, teaching and healing people. People loved the way He taught. His stories were interesting; they made His ideas easy to understand and remember. Crowds of people gathered around to hear Jesus teach and to be healed.

Many people believed Jesus was the Messiah, but there were some people who did not believe. The Jewish leaders did not like the things Jesus said when He taught. They were upset about the crowds of people who came to see Jesus.

The priests, rabbis, and Pharisees had power, and they did not want to give that up. They were afraid that if the people kept listening to Jesus, no one would listen to them anymore. They were jealous.

So they determined to stop Him. They sent spies to watch Him, to try to catch Him breaking one of their many laws. Then they could convince people He was wrong.

Jesus knew what the spies were up to. But since they were listening (even though they just wanted to trap Him), He decided to try to teach them about God's love too.

Jesus told a story we call "The Prodigal Son." You've probably heard it—it's the one about the son who left home and wasted all his money, then came dragging home and his father was so happy to see him. The story has a second part about a jealous older brother. Jesus told that part for the Jewish leaders who were spying on Him.

In the story the brother was invited to the party. Jesus was inviting the leaders to join God's kingdom. Jesus wanted to save everyone—even His enemies.

Blind Leaders

Jesus wanted to save the Jewish leaders, but He did not ignore the wrong things they were doing. In fact, He let them have it. He told them they were hypocrites and snakes and cheaters, and He warned His followers to not be like them.

When the Jewish leaders asked Him why He didn't follow their rules, He asked them why they followed those rules instead of following God's rules.

When His followers told Him that the leaders got angry when He talked to them like that, Jesus answered, "Stay away from the Pharisees. They are blind leaders. And if a blind man leads another blind man, then both men will fall into a ditch" (Matthew 15:14).

The Jewish leaders often tried to trick Jesus into saying something they could use to get Him in trouble. But He always knew what they were up to, and He answered them in ways they didn't expect—ways that left them speechless and amazed.

Once the spies asked Jesus if they should pay taxes to Caesar. They figured they had Him trapped with this question. If He answered no, they could tell the Roman authorities and have Him arrested. If He answered yes, the people would get mad because they felt the tax was an insult to God.

Jesus said, "'Whose name is on the coin? And whose picture is on it?' They said, 'Caesar's.' Jesus said to them, 'Then give to Caesar the things that are Caesar's. And give to God the things that are God's'" (Luke 20:25). The spies were speechless and amazed.

They show honor to me with words. But their hearts are far from me. The honor they show me is nothing but human rules they have memorized. Isaiah 29:13.

The Wicked Farmers

The Jewish leaders were angry that the people were listening to Jesus instead of to them. When Jesus was teaching in the Temple, some of them came up to Him and demanded, "Tell us! What authority do you have to do these things?" (Luke 20:2). Jesus didn't answer their question. But He did tell them this story.

A man rented his vineyard to some farmers, but when he sent a servant to get his share of the grapes, the farmers beat the servant and sent him away with nothing. The man sent many more servants, but each time the servants were beaten or even killed.

"The owner of the vineyard said, 'What will I do now? I will send my son whom I love very much. Maybe they will respect him!'" (verse 13). But they didn't—the farmers killed the son. Jesus asked His listeners, "What will the owner of the vineyard do? . . . He will give the vineyard to other farmers" (verses 15, 16).

The vineyard stands for the nation of Israel. The owner stands for God. The servants are God's prophets. The son was God's Son, Jesus Himself.

And Jesus was telling the Jewish leaders that they were the wicked farmers. God had given them the responsibility of taking care of the vineyard, but they wanted to take it over. They weren't even willing to listen to God's Son. And God was going to take the vineyard away from them.

The leaders could have said, "You're right! We're sorry." But they didn't. They only got angrier. They wanted to arrest Jesus at once, but they were afraid of the people.

Come to the Feast

Jesus told another story to show that things were going to change for God's chosen people: A king invited some people to a wedding feast. But the people refused to come. He sent more servants to say that everything was ready, but they still wouldn't come. Some of them went to work instead. Some of them beat the servants up.

This made the king angry. But he wasn't about to waste a perfectly wonderful party. So he sent his servants to "'go to the street corners and invite everyone you see.' . . . And the wedding hall was filled with guests" (Matthew 22:9, 10).

What did this story mean? God (the king) had invited the Jews to be His people, but they had refused. They had ignored the prophets (the servants). So God was going to invite other people, non-Jewish people, to join God's kingdom (come to the party).

Do you remember the story of the good Samaritan, found in Luke 10:30-37? When Jesus told this story, His listeners were shocked. This story was about a Samaritan—the Jews hated the Samaritans. But that wasn't the worst of it—in the story the Samaritan was the hero. And the Jewish leaders in the story behaved badly.

Jesus wanted the Jews to know that things were not going to turn out the way they had always planned. They thought that only Jews would sit down at the feast. But Jesus said that just being Jewish was not enough.

You have to accept the invitation. You have to come to the table.

People will come from the east, west, north, and south. They will sit down at the table in the kingdom of God. Luke 13:29.

The Savior of the World

Jews and Samaritans were bitter enemies; they wouldn't even talk to each other. The Jews pretended that the Samaritans were invisible. But Jesus didn't. He walked right through Samaria, dragging His reluctant disciples along.

At noon, they came to a well. Jesus sat down, and the disciples went into the village to buy some food. Along came a woman from the village to fill her jar with water. She was a Samaritan; she pretended Jesus was invisible.

Jesus said, "Please give me a drink" (John 4:7). The woman was astonished. It was the custom to give travelers water, but a Jew wouldn't have accepted it from her, so she thought there was no point in offering. She said, "I am surprised that you ask me for a drink. You are a Jew and I am a Samaritan" (verse 9). She was honest.

So was Jesus. He told her that if she knew who He was, she'd ask Him for a drink and He'd give her living water. She didn't know what He meant. She was curious.

Jesus said, "Whoever drinks the water I give will never be thirsty again" (verse 14). She heard Jesus say "whoever." That included her—a Samaritan. She was thirsty.

She wanted that Water. She was beginning to understand. She said, "When the Messiah comes, he will explain everything to us" (verse 25). And Jesus said, "I am he."

The woman ran back to the village and told everyone to come and see. They came and listened to Jesus teach for two days. The villagers said, "We know that this man really is the Savior of the world" (verse 42). They were right. Jesus is the Savior of Jews, Samaritans, everyone. He is the Savior of the world.

Miracles

There are lots of stories about miracles in the Bible. The Red Sea parted so the children of Israel could escape from the Egyptians. The walls of Jericho fell down when the Israelites shouted. The lions ignored Daniel. Miracles were special signs that showed God was taking care of His people.

So they ate the bread of angels. He sent them all the food they could eat. Psalm 78:25.

When Jesus was on earth He performed miracles. The miracles showed that God had sent the Redeemer to take care of His people. In many of the miracles people were healed, but there were also miracles that showed that Jesus had power over nature.

Once Jesus and His disciples had gone someplace quiet to try to get some rest. But word got around where He was, and crowds of people came to hear Him teach and to be healed. Late in the afternoon the disciples told Jesus He should send the people away so they could buy something to eat.

"But Jesus answered, 'You give them food to eat'" (Mark 6:37). The poor disciples were stunned. There had to be at least 5,000 people there. They stammered, "We can't buy enough bread to feed all these people!"

But Jesus wasn't worried about the fact that they didn't have any food or any money to buy food. The people were hungry. They needed to eat.

The disciples found a boy with five loaves and two fish in his lunch. Jesus thanked God for the food and began dividing it up. Everybody had plenty to eat. It was a miracle. Jesus took care of the people.

Storms

One day Jesus and His disciples were in a boat in the middle of the lake when a terrible storm blew up. The boat began to fill with water, and they were in danger of sinking. The disciples were really scared. And what was Jesus doing? He was sleeping. The disciples started yelling, "Master! Master! We will drown!"

Jesus got up and spoke to the wind and the waves. The wind stopped. The lake became calm. The disciples said to each other, "What kind of man is this? He commands the wind and the water, and they obey him!" (Luke 8:25).

Jesus is in charge. He knows about storms.

Sometimes in your life bad things will happen. It's as if you're sailing along when BOOM, a storm hits. What should you do? You are in trouble. You need help.

Remember, Jesus is there. He is in the boat with you. He knows about storms. Ask Him for help.

That probably makes sense now while you are sitting here calm and safe, reading this. But when you are in the middle of something terrible, it's easy to panic. You can get so busy trying to keep the boat from filling with water, that you forget Jesus is there.

So don't wait until you are in trouble. Become good friends with Jesus now. Then, when there is trouble, you will naturally turn to Him for help. You will remember that He is there. You will remember that He is in charge.

Jesus knows about storms. He can get you safely through the storm.

In His Right Mind

After the stormy night on the lake, the disciples landed the boat in an area where non-Jews lived. As they walked away from the boat, they heard a terrifying howl. Near the shore there were caves—in those days caves were used as graves. From one of these caves came a shriek that didn't even sound human. And rushing from a cave came a wild man.

With authority and power he commands evil spirits, and they come out. Luke 4:36.

The disciples were still feeling a little shaky from their wild night on the water. So you can't really blame them for running back to the boat as fast as they could. As they pushed the boat into the water they turned and saw that Jesus was still standing on the shore. The wild man was dangerously near. His hair was long and matted; his eye were horribly blank; all that he was wearing were some broken chains hanging from his wrists.

But Jesus wasn't afraid. Jesus loved this man and wanted to help him. He knew that Satan had control of his life. Jesus healed the man by commanding the evil spirits to leave. The evil spirits asked Jesus if they could go into a nearby herd of pigs instead. Then the pigs ran into the lake and were drowned.

The pig herders ran into town and told everyone. "So people went out to see what had happened. They came to Jesus and saw the man who had had the many evil spirits. The man was sitting there, clothed and in his right mind" (Mark 5:14, 15). But the people weren't happy about it—they were afraid. They asked Jesus to leave.

The man begged Jesus to let him come with Him. But Jesus needed the man to stay and tell others his story. So he stayed and told everyone what Jesus had done for him. And when Jesus came back, the people were ready. Thousands came to hear Him teach.

279

The Sheep and the Goats

I was hungry, and you gave me food. I was thirsty, and you gave me something to drink; I was a stranger and you brought Me together with yourselves and welcomed and entertained and lodged Me; I was naked and you clothed Me; I was sick and you visited Me with help and ministering care; I was in prison and you came to see Me. Matthew 25:35, 36, Amplified.

The disciples wanted to know what it would be like when Jesus came again, so He told them a story. He started out by saying that the King would come in great glory. The disciples liked the sound of this—they were hoping Jesus would take over the world as king and give them important jobs. But that's not how the story turned out.

Jesus said that the King will gather all the people of the world and "put the sheep, the good people, on his right and the goats, the bad people, on his left" (Matthew 25:33). Then the King will tell the good people to come receive God's kingdom. This was just how the disciples thought the story should be going. But then the plot took a turn.

Jesus said today's Bible text. The disciples were confused. Surely the King's "good" people would be rich or religious—not people who gave Him a drink. The sheep in the story were confused too. They couldn't remember doing any of that. The King explained, "Anything you did for any of my people here, you also did for me" (verse 40).

Then the King told the goats almost exactly the same thing. Almost. "I was thirsty, and you gave me *nothing* to drink" (verse 42). The goats were even more surprised. They would've given the King a drink if He'd asked them. And the King explained, "Anything you refused to do for any of my people here, you refused to do for me" (verse 45).

We show our love for Jesus by loving each other. When people need help, "sheep" just help, without even thinking about it, without expecting a reward. We just do it.

Get Ready

There are different ways to study for a spelling test. Maybe you write each word three times. Maybe you write the words in a sentence. Maybe your mom tells you the word and you spell it out loud. You know.

So always be ready.
Matthew 25:13.

But on Friday morning, when your teacher tells you it's time to take the test, it is too late to study any more. If you are not ready, too bad.

Jesus told a story about 10 girls who got ready for a wedding. There was going to be a procession from the bride's house to the groom's house, and the girls wanted to join in. Because this was a night wedding, the girls brought oil-burning lamps so they could see.

If you've ever been to a wedding, you know that they don't usually start on time. Evidently weddings didn't start on time back in Bible times either, because the girls had to wait so long they fell asleep. When someone called that the procession was coming, they woke up and saw that their lamps were going out. Five of the girls had been smart—they had brought extra oil for their lamps in case this happened. They poured the oil into their lamps and were ready to go. But the other five girls didn't have extra oil. They had to go look for some. By the time they got back, the procession had passed them by. They missed the wedding because they weren't really ready.

Jesus told this wedding story to help us see how important it is to be ready. Jesus wants us to be ready when He comes to take us to heaven. Jesus wants you to choose to follow Him now. You need to get to know Jesus now. Don't wait to get ready.

Making an Entrance

Shout for joy, people of Jerusalem. Your king is coming to you. He does what is right, and he saves. He is gentle and riding on a donkey. Zechariah 9:9.

It was almost time for Passover. People were traveling to Jerusalem to sacrifice their Passover lambs. Jesus, the Lamb of God, knew it was time for Him to sacrifice His life to redeem the world.

The Jewish leaders had given orders that "if anyone knew where Jesus was, he must tell them. Then they could arrest Jesus" (John 11:57). The safe thing would be for Jesus to stay away from Jerusalem, or maybe sneak in quietly. That's not what He did.

He asked His disciples to bring Him a donkey. By the time they returned, a crowd had begun to gather. As Jesus sat on the donkey and it began to walk, the excitement grew. The people remembered the prophecy in today's Bible text. Word began to spread that this was the Messiah. People spread their coats on the road, they cut tree branches and waved them, they shouted and sang as if they were welcoming a king.

The disciples could hardly believe it—finally Jesus was doing what they'd wanted Him to do all along. He was acting like a king. More and more people joined in. The Jewish leaders tried to get people to be quiet and go home, but no one listened to them.

When the procession got to the top of a hill outside the city, everyone stopped to gaze at its beauty. Then they turned to stare at Jesus. He was crying. He was sad because the people who had rejected Him over and over were about to reject Him again. Now they were shouting, "Hosanna!" But soon they would be shouting, "Crucify Him!"

The True Sacrifice

Let's say you are making your bed and you want to put a clean pillowcase on your pillow. Would you just put the new pillowcase on over the old pillowcase? No. First you take the old pillowcase off; then you put the clean one on. You get rid of the old and replace it with the new.

So God ends the first system of sacrifices so that he can set up the new system. Hebrews 10:9.

Jesus rode into Jerusalem at Passover time. During this Passover things were going to change. The Jews had always celebrated Passover by sacrificing a lamb to help them remember that God had delivered them from slavery in Egypt. It also was supposed to help them remember that the Redeemer would come to deliver them from sin.

And now, during this Passover, the actual Lamb of God was going to be sacrificed. God's plan was moving forward. It was time to get rid of the old and replace it with the new. Jesus had come to replace the old system of sacrifices. Jesus was the new sacrifice, the new system. This Sacrifice would happen once and would last forever.

The Jews had been celebrating Passover the same way for hundreds and hundreds of years. It had become a tradition, a holiday, a custom—many people didn't really think about what it all meant anymore. They just did it. They came to Jerusalem. They bought the lamb. They sacrificed the lamb. Maybe some people even treated it as a business deal—they were paying for forgiveness and trying to buy a blessing.

Jesus had to get rid of the old system in order to replace it with the new system.

Cleaning House

This is because my Temple will be called a house for prayer for people from all nations. Isaiah 56:7.

After Jesus rode into Jerusalem, He went to the Temple. He was not pleased by what He saw.

He saw animals. Because many people traveled great distances for Passover, they didn't bring animals to sacrifice. So the priests allowed dealers to sell animals in the outer court of the Temple. It was noisy and confusing and it didn't smell very good, either.

He saw moneychangers. The priests would accept only the Temple shekel. So people with a different kind of money had to exchange it for Temple shekels at the moneychanging tables. The moneychangers charged high rates. They were noisy too.

He saw what was happening in the holy Temple that had been built as a place to worship His Father. He saw that the priests were earning money from all this business instead of stopping it. He saw poor people buy overpriced sacrifices so their sins could be forgiven. He saw people buy, sell, cheat, without a thought as to where they were.

"He threw out all the people who were buying and selling there. He turned over the tables that belonged to the men who were exchanging different kinds of money" (Matthew 21:12). Money, animals, and people scattered everywhere. Nobody argued.

Then they were gone. It was quiet. Jesus was left alone with His disciples. But not for long. Sick people crept up to Jesus. People tiptoed in to listen to Jesus teach. Children climbed onto His lap. It was peaceful. But the priests were not happy, not at all.

The Terrible Truth

The Jewish leaders were angry that Jesus had made such a scene in the Temple, chasing everyone out. They were jealous that the people were listening to Jesus instead of to them. They were worried that they were losing their power. "They began trying to find a way to kill Jesus" (Mark 11:18).

They tell you to do things, but they don't do the things themselves. Matthew 23:3.

They tried and tried to trap Him with trick questions. But His answers were always so good that the people became even more impressed with Jesus and less impressed with the Jewish leaders. So after a while none of the leaders were "brave enough to ask Jesus any more questions" (Matthew 22:46).

But Jesus was brave. Even though He knew they were trying to figure out a way to kill Him, He didn't try to avoid them. He kept telling them the truth about themselves.

In Matthew 23 Jesus tells the terrible truth over and over. Seven times He says, "How terrible for you, teachers of the law and Pharisees!" Then each time He confronts them with ways that they are bad examples for the people. Jesus tells them that they close the door of heaven to people. That they are evil missionaries who make people fit for hell. That they teach people how to get out of keeping promises. That they focus on little things (such as paying tithe on a dill plant), but ignore the important things (such as being fair). That they are like dishes that have been washed on the outside but are still dirty on the inside, or like tombs that have been whitewashed on the outside but are still full of bones. He told them they were hypocrites. He told them they would be sent to hell.

He was brave. He told the truth.

285

Like a Chicken

He will protect you like a bird spreading its wings over its young. Psalm 91:4.

Jesus was very brave. But He said that He wanted to act like a chicken.

That sounds odd to us. When we call someone a chicken, we mean that they are afraid. But that's not what Jesus meant.

When Jesus told the Jewish leaders "How terrible for you!" He was angry, but He was also very sad. He remembered how the people had rejected the prophets over and over.

So Jesus spoke to the city, as if He could talk to all the people who had ever lived there: "Jerusalem, Jerusalem! You kill the prophets and kill with stones those men God sent to you. Many times I wanted to help your people! I wanted to gather them together as a hen gathers her chicks under her wings. But you did not let me" (Matthew 23:37).

When a mother chicken senses that there is danger, she calls her chicks to her. She hides them under her wings until the danger is past. If they run to her when she calls, if they snuggle quietly under her wings, if they obey and trust her, they will be safe.

Again and again God had called the people to Him. But He would not force them to come. People can choose whether or not they want to obey. He could only call and call, with His wings spread out, hoping that His people would come to Him and be saved.

Once again Jesus, the mother hen, was calling. Would the leaders come? It was not too late. Would the people come, or would they turn on Him at the first sign of trouble? Would His disciples come, the people closest to Him, the ones who knew Him best—or would they abandon Him, deny Him, betray Him?

Giving Everything

God loves the person who gives happily.
2 Corinthians 9:7.

Jesus was tired. He went into the courtyard of the Temple and sat down to rest. He just sat, watching the people bringing their offerings. Because it was Passover there were lots more people than usual. And the rich people were putting on quite a show.

They would sweep into the courtyard with lots of money and maybe even with a servant to carry it for them. They would make a big deal about deciding how much money went into each offering box. Then they would drop the coins into the boxes with a great deal of clanking and grandly march out of the courtyard. Jesus was not impressed.

Jesus saw a poor widow creep up to the money box, slip in two very small copper coins, and hurry away. She was shy and embarrassed by her tiny gift, but she wanted to give an offering to God.

Jesus told His disciples, "This poor widow gave only two small coins. But she really gave more than all those rich people. The rich have plenty; they gave only what they did not need. This woman is very poor, but she gave all she had" (Luke 21:3, 4).

Both of those coins together were worth less than a penny. But Jesus said she gave more than the rich people. How can that be? Their hundreds were worth a lot more than her little coins. Yes, but she gave all she had. She gave everything. They just gave some. And "everything" is more than "some."

She was willing to give everything to God. She loved with all her heart, soul, and mind. And thousands of years later, we still talk of it; we are still impressed.

Preparations

This was a time when the Jews always sacrificed the Passover lambs. Jesus' followers came to him. They said, "We will go and prepare everything for the Passover Feast. Where do you want to eat the feast?" Mark 14:12.

The Jewish leaders were losing their power over the people. They had to do something about it. They met at the high priest's palace. "At the meeting, they planned to set a trap to arrest Jesus and kill him. But they said, 'We must not do it during the feast. The people might cause a riot'" (Matthew 26:4, 5). The leaders prepared to kill Jesus.

But then Judas showed up and offered them a way to solve their problem. Judas was one of the 12 disciples, one of Jesus' best friends, one of His closest followers. "He said, 'I will give Jesus to you. What will you pay me for doing this?' The priests gave Judas 30 silver coins. After that, Judas waited for the best time to give Jesus to the priests" (verses 15, 16). Judas prepared to betray Jesus.

Meanwhile, the disciples got ready for the Passover feast. Peter and John came to Jesus and told Him they would get things ready. They asked Him where He wanted to have the feast. Jesus told them to follow a man carrying a jar of water. When he went into a house, they were to ask there about a room where they could have the Passover meal.

Everything happened just as Jesus had said. They were shown a large room upstairs. They brought the food there. The disciples prepared to celebrate Passover.

That evening people all over Jerusalem gathered together to eat the Passover feast. Jesus was glad for these last peaceful moments as He prepared to die.

Our Example

In Bible times people wore sandals. Whenever they went anywhere their feet got dirty because the roads were dusty. When people had a party it was the custom to provide water and a towel so guests could get their feet cleaned up. You've seen pictures of the way people dressed back then. It was hard for them to try to wash their feet with all those clothes on, so someone would wash their feet for them. It was a messy, unpleasant job. They made a servant do it.

I, your Lord and Teacher, have washed your feet. So you also should wash each other's feet. I did this as an example for you. John 13:14, 15.

At this last Passover feast Jesus ate with His disciples, there was water and a towel, but there was no servant. None of the disciples were willing to wash anybody's feet. They were busy arguing about who would be the greatest leader in the kingdom they thought Jesus was going to set up. How could you be thought of as a leader if you were acting like a servant?

Jesus showed them how. He washed their feet. They were confused—why was their Master doing servant's work? When Jesus was done He told them why. It's today's Bible text. Jesus wanted them to know that the best kind of greatness is the greatness of helping people.

We want to remember this, so sometimes at church we wash each other's feet. Maybe you've seen it. We wash each other's feet because we want to remember how important it is to help each other and love each other. We follow Jesus' example.

New Symbols

Do this to remember me. Luke 22:19.

As Jesus and His disciples ate their Passover meal, Jesus wanted to show the disciples that things were going to change. Up until now people had been looking forward to the Redeemer. Now the Redeemer was here. After He died, the old agreement between God and the children of Israel would be finished. God would make a new agreement with His people.

"Jesus took some bread. He thanked God for it and broke it. Then He gave it to his followers and said, 'Take it. This bread is my body'" (Mark 14:22).

The special Passover bread had always been a symbol of when God rescued the children of Israel from Egypt. Now Jesus was showing the disciples a new symbol for the bread. From now on the bread would be a symbol of when Jesus had died to rescue His people from sin.

Then Jesus passed around a cup; the disciples each took a sip. Jesus said, "This is my blood which begins the new agreement that God makes with his people. This blood is poured out for many to forgive their sins" (Matthew 26:28).

The Passover wine had always been a symbol to help them remember their freedom from Egypt. Now it would be a symbol to help us remember that Jesus has given us freedom from sin.

We want to remember this, so sometimes at church we celebrate the Lord's Supper. We eat the bread and drink the grape juice together. And we remember.

The New Agreement

The old agreement between God and the children of Israel was based on the law. When God gave them the Ten Commandments He told them, "Obey me and keep my agreement. Do this, and you will be my own possession" (Exodus 19:5). To keep the old agreement, the people had to obey God's law.

It is not written on stone tablets. It is written on human hearts.
2 Corinthians 3:3.

Then God sent Jesus, the Messiah, to redeem the people from sin. The old agreement was finished. That part of God's plan was complete.

At the last supper Jesus ate with His disciples, He told them about the new agreement that God was making with His people. "I give you a new command: Love each other. You must love each other as I have loved you. All people will know that you are my followers if you love each other" (John 13:34, 35).

The new agreement is based on love—God's love for us, our love for God, our love for each other.

Do we love each other because that's the way to earn salvation, to earn God's love? No. We don't have to earn salvation—Jesus has already redeemed us. We don't have to earn God's love—He has always loved us.

We love each other so that people will know we are Christians, so that they will see God's love in us. We love each other because Jesus loved us. He is our example. We love each other "as I have loved you."

How did He love us? He gave everything. He forgave everything.

Learn It by Heart

Are you learning about the metric system? It's wonderfully logical. Once you know a few basic terms, you can figure out what the words mean. For instance, *centi-* means "hundred." Whenever you see a word with *cent* in it, it probably has something to do with a hundred. There are 100 *cents* in a dollar. A *century* is 100 years. Can you figure out what a centipede is if I tell you that *pede* means "foot"?

If you had a vocabulary test on the metric system, you could memorize each word. Or you could just remember that *kilo* means a thousand times bigger and *milli* means a thousand times smaller, etc. Then you'd be able to figure out what the words mean from looking at the parts. You would also be learning to understand the system.

Memorizing and learning are not the same thing. Let's say you need to memorize today's Bible text. You could just memorize it, word for word. Then you could put a star on the memory verse chart. But you'll have to do more if you want to *learn* it.

Get out your Bible and turn to John 13. Let's see who's speaking. Look at verse 33—it's Jesus. To whom is He talking? Look at the beginning of the chapter—it's His disciples. There are so many more things you could learn about this verse. Remember what the disciples had just been doing instead of loving each other? Arguing over who was the greatest.

You can learn by memory (millimeter, centimeter, decimeter, meter). Or you can learn to understand. (*Centurion?* He must be the commander of a *hundred* people.)

Memorizing is good. Understanding is better. Learn it by heart.

All You Can Eat

Love never ends.

1 Corinthians 13:8.

Some people think love is like pie. They pass it out in little slices or they save it for later. They are stingy with it because they don't want to use it up.

But love is not like pie. Love doesn't run out. You don't need to save it or be stingy with it or worry about using it all up.

Do you remember that story about Elijah the prophet and the time of no rain (1 Kings 17)? The jar of flour and the jug of oil did not get used up. Every day there was enough so that Elijah and the widow and her son could eat. The flour and oil that never run out—that's what love is like.

Jesus tells us, "You must love each other as I have loved you" (John 13:34). The reason love doesn't run out is that it comes from Jesus. He just keeps pouring it out. He loves us with no limit.

And there's more. Love doesn't disappear when you give it away. It grows. Let's say you give your mom a hug. Then she might give it to your brother and he might give it to your dad and he might give it to your grandma and she might give it to your cousin. Who knows how far that hug will travel?

So we can love as much as we want. We can give a hug anytime it seems like a good idea. We can tell people we love them and show them that we love them. We can spend all our kisses, and still there will be more.

Love never ends.

A Helper

I will ask the Father, and He will give you another Helper.
John 14:16.

So Jesus has given us a new command: to love each other as He loved us. Does that mean we don't need to obey the old commandments anymore?

No. We still need the Ten Commandments. They show us how to love God and love each other. They are very helpful.

In fact, if you look a little further at what Jesus said to His disciples at that last supper, you will see that Jesus still expects us to obey the commandments. Look at John 14:15: "If you love me, you will do the things I command." When we obey God, we show our love for Him.

You can say, "I love my classmates." But if you cheat them or bully them, the words won't be true. You can say, "I love my family." But if you tease your brother or sass your mother, the words won't mean much. We show love by what we do.

Jesus' new command is that we should love others as He loved us. Is this even possible? No, not if we try to do it on our own. But look at today's Bible text. We have help. Jesus promised to send us a Helper—the Holy Spirit.

The Holy Spirit helps us love. The Holy Spirit helps us love without thinking of ourselves. He helps us love without limit. He helps us love others as they are, in spite of their faults, forgiving their faults. The Holy Spirit helps us love others as Jesus loved us.

Jesus has given us a very difficult new command. But He has given us the Holy Spirit to show us what to do and to help us get it done.

Betrayed

"Aren't you also one of that man's followers?" John 18:17.

Peter was one of Jesus' best friends. It's true that he had a lot of faults. He often said the wrong thing at the wrong time. He often did things without thinking about them first. But Peter loved Jesus, and Jesus knew it. Peter wanted to do the right thing, even if it didn't always turn out that way.

At the Last Supper Jesus told His disciples that He would be leaving soon. And Peter blurted out, "Where are you going? Why can't I follow you now? I am ready to die for you!" (John 13:36, 37). And Jesus said, "Will you really die for me? . . . Before the rooster crows, you will say three times that you don't know me" (verse 38).

And that's what happened. After supper Jesus and His disciples left the room and went to a garden to pray. Judas, the disciple who had made a deal with the Jewish leaders, led a group of soldiers and guards to Jesus. And Jesus was arrested.

Jesus was taken to the high priest's house. Most of the disciples had run away, but Peter followed and tried to sneak into the courtyard. A girl at the door thought she recognized him as one of Jesus' followers, but Peter said he wasn't.

Peter pushed his way through the crowd to warm up by the fire. Some of the servants standing around asked if he was one of Jesus' followers. Peter said he wasn't.

Then one of the high priest's servants said, " 'Didn't I see you with him in the garden?' Again Peter said it wasn't true. Just then a rooster crowed" (John 18:26, 27).

Then Peter remembered what Jesus had said. And he began to cry.

Trial

"What should I do with Jesus, the one called the Christ?"
Matthew 27:22.

At the high priest's house more and more people gathered to see what all the excitement was about. The Jewish leaders who had arrested Jesus "tried to find something false against Jesus so that they could kill him. Many people came and told lies about him. But the council could find no real reason to kill Jesus" (Matthew 26:59, 60).

The priests and leaders were nervous. What they were doing was illegal—a secret trial, in the middle of the night. For now they had the crowd of people on their side. But they needed to get rid of Jesus quickly while the crowd was excited and angry.

The high priest tried again. He asked Jesus, "'Tell us, are you the Christ, the Son of God?' Jesus answered, 'Yes, I am'" (verses 63, 64).

The high priest became so angry he began to tear his clothes. He told the mob Jesus had spoken blasphemy. They shouted, "He is guilty, and he must die" (verse 66).

They wanted to kill Jesus immediately, but they had to get permission from the Romans first. They took Jesus to Pilate, the Roman governor. Pilate didn't want anything to do with this—he couldn't find anything wrong with Jesus. He finally sent Jesus to Herod the king. Herod asked Jesus some questions, but then he lost interest and sent him back to Pilate. Pilate was tired of this. He told the crowd he wanted to let Jesus go free. "But they continued to shout. They demanded that Jesus be killed on the cross. Their yelling became so loud that Pilate decided to give them what they wanted" (Luke 23:23, 24). Pilate gave permission for Jesus to be killed.

Jesus Fulfills God's Plan

Pilate told the Roman soldiers to take charge. They took Jesus to the place outside the city where criminals were executed. As they nailed Him to a cross, Jesus prayed, "Father, forgive them. They don't know what they are doing" (Luke 23:34).

Many people were there. The mob from the night before was still around, jeering at Jesus. The Jewish leaders were there. They "made fun of Jesus and said, 'He saved other people, but he can't save himself!'" (Matthew 27:41, 42). Even the soldiers and one of the other criminals shouted insults at Jesus.

But not everybody was being mean. Some of Jesus' friends were watching from a distance. It was dangerous, but they couldn't bear to stay away. A few friends were brave enough to come close. Jesus' mother was there, and His beloved disciple John.

At 3:00 in the afternoon, Jesus cried, "My God, my God, why have you left me alone?" (Mark 15:34). All the sins of the world were laid on Jesus, the Lamb of God. Jesus was being sacrificed to redeem us from our sins. These sins were separating Jesus from His Father. That's why He felt alone. That was the hardest thing for Him to bear.

Satan did not want Jesus to die for our sins. He tried to get Jesus to give up and come down off the cross. But Jesus knew He was following God's plan.

Jesus said, "It is finished." The sacrifice was complete. God's people had been redeemed. Jesus bowed His head and died.

He willingly gave his life. He was treated like a criminal. But he carried away the sins of many people. And he asked forgiveness for those who sinned. Isaiah 53:12.

297

Jesus Is Alive

Now it was finished. Jesus' work was done.

"A man named Joseph from Arimathea was brave enough to go to Pilate and ask for Jesus' body" (Mark 15:43). Joseph wrapped the body in cloth and buried Jesus in a tomb—a cave cut into a wall of rock. A large stone was rolled to cover the entrance.

Now it was Sabbath. Jesus rested.

It was a very sad Sabbath for Jesus' followers. They were so upset that they didn't remember that Jesus had told them that He would die, that this was God's plan. They were worried and scared.

So were the Jewish leaders. They had heard Jesus say He would rise from death after three days. They did not have a restful Sabbath. In fact, they broke the Sabbath. They went to Pilate and asked him to send soldiers to guard the tomb. They said they were worried that Jesus' disciples would steal His body and then claim that He'd risen from death.

They sealed the tomb and put soldiers there to guard it. But it didn't make any difference. They could keep thieves out, but they couldn't keep Jesus in.

Very early on Sunday morning there was an earthquake. Even though the sun wasn't up yet, it got very, very bright. An angel rolled the stone away from the tomb.

Jesus was alive.

He Is Not Here

At dawn on that first Easter Sunday, some women made their way to Jesus' tomb. They were bringing sweet-smelling spices to prepare Jesus' body for burial—it was one last thing they could do for Jesus.

You can be sure that I will be with you always. Matthew 28:20.

When they got there, they were confused. The large stone had been rolled away. They looked inside and saw an angel, who told them, "Don't be afraid." (It seems like angels always have to say that.) "He is not here," the angel said. "He has risen from death as he said he would" (Matthew 28:5, 6). The angel told them to go tell the others.

The women ran to tell the disciples what had happened. "But they did not believe the women. It sounded like nonsense" (Luke 24:11).

Peter and John had to go see for themselves what was going on. They both ran to the tomb. John got there first and peeked inside; then Peter rushed up and charged right in. They saw that the tomb was empty except for the cloth that had been wrapped around Jesus' body. Peter and John believed.

Mary Magdalene was the first person to see Jesus after He had risen from the dead. She thought He was the gardener—her eyesight was all blurry because she had been crying so much. Then Jesus spoke her name, and she knew it was Him.

Jesus came to see His followers several times. Now when He talked to them, they listened better. Slowly they began to understand what He had been trying to teach them. Jesus helped them understand what had happened and what was going to happen next.

God's Plan for Peter

Jesus' disciples left Jerusalem and went to Galilee. One night several of them decided to go fishing on the lake, like they used to before they'd met Jesus. That morning, as they were coming back to shore, they saw Jesus on the beach. He was making them breakfast. The disciples were happy to see Him. They headed for shore, but the boat wasn't moving fast enough for Peter; so he jumped in the water and swam to Jesus.

After breakfast, Jesus asked Peter, "Do you love me?" Peter answered, "Yes, Lord, you know that I love you." Then Jesus said, "Take care of my sheep" (John 21:16).

Jesus asked Peter the same question again and then again. Three times. And three times Peter answered that he loved Him. Three times to make up for the three times in the courtyard when he said he didn't know Jesus. Jesus gave Peter the chance to take it back, to tell the truth. Peter knew that Jesus forgave him.

And three times Jesus gave Peter an assignment: Take care of My sheep. He had already called Peter to be a fisher of men. Now Peter was to be a shepherd, too. Part of his new job would be to take care of Jesus' followers. Once again Jesus said, "Follow me!" (verse 19).

Peter was ashamed that he had denied Jesus. But he never denied that he had messed up. He was brave enough to tell others about it. He told people that he knew Jesus would forgive. He told people that he knew Jesus could change lives. He told everyone the truth: that he knew Jesus, that he loved Jesus, that Jesus was the Redeemer.

Keep Your Balance

He stood me on a rock. He made my feet steady. Psalm 40:2.

Do you remember when you were learning to ride a bike and you tipped over a lot? A bike tips over because it has only two wheels and it is unstable. That means you have to balance it when you ride it. The secret to balancing a bicycle is to keep it moving forward.

Let's say you're riding your bike down the street and you see a friend. You want to talk to your friend, so you start to slow down. When your bike stops you have to take at least one foot off the pedals and put it on the ground to balance the bike, or else you will tip over, and your friend will think you're strange.

There are two things to do if you don't want to tip over: (1) you have to keep moving to keep your balance; (2) you have to put your feet on the ground when you stop.

These are good rules to remember. They are helpful for other things besides riding bikes—such as school, and getting along with people, and deciding how to spend your time. These things don't stay the same; they are always moving and changing. You have to keep your balance. And when you stop to look around and get your bearings, you need to be on solid ground. You need to know who you are and where you are going.

Jesus can keep you on solid ground. Jesus can keep you balanced. Nobody tipped over more than Peter, but Jesus just kept picking him up and putting him back on. Peter's real name was Simon, but Jesus called him Peter—which means "rock." And through Jesus' patience and forgiveness and love, Peter grew to be as steady as a rock.

Our Assignment

Go everywhere in the world. Tell the Good News to everyone. Mark 16:15.

Forty days after His resurrection Jesus came to see the disciples one last time. Jesus said that He was going back to heaven, but He reminded them that He had promised to send a Helper. The Holy Spirit would give them power. Why would they need power? Jesus had a job for His followers.

Jesus told them, "The Holy Spirit will come to you. Then you will receive power. You will be my witnesses—in Jerusalem, in all of Judea, in Samaria, and in every part of the world" (Acts 1:8). Jesus wanted them to tell everyone about God's plan.

Jesus raised His hands and blessed them. Then He began to rise into the sky, higher and higher, until He was hidden from sight in the clouds. His followers stood there, looking up, hoping for one last glimpse. Suddenly two angels stood beside them and asked, "Why are you standing here looking into the sky? You saw Jesus taken away from you into heaven. He will come back in the same way you saw him go" (verse 11).

Jesus' work on earth was complete. The Son of God had gone back to His Father. Now His followers needed to begin their work. They needed to stop standing around, staring into the sky, and start telling everyone the good news about Jesus.

This time they weren't sad that He was gone. The Bible says they "went back to the city very happy" (Luke 24:52). Now they understood who He was and what had happened. Jesus had promised to be with them always. The Holy Spirit would give them power. The angels had said that He would come back. Now they understood the plan.

Pentecost

Before Jesus went back to heaven, He told His followers to wait in Jerusalem until they received power from the Holy Spirit. So they waited—worshiping at the Temple, talking together about the amazing things that had happened, and praying.

Now Jesus has poured out that Spirit. This is what you see and hear. Acts 2:33.

Fifty days after Passover, the Jewish people celebrated Pentecost, a harvest festival. More people came to Jerusalem for Pentecost than any other festival. This Pentecost there was going to be a harvest like never before—a harvest of new believers. This was the birthday of the new Christian church.

On this Pentecost, 10 days after Jesus had gone back to heaven, about 120 of Jesus' followers were praying together. Suddenly they heard a sound like wind and saw something that looked like fire. "They were all filled with the Holy Spirit" (Acts 2:4). They were filled with courage—they could face danger knowing that God would be with them. They were filled with wisdom—they knew that the Holy Spirit would guide them and help them know what to say. They were filled with joy—they had known Jesus and had been chosen to help finish His work.

The Holy Spirit gave them the power to speak in different languages. People from all over the world were in Jerusalem, and they were amazed to hear their own language. They were curious—so Peter began to preach about Jesus and God's plan.

Many people listened to Peter's sermon and believed and were baptized. The gift of the Holy Spirit had come. The believers had begun to share the good news.

Peter Preaches

Peter heard Jesus' assignment to tell the good news, and that's what he did—every chance he got, he told everyone who would listen about Jesus.

One day Peter and John went to the Temple. Sitting by the gate was a man who couldn't walk. He was asking people for money as they went into the Temple. When he asked them for money, Peter answered with today's Bible text. And what was the "something else" that Peter gave him? He told him to stand up and walk. Then he grabbed him by the hand and hauled him to his feet.

"Immediately the man's feet and ankles became strong. He jumped up, stood on his feet, and began to walk. He went into the Temple with them, walking and jumping, and praising God" (Acts 3:7, 8).

It was time for the afternoon prayer service, so lots of people were at the Temple. They recognized the man—they'd seen him by the gate every day. Now he was jumping and running around the courtyard. The people were amazed.

Can you guess what Peter did? He began to preach. He explained that the man had been healed through the power of Jesus. And Peter gave the crowd "something else." He told them the good news about Jesus, which is a lot more valuable than silver or gold.

And then he got arrested. The Jewish leaders were not happy that Peter was preaching about Jesus. Can you guess what Peter did? That's right. He preached to them.

The Church Grows

Peter and the other disciples were now called apostles; they were leaders of the new believers and the new church. They all believed the same thing—that Jesus was the Messiah. They all did the same thing—they told everyone the good news. They prayed together. They all got along. They took care of each other.

Should we obey you or God? We cannot keep quiet. Acts 4:19, 20.

The apostles continued to preach, even though the Jewish leaders had ordered them to stop. So they were put in jail. "But during the night, an angel of the Lord opened the doors of the jail. He led the apostles outside and said, 'Go and stand in the Temple. Tell the people everything about this new life'" (Acts 5:19, 20).

Did the apostles tell the angel, "We can't; the Jewish leaders told us not to"? Of course not. They went straight to the Temple and began to preach.

When the Jewish leaders went to the jail to bring them to trial, the apostles were nowhere to be found. Everyone was confused—the jail was locked, the guards were standing at the doors, but the jail was empty. Then someone reported that they were teaching at the Temple. The apostles were dragged back into court.

The Jewish leaders were so angry they were ready to kill the apostles. But a Pharisee named Gamaliel told them to be careful: "If their plan comes from men, it will fail. But if it is from God, you will not be able to stop them" (verses 38, 39).

So the apostles got a beating and a warning to stop preaching. Did they stop? No. They obeyed God. "More and more people were being saved every day" (Acts 2:47).

305

A Dream Teaches Peter

You are all the same in Christ Jesus. Galatians 3:28.

At first the apostles stayed in Jerusalem and preached to the people there. But as the Jewish leaders made it more and more difficult, the believers began to travel to other towns to spread the good news.

Peter was in Joppa, staying with friends. While lunch was being prepared, he went up on the roof to pray. While he was praying, God sent him a dream. In this dream a big sheet full of animals came down from heaven. A voice told Peter, "Get up and eat."

Peter was hungry, but not that hungry. The Jews had strict laws about food. They were allowed to eat only certain kinds of animals. The animals in this dream were not the kind they would eat. There was no way Peter was going to eat them. He said, "No."

The voice said, "God has made these things clean" (Acts 10:15). The sheet was lowered twice more. Peter was shocked and confused by this dream. What did it mean?

While he was trying to figure it out, some men knocked at the gate. They wanted Peter to come see their friend Cornelius. An angel had told Cornelius to send for Peter.

Then Peter began to understand what his dream had meant. The Jews believed that God belonged to the Jews only. Cornelius was not a Jew. The animals in the dream were symbols for the non-Jews. God wanted to show Peter that everyone needed to hear about Jesus—not just the Jews. God wanted Peter to preach to everyone.

Peter went to see Cornelius, preached to his family and friends, and baptized them. When he got back to Jerusalem, he told the other believers what he'd learned.

God's Plan for Paul

Life got very difficult for the believers in Jerusalem. The Jewish leaders were doing their best to destroy the new church—searching for Christians, dragging them to court, throwing them in jail, and even putting them to death.

But something happened to me on my way to Damascus. Acts 22:6.

There was one man named Saul who tried especially hard to get rid of the Christians. Even after most of them had fled from Jerusalem, Saul wasn't satisfied. He wanted to chase them down. He decided to go after the Christians in Damascus.

Saul was intelligent and religious and dedicated. He was an important leader, eager to defend the Jewish religion. But things didn't turn out the way he'd planned.

As he got near to Damascus, suddenly a light flashed. Saul fell to the ground. He heard a voice say, "Saul, Saul! Why are you doing things against me?" (Acts 9:4). The light was so bright Saul couldn't see who was talking. He asked, "Who are you?"

"The voice answered, 'I am Jesus. I am the One you are trying to hurt'" (verse 5). And Saul knew he was in big trouble. In an instant he realized that everything he had believed was wrong. In that instant Saul turned away from the wrong and surrendered to Jesus. Jesus told Saul, "I want you on my side," and Saul joined up immediately and totally.

At first the other believers were suspicious, but they baptized him and learned to love him and accept him. He had been one of the church's worst enemies, but Jesus called him to become one of its greatest leaders. Saul was changed. He was so different that people began calling him by his other name, Paul.

Converted

Have you ever made bread? You take flour and yeast and water and other stuff. You mix them together in the right order and in the right way, and you get bread. It makes the house smell great while it's baking. And if things work out, the bread is good to eat, too.

It's not like making mudpies. (Well, it's a little like making mudpies.) When you make mudpies, you mix the dirt and the water and you play around with it and squish it and pat it. But then there is a big difference (besides the fact that you cannot eat your mudpies). After you quit playing with your mudpie and go inside and wash your hands real good, the mudpie sits there and dries out, and after a day or so it turns back into dirt.

That's the difference. If you mix dirt and water, eventually the water will evaporate and you'll have just dirt again. The ingredients come apart.

But when you make bread, and you mix the flour and yeast and water and other stuff, they stay mixed. It is impossible to take them apart again. When you mix them together, they change into something new—bread.

When Paul was converted, it wasn't a "mudpie" kind of thing. It was bread. He never went back to the way he was before. He was made new. He spent the rest of his life traveling through many countries, telling everyone that he was a changed man and that it was Jesus who changed him.

Missionary Journeys

Paul began traveling from city to city, through many countries, telling everyone who would listen the good news about Jesus. Paul became a missionary.

Paul sometimes followed a system when he went to a new city. First he went to the Jewish synagogue on Sabbath and began preaching about God's plan to redeem His people. He told the Jews that Jesus was the Messiah and that He had come as part of God's plan to die for our sins.

Usually some people would be interested, and they would ask Paul to tell them more on the next Sabbath. They would tell all their friends to come hear, and there would be big crowds to hear Paul preach.

And then usually the Jewish leaders in the city "became very jealous. They said insulting things and argued against what Paul said" (Acts 13:45). Then, often, there would be trouble. Sometimes Paul could stay for a while and teach the non-Jews, but often the Jewish leaders would be so upset that Paul would have to leave.

However, Paul usually managed to start teaching about Jesus before he had to leave. And some people believed. Those people would start a church and begin telling others what they had learned about Jesus. Many of those people would believe, and they would tell others. Then those people told others—and that's how the good news about Jesus began to spread around the world.

Because we loved you, we were happy to share God's Good News with you.
1 Thessalonians 2:8.

Love, Paul

*I have written to
you very openly
about some things
that I wanted you
to remember.
Romans 15:15.*

Because Paul often had to leave town suddenly, a new church would have to struggle to grow on its own. Paul worried that he hadn't had time to teach them properly; he worried that they might get wrong ideas. So he wrote them letters. He wrote letters to help churches in trouble. He wrote letters to strengthen the new Christians.

Well, Paul didn't actually write the letters. In those days people often used a scribe to do the writing. Paul spoke the words, and the scribe wrote them down. Some people think his eyesight was so bad that he couldn't see well enough to write.

But he could talk. When he heard that a church was having problems, he would worry and think about it. Then he'd call in his scribe and begin to talk. It's not hard to imagine him pacing the floor, waving his arms, shaking his finger to make a point. Paul talked and talked to his friends as if they were there with him.

And no doubt the poor scribe would be writing as fast as he could, trying to keep up with all the words.

When the people in the church received a letter from Paul, they read it and saved it and passed it around to other churches so they could read it. And many times those churches would copy the letter so they could read it over and over, and those copies were passed around. Now we can read those letters in our Bibles—letters from our good friend Paul, setting us straight, urging us to repent, encouraging, teaching, sending his love.

Starting a Car

Do you know how to start a car? You just put in the key and turn it. It's simple.

But if you want to find out more about what it takes to start a car, there is lots more you can learn. For instance, the place where you put the key is called the ignition. *Ignite* means "start on fire." Does that seem like something you want to do when you're starting a car? No? Actually, it is. Sort of. When you turn the key, the battery in the car makes an electric spark. Inside the engine, that spark makes the gasoline explode. "Explode" doesn't seem like something you want to happen either. But actually, it is. That explosion is just the right size. It happens in just the right place. The explosion creates the power for the machinery that makes the car's wheels turn.

All that machinery involves cylinders and pistons and crankshafts, to name just a few important engine parts. There is lots you can learn about how a car works.

Do you know how to become a child of God? You just have to ask. It's simple.

But if you want to find out more about it, there is lots more you can learn. You can learn about how God's power can ignite your soul. You can learn how God's spark in you can explode at just the right time in just the right place. You can discover how you and God can work together to move the wheels of His plan for the world. You can find out about belief and forgiveness and faith, to name just a few important ideas.

Look at today's Bible text. There is lots you can learn about God's plan.

There are many other things that Jesus did. If every one of them were written down, I think the whole world would not be big enough for all the books that would be written. John 21:25.

God's Plan for You

Your plans for us are many. If I tried to tell them all, there would be too many to count. Psalm 40:5.

There has always been a plan. When God created our world, He planned for everything to be good and for everyone to be happy. When Adam and Eve sinned and rejected that plan, God had a plan to redeem the world—He would send His Son to take our punishment for us. When Jesus came to earth, He was following God's plan.

From the beginning, God has wanted us to know about His plan. The Bible tells us many stories about God's plans for different people and what happened when they followed the plan—or didn't follow it.

God had a plan for Noah. "Noah did everything that God commanded him" (Genesis 6:22), and his family was saved on the ark.

God had a plan for Abraham. God made an agreement with Abraham and promised to bless him with many descendants. And Abraham discovered that nothing is too hard for the Lord.

God had a plan for Moses. Even though Moses had all kinds of excuses for not following God's plan, God patiently taught him to be a great leader.

God had a plan for Samuel and Elijah and Isaiah. They said yes, they would be God's prophets. And they faithfully spoke God's words to His people.

And God has a plan for you. God wants you to know how much He loves you. He wants you to share that love with others. He wants you to choose to follow His plan.

God Wants You to Be Happy

From the very beginning, God planned for us to be happy.

Being with you will fill me with joy. Psalm 16:11.

When He created the world, God filled it with everything we would ever need. And it was very good. But even if we have every good thing in the world, that is not all we need to be happy.

God gave His people the law. The law tells us how we should live and what we should do to be happy. But even if we could keep every law there ever was, that is not all we need to be happy.

We need more than things. We need more than rules. We need to know God.

Jesus said we don't need to worry about things. "Don't worry and say, 'What will we eat?' or 'What will we drink?' or 'What will we wear?' All the people who don't know God keep trying to get these things. And your Father in heaven knows that you need them. The thing you should want most is God's kingdom and doing what God wants. Then all these other things you need will be given to you" (Matthew 6:31-33).

Jesus said the most important law is "Do for other people the same things you want them to do for you" (Matthew 7:12). But the only way to find happiness in this golden rule is to understand what God has done for you. We do for others because He did for us.

Happiness is knowing how much God loves you. If you want to be happy, get to know God. God wants you to be happy. God wants to be friends with you.

God Wants You to Love Yourself

This is how we know what real love is: Jesus gave his life for us. 1 John 3:16.

God wants you to know how much you are worth. Jesus explains this by talking about sparrows. In Bible times little wild birds were sold in the marketplace. They weren't expensive—you could buy two sparrows for one penny. The bird sellers even had a special bargain: "When five sparrows are sold, they cost only two pennies" (Luke 12:6). If you were willing to spend another penny, you could get one extra sparrow for free. That meant that the extra sparrow wasn't worth any money.

But even though people might think these little birds are worthless, God doesn't. "God does not forget any of them," Jesus says (verse 6). God knows all the birds. They are all valuable to Him—even the little one who is thrown in for free.

And, Jesus says, "You are worth much more than many sparrows" (verse 7).

You are valuable. You are worth so much that Jesus paid for you with His life. You are special. No one looks or acts exactly like you. No one can replace you.

It is important for you to remember that you are valuable. When you do, we say that you love yourself. That might sound kind of weird—people who love themselves aren't fun to be around. But that's if they love only themselves. You need to love others as well as yourself. And in order to love others, you must first love yourself.

God wants you to be happy. You can't be happy if you don't love yourself. It's not always easy. People may not always treat you as though you are valuable. But you are. You are special. Don't forget.

God Wants You to Love Your Family

Do you remember Naomi? She was Ruth's mother-in-law. During her life her family took many different forms. When she got married, her family had just two people—Naomi and Elimelech. Then it was four—they had two sons. Then it was six—the sons got married. Then Elimelech and the sons died, and it was three. Then just Naomi and Ruth went to Bethlehem. Then it was three again when Ruth married Boaz. And last we hear, the family has four people, with Naomi, Ruth, Boaz, and Baby Obed.

A rope that has three parts wrapped together is hard to break. Ecclesiastes 4:12.

There are many different kinds of families. God gave us families because He wants us to be happy. You are an important part of your family.

Naomi was a valuable part of her family. Something about her made Ruth want to stay with her and not go back to her own people. Naomi made a difference.

You are a valuable part of your family. Your family needs you. You can make a difference. The things you do can make your home a happier place. You can be thoughtful. You can be kind. You can follow the rules.

Families take care of each other. Ruth and Naomi took care of each other. Your family takes care of you. And you must do your part to take care of your family. You can be helpful. You can work together. You can learn from each other.

Look at today's Bible text. What do you think it can mean? Your family is like a rope with three parts: you, your family, and God. When all three parts are wrapped together, that rope is very strong. God wants you to be happy at home.

God Wants You to Love Others

We love because
God first loved us.
1 John 4:19.

Your probably noticed. Whenever Jesus taught, He used one word over and over: *love*. Love God. Love your neighbor. Love each other. Love your enemies.

Sometimes that's easy. Sometimes it's not.

It's easy to love your family, most of the time. They love you and think you're wonderful. They take care of you and celebrate your birthday.

It's easy to love your friends, usually. They share and listen and understand. They like the same things you do. It's important to love your friends—but everyone does that. As Jesus pointed out, "If you are nice only to your friends, then you are no better than other people" (Matthew 5:47).

But it's hard to love people who are not lovable. They whine. They tattle. They won't share or take turns. If we are going to love our enemies, we have to learn to love with our brains instead of our feelings. When we love in this way, we treat people kindly, even if they treat us badly.

Sometimes when you try to love someone you don't like very much, eventually you discover that you do like them after all. Sometimes when you are nice to someone, they will start being nice too. It's wonderful when that happens. But it doesn't always work that way. And if you are nice and they're still mean, you just keep on loving.

It's not easy to love your enemies. In fact, you couldn't do it at all if Jesus didn't help you. Fortunately, that is exactly what He wants to do.

God Wants You to Be a Good Example

In Bible times most people lived in houses with only one room and one window. At night their only light came from a lamp made of a small dish of oil with a wick floating in it. It only gave about as much light as a candle, but when that little lamp was put on a stand, its light shone everywhere in the house.

People don't hide a light under a bowl. They put the light on a lampstand. Then the light shines for all the people in the house. Matthew 5:15.

When Jesus told the little story in today's Bible text, the people listening must have been amused. Why would anyone put a light under a bowl? A light is meant to be seen and to help you see. The whole point of having a lamp is for it to give light.

And that was Jesus' point. You are a light. Don't hide it. Shine. How can you let your light shine?

Your light shines in the way you treat your family, your friends, your neighbors. You let your light shine in the everyday things you do. When you help carry in the groceries. When you are a good loser or a good winner. When you smile and say hello.

Your light shines when you help others. You can be kind to people who are lonely or sad or in trouble. You can be thoughtful of what other people want. You can give to people who don't have enough.

You let your light shine by being a good example. People notice. You can be the light that helps others do the right thing. You can be a leader. You can be the light that helps others find Jesus.

God Wants You to Witness

Everywhere in the world that Good News is bringing blessings and is growing. Colossians 1:6.

One of the last things Jesus told His disciples before He went back to heaven was "Go everywhere in the world. Tell the Good News to everyone" (Mark 16:15).

Now, this is a very big assignment. You can't do this all by yourself—nobody could. But you don't have to do it by yourself. Just do your part.

Most likely, at your age you are not free to travel the world and preach. You have to go to school. Does that mean that right now you can't help spread the good news? No. We can all help with this assignment, even if we never leave home. You know you can be a good example to the people you meet. But you can also help tell the world the good news.

You can learn about missions and missionaries. The more you know, the more you can help. You can pray for them. You can give money to mission projects. You can be proud of your missionaries.

You can learn about the people of other countries and the way they live. When you understand better, you can help better. There are plenty of people who are poor and sick and hungry. There are plenty of disasters—earthquakes, floods, famines, wars. People who are suffering need help from the rest of the world.

You can help. Jesus will help you help. "You can be sure that I will be with you always" (Matthew 28:20).

RSVP

Have you ever gotten an invitation to a party? When you open the invitation, first you look to see who the party is for. Next you check to see what day it will be, to make sure you can go. But before you start to think about what present you will bring or what you will wear, you probably need to do one thing: Check to see if it says RSVP.

Come and share my happiness with me.
Matthew 25:21.

Do you know what RSVP stands for? *Répondez s'il vous plaît.* It's French. It means "let us know if you want to come or not." You can see that it is much quicker to write RSVP instead of all that. People need to know how many are coming to their party so they can make plans and have enough cake. So they ask their guests to RSVP.

There are lots of invitations in the Bible. When Jesus first started to teach, He chose some followers. When He invited them, He said, "Come follow me" (Matthew 4:19). Jesus invites you to follow Him, too.

When people brought their children to Jesus so He could bless them, His followers tried to shoo them away. Jesus said, "Let the little children come to me. Don't stop them" (Matthew 19:14). Jesus invites you to receive His blessings, too. Jesus especially invites children.

So you have the invitation. Now you need to RSVP. You need to let Jesus know whether you will accept His invitation or not. When you pray, let Him know that you want to follow Him. Let Him know that you want to share His happiness. Let Jesus know that, more than anything else, you want to come to His party.

Believe

One time Paul and his friend Silas got in trouble for preaching; they were thrown into jail. They were praying and singing when all of a sudden there was an earthquake. The door of the jail broke open. The chains fell off the prisoners. They were free.

The jailer came running; he thought all the prisoners had escaped. He knew he'd be killed as punishment for letting them escape. But Paul shouted, "We're still here!"

The jailer was shaking with fear. He had heard Paul and Silas singing—he wanted whatever they had that made them happy even though they were in jail. Right there in the middle of the disaster, he asked them how he could be saved. And they told him, "Believe in the Lord Jesus and you will be saved" (Acts 16:31).

When they told him to believe, they didn't just mean to believe that God exists. They didn't want him to just believe *in* God; they wanted him to believe God. Believe God when He says He loves you. Believe Jesus died for you. Believe God has a plan for your life—and you want to follow that plan. This kind of believing changes everything.

The jailer believed, and his life was changed. He took Paul and Silas to his house. He fed them and washed their wounds. Paul and Silas taught the jailer and his family about Jesus; they believed and were baptized and were very happy.

You can accept Jesus' invitation. You can believe. You can choose to follow God's plan for your life.

The Gift of Grace

Did you ever receive an offer for a free gift? Did it sound suspicious to you? Did you wonder why the person offering it needed to say it was free? If it's really a gift, then of course it's free; that's what "gift" means. It kind of makes you wonder if maybe it isn't really a gift after all. What's the catch?

You have been saved by grace because you believe. You did not save yourselves. It was a gift from God. Ephesians 2:8.

Some people are suspicious of the gift of salvation. They can't believe it's really free. They hear that we should love each other— and they assume that *if* they love others, *then* they will be saved. They think they can earn salvation by loving. They don't understand that Jesus has already saved us. We love because we are saved. We aren't saved because we love.

Your salvation is a gift. What's the catch? Well, like any gift, it can be yours only if you reach out and take it. And then don't be surprised if your life totally and completely changes. Salvation isn't something you accept in theory. It is something you believe with all your heart, soul, mind, and strength.

God has invited you to the party. Not because you have earned an invitation by being so good. Not because you deserve to come. Not because of something you've done. You are invited because it just wouldn't be the same without you. Because He loves you. Because He wants to be with you.

We call it grace. Grace is something you are given.

Bonding Agents

They will come and join themselves to the Lord. They will make an agreement that will last forever. Jeremiah 50:5.

Your may know someone who has eaten paste. It doesn't seem like a good idea—what if it glued their insides together? Actually, it wouldn't. Paste is good for sticking paper together; however, it dissolves in water. If you broke a dish and tried to put it back together with paste, the dish would fall apart the next time you washed it.

Glue is stronger. It's made from the skin and bones of animals. (Bet you never eat glue again!) When you glue two pieces of wood together, the glue fills in the tiny holes on the wood's surface. When the glue dries, it holds the two pieces together.

Mucilage is made from plants. (If you've ever seen mucilage, you'll understand why no one would ever want to eat it!) Mucilage is great for gluing paper together, because if you change your mind you can lift the pieces apart and reposition them.

Paste, glue, and mucilage are "bonding agents" because they join or bond things together. Bonding agents are useful around the house for fixing things and making things. Each type is good for a certain task. But none of them can fix a broken heart.

Jesus can. Jesus came to earth "to bind up the brokenhearted" (Isaiah 61:1, NIV). People can come to Jesus and He will mend their broken hearts. Look at today's Bible text. You can bind yourself to Jesus. His love is a bonding agent that is stronger than super strong. It is everlasting.

And Jesus asks you to share His love. You can bring others to Jesus so He can bind up their broken hearts. You can become a bonding agent for Him.

Excuses, Excuses

What's the first thing you do when you get caught making a mistake? If you're like many people, you try to think of an excuse. It's not my fault. It was slippery. I couldn't help it. There wasn't enough time. The devil made me do it.

It's human nature to make excuses. It's usually pretty easy to think one up.

But excuses do more harm than good. When you make an excuse, you try to put the blame somewhere else. You don't admit that you messed up. And if you won't admit your mistakes, how can you possibly ask for forgiveness? How can you be forgiven? How will you do better next time?

Making excuses can become a bad habit that's really hard to break. Don't start. A grown-up who won't take responsibility for mistakes is an even bigger pain than a kid who makes excuses.

Have you ever wondered what today's Bible text means? Why do we need to confess, anyway? God already knows everything that we've done.

When you confess your sins to God, you are not telling Him anything new. He knows it all already. Confessing is more than just informing. It's more like admitting.

When you confess your sins, you are admitting that you are a sinner. You are admitting that you need Jesus to save you from sin. You are asking Him to forgive you and help you be good. When you confess your sins, you let Jesus build a bridge over sin—a bridge between you and God.

But if we confess our sins, he will forgive our sins. I John 1:9.

323

Why Soap Works

Has this ever happened to you? Your mom tells you to wash your face, so you do it. Then she looks at you and tells you to wash it again, with soap. Have you ever wondered why sometimes you can get away with just washing with water, but other times you have to use soap? It's because of oil. Some dirt has oil in it.

If the dirt doesn't have oil in it, then water can easily wash it away. The water just mixes with the dirt, soaks it up, and carries it away. However, if the dirt does have oil in it, there is a problem. Water won't mix with oil. It can't wash it away.

That's where soap comes in to save the day. Soap is able to mix with both water and oil. First the soap mixes with the water and goes out in search of the oily dirt. Then it surrounds the dirt and attacks it (sort of), pulling it apart and breaking it into tiny bits. Once the oil is in such tiny bits, the water is able to dissolve the dirt and carry it all away.

Sometimes we say that getting rid of sin and being forgiven is like being washed. But when we ask God for forgiveness, we also need to promise to try not to make those mistakes again. That's the "soap" part of this kind of washing.

Look at the first sentence of today's Bible text. Perhaps that's the "water" of the washing—when we ask for forgiveness. Now look at the rest of it. Perhaps this is as if God is telling us to go back and use soap this time.

Jesus will help you be clean. He promised. Ask Him to forgive you and ask Him to help you do better. He will. It's like soap and water.

In Hot Water

Some things get softer when you cook them and other things get harder. What happens when you put macaroni in boiling water? It gets softer. What happens if you put an egg in boiling water? It gets harder. What happens if you put a potato in a hot oven? Softer. Cookie dough in a hot oven? Harder.

God is our protection and our strength. He always helps in times of trouble. Psalm 46:1.

It all has to do with chemistry and what the different foods are made of. Fruits and vegetables contain mostly carbohydrates. Their firm structure dissolves in the heat. Eggs contain protein. Those molecules weld together when they get hot.

Sometimes when people get into trouble we say they are in hot water. Both "trouble" and "hot water" are uncomfortable places for people to be.

Different people behave differently when they get into hot water—just like food. Some people fall apart. Their structure dissolves in the heat. They can't handle it. Other people get stronger. They are able to pull themselves together and tough it out.

It all depends on what they're made of—their structure, their foundation. Remember the wise man who built his house on a rock (Matthew 7:24)? The wise man is strong because Jesus is strong. Build your foundation in Jesus. Follow Jesus.

And what should you do when you get into hot water? The Bible says, "If one of you is having troubles, he should pray" (James 5:13). Praying can bring you close to Jesus. His strength will weld together with yours. Together you will survive the hot water, stronger than ever.

325

We Are Family

Prairie dogs are not dogs. They don't look or act like dogs. Their name comes from the barking noise they make. They're noisy critters—they chirp, whistle, and call.

One of the coolest things about prairie dogs is the way they build towns. Prairie dog towns are like people towns, only they are underground. There are long tunnels, like roads, leading to neighborhoods of family burrows. Each prairie dog family builds a burrow, which is like a house. Each burrow has a main tunnel, which is like a hallway, leading to different little rooms. There are sleeping rooms, a nursery, and a toilet. And up near the entrance there is a room where they listen to see if it's safe to go outside.

Prairie dogs like to go outside to eat and play with each other. Prairie dogs really like to be with other prairie dogs. That's why they live in families, that's why the families live in neighborhoods, and that's why prairie dogs build towns. They look out for each other. They keep each other company.

That's why people have families and live in towns, too. We need each other.

The Bible talks about a special kind of family—the family of God. In this family, God is the Father and we are His children. Other people who love God are our brothers and sisters. This is a big family.

It's important to get together with our family. That's one reason we go to church. We keep each other company. We take care of each other.

The Family of God

God has given you your family. You are a valuable part of your family. Families do things together and take care of each other.

You also belong to another much bigger family—the family of God. You are a valuable part of the family of God. God promises to be with you, just like He promised Abraham. Jesus calls you to follow Him, just as He called Peter and John. God asks you to be on His side, just as He asked Paul to be on His side. God has plans for you. He wants you to be a part of His family.

In the family of God we do things together. One of the most important things we do together is to meet together for church. At church we worship our Father with our brothers and sisters. We sing and pray together; we learn and listen and give.

Church is a place you can go to be with people who believe the same things you believe—people who love Jesus. You can feel at home there. You don't have to worry that people will make fun of what you believe. You can feel comfortable at church because you know that the people there love you and want you to be there. Church is a wonderful place to make friends.

You can also help others be comfortable in church. Families take care of each other. You can do your part to make sure that everyone who comes to church feels welcome and loved and valuable—a part of the family.

When we have the opportunity to help anyone, we should do it. But we should give special attention to those who are in the family of believers. Galatians 6:10.

We Are His Hands

The church is Christ's body. The church is filled with Christ, and Christ fills everything in every way. Ephesians 1:23.

When Jesus was on earth, He taught people about God. He healed the sick and fed the hungry. He helped people who were in trouble.

But now Jesus is in heaven. He has asked us to help Him. He is counting on us to tell people the good news about how they have been saved from sin. He depends on us to help when someone is hungry or in trouble.

Since Jesus is not here, we are His body. When we help others, we are His hands. When we tell others about God, we are His voice.

It was Paul who came up with this idea—that the church is the body of Jesus. Paul wrote that Jesus is the head of the church and the church is the body. The head must have a body through which it can work.

Let's say a scientist finds a cure for a disease. Is that enough? Will people start getting well now? No. People have to be told about the cure before it can start helping. Doctors must learn about the cure before they can start using it to help people get well. The cure is there—but the scientist needs help to let the world know about it.

Jesus has the cure for sin. But people have to be told about it. People need to hear about what He did for them. They need to experience His love, His forgiveness, and His grace. This news must be spread. That is the job of the church.

That is our job. God's plan for our world is in our hands. It depends on us.

Lots of Parts, Working Together

When Paul was traveling as a missionary, he spent some time in Corinth. Later he heard that there was trouble in the church he had started there—people weren't getting along. So Paul wrote them a letter. He told them that if they wanted to solve their problems, they were going to have to learn to love each other. He told them that if they didn't have love, then they had nothing.

There are many parts, but only one body.
1 Corinthians 12:20.

Paul thought of a way to explain that they needed to work together. He wrote that the church is like a body. A body has many different parts—so does the church. What are the parts of the church? People! The church is made up of people. They are all different. They are all important.

A body has many different parts, but all the parts work together. For example, your mother says, "Here is some ice cream." Your ears hear her voice. Your ears tell your brain. Your brain decides that is good and tells your hand to reach for the ice cream, your voice to say "Thank you," and your mouth to start eating. It's a good system.

The parts of the body don't fight with each other. Your hand doesn't get jealous of your mouth and throw the ice cream at your ear. Each body part does the work it's supposed to do. They get along.

That's how Jesus wants the church to behave. There are many different people in the church. We all have different jobs. Each of us needs to do the work we're supposed to do. We need to work together.

Making Toast

*It is good and pleasant
when God's people live
together in peace!
Psalm 133:1.*

Have you ever wondered how a toaster knows when the toast is ready? The secret is the bimetal switch—a special switch made of two metals. Metal expands when it gets hot; however, different kinds of metal expand different amounts. The people who invented toasters took one metal that only expanded a little when it got hot and one metal that expanded more. They stuck the two pieces of metal together. When this new bimetal plate gets hot, it bends!

When you push the lever to start the toaster, the heat turns on. The heat toasts the bread, and it also makes the bimetal switch get hot. As the bimetal switch gets hotter, it starts to bend. The switch bends over and pushes a hook away. The hook releases a spring, which pushes the toast up and turns off the heat. As it cools down, the bimetal switch goes back to its unbent shape.

The bimetal switch works because, even though the two pieces of metal are different, they work together. People need to learn to work together like that. People are different. They have different ideas. They have different ways of doing things and different ways of thinking. This is good—if they are willing to work together.

Look at today's Bible text. The next verse says, "It is like having perfumed oil poured on the priest's head and running down his beard." Well, that's good and pleasant, no doubt. But maybe we could also say: When God's people live together in peace, it's like two different metals bending together to make the perfect piece of golden toast.

Rubber Bands

Do you know how to shoot a rubber band? Make a "gun" shape with one hand. Hold one end of the rubber band in the crook of your little finger. Stretch the rubber band around the back of your thumb and hook the other end on the tip of your pointer finger. Point at your target, then let go with your little finger. It might take a little practice.

Show mercy to others; be kind, humble, gentle, and patient. Colossians 3:12.

The rubber band shoots because you stretch it—and when you let go, it snaps back into shape. Rubber is a material with molecules that change shape easily. The rubber molecules have strings of carbon atoms in a zigzag pattern. They can be stretched any which way; then they snap back into the original shape.

Rubber is flexible. That's why it's so useful. People need to be flexible too—in the way they think and behave toward others.

There are some things you can't be flexible about. "Don't shoot rubber bands at people" is an inflexible rule. But other times you need to be flexible. If your mom asks if you want ice cream and you say, "Yes! Chocolate!" but all she has is vanilla, you'll have to be flexible. You can have vanilla or you can have none, but you can't have chocolate.

You can't always get what you want. You can't always have your own way. Be flexible. Stretch. And after you are all stretched out, do you know what returns you to your normal shape? Love. "Love patiently accepts all things" (1 Corinthians 13:7).

Love is like a rubber band. And so, we hope, are you.

Super Ants

Each part of the body does its own work. And this makes the whole body grow and be strong with love. Ephesians 4:16.

Have you ever seen an ant dragging something absolutely huge? (Well, it's huge compared to the ant.) Ants can carry things like a piece of cracker or a dead bug over huge cracks in the sidewalk. (Well, they must seem huge to the ant.)

If we were able to carry things that much bigger than us, we could carry cars and small buildings. Do ants have supermuscles that are a lot stronger than human muscles?

No. Ant muscles are no stronger than human muscles. Ants use their muscles differently. Ants don't weigh a lot, so they aren't affected much by gravity. (Humans are.) Ants don't need to use many of their muscles to hold themselves up. (Humans do.) Ants can use most of their muscles for hauling stuff around. (Humans can't.)

Another reason ants can haul incredible loads is because they work in teams very, very well. They know how to work together so that whatever they're carrying as a team is balanced perfectly on all of their backs. They know how to walk in step so that as many legs as possible will be on the ground to bear the weight of the load.

We can't carry cars and buildings by ourselves. But we can do amazing things when we work together. When we cooperate, things have a better chance of working out.

We need to cooperate with each other to get things done and we need to help each other.

When people cooperate, they can do a lot. But when Jesus helps too, incredible things can happen. Jesus can help you learn to cooperate with other people. Jesus can help your team really make a difference.

Quilting Party

Do you have a patchwork quilt? It's a special blanket made of different colors and shapes sewn together. Years ago people made them mostly because they didn't want to waste any leftover scraps of fabric. But now people make them because it's fun and because they're beautiful.

Quilts are beautiful because of the patterns the colors and shapes make. The contrasts between the colors make the patterns stand out. If the patchwork pieces were all the same, it might as well be a plain blanket. The different colors look good together.

Our church family is like a quilt. It's made of different people who are good at different things. It's the different people working together that make it so beautiful.

God's people work together. But we don't do the same work. The church needs lots of different kinds of people because there are lots of different kinds of work. Some people are good leaders. Some people are good at helping others. Some people are good at making others feel welcome. Some people are good at putting things in order. Each of us is good at something. It's good that we're all different.

It's a wonderfully warm quilt that God has designed. There's a place in the design for you. Your special colors and talents help make the quilt beautiful. And what is the thread that stitches you together with all the other people in the patchwork? Love. God's love is the thread that "holds [us] all together in perfect unity" (Colossians 3:14).

There are different ways to serve; but all these ways are from the same Lord.
1 Corinthians 12:5.

333

Gifts for Everyone

We all have different gifts. Each gift came because of the grace that God gave us. Romans 12:6.

Some people can take singing lessons and practice an hour a day and, to be perfectly honest, they still don't sing all that well. Other people just open their mouths and out comes the most glorious music. Some people study their spelling words every night and still get some wrong on the test. Others never study and get perfect scores.

It's talent. Some people are talented singers. Some people are talented spellers. Other people are really good at playing baseball or growing flowers or giving speeches. It's more than average. It's more than practice. It's something extra—a gift from God.

The Holy Spirit gives different gifts to different people. These gifts help us help others. Some people are good listeners—people who have problems or are in trouble feel better after talking to someone who has the gift of listening. Some people are good at sharing—they just seem to know when and how to give.

The Holy Spirit gives us gifts so we can tell others about Jesus. Some people are good teachers—they are patient and know just the right way to share an idea. Some people are good preachers—they tell good stories and know the right words to help people want to know Jesus.

The Holy Spirit gives everybody a gift. He has a gift for you. What do you think it could be? Perhaps you have the gift of cheerfulness or helpfulness. Maybe you are sympathetic or friendly. Maybe you can encourage others. Open your gift and use it.

Use It or Lose It

Jesus told a story about a man who was going on a trip. He called his three servants and gave them coins to take care of while he was gone. He gave one servant five coins, the next servant two coins, and the last servant one coin. (See Matthew 25:14-30.)

The servant with five coins used those coins to double his money. So did the servant with two coins. But the servant with one coin dug a hole and buried his coin.

When the master returned, he called his servants. The first servant showed him his five coins and the five coins he'd earned. The master said, "You did well." The next servant showed him that he'd earned two more coins. He was told, "You did well." But the third servant said, "I hid your coin in the ground. Here it is." The master threw the servant out. He hadn't given him the coin so he could bury it. He wanted him to use it.

Jesus told this story to show us that we must use our gifts from the Holy Spirit. The servant who hid his coin was not fired because he'd lost the coin. He was fired because he didn't even try. Even if he'd tried to do something with it and failed, that would have been better than doing nothing at all.

This story also shows that we all receive different gifts. The master was as pleased with the servant who ended up with four coins as he was with the servant with 10. God doesn't ask us all to be equal in talent. But He does ask us to do our best with what we have. When we use whatever gifts we have been given, they will grow and become stronger.

Be good servants and use your gifts to serve each other.
1 Peter 4:10.

Fruits of the Spirit

Paul heard that there was trouble in the churches he had started in Galatia. Some new teachers were spreading false ideas. They were saying that a person needed to keep all the Jewish laws in order to be saved.

Now, what's wrong with that? It's good to keep the law, isn't it? Of course it is. But what these teachers really meant was that you could save yourself if you kept the law. That's wrong. That's very wrong. If we were able to save ourselves, we wouldn't need Jesus. The whole point of everything Paul taught was that we need Jesus.

So Paul wrote the Galatians a letter. He made sure they understood that they could not save themselves by following the law. He wanted them to realize that it was the Holy Spirit—not the law—that would help them do the right thing.

Then Paul got an idea. He told his friends that they were kind of like a tree—a fruit tree. He said that the Holy Spirit will help you grow wonderful fruit—fruits of the Spirit. What kind of fruit is that? Love is first, of course. Love is the sweetest fruit of all. Then "joy, peace, patience, kindness, goodness, faithfulness, gentleness, self-control" (Galatians 5:22, 23). The Holy Spirit can help you be like Jesus.

Paul wanted his friends to be happy knowing Jesus. He knew that trying to follow the law couldn't make them happy. Paul had been very good at keeping the law before he had met Jesus, and he hadn't been happy. Living a life filled with these fruits of the Spirit—that would make them happy.

Love

The Corinthians were arguing about which gift of the Spirit was the most important. Paul had to write them a letter.

Some of them were arguing that the gift of speaking was the most important gift of the Spirit. Paul told them that even if they could speak as beautifully as an angel, if they didn't have love it was just a bunch of noise. Words mean nothing without love.

Some were saying that the gift of prophecy was the most important. Paul told them that even if they knew all of God's secrets, if they didn't have love, it wouldn't matter. Faith without love? Nothing. Offerings without love? Worthless.

Then Paul wrote today's Bible text. Many people think it is the best thing ever written about love. When you read this list of what love is and what love isn't, you may wish you knew someone like that. You do—Jesus. Read it again now and see how it describes Jesus exactly. When you read this list you may wish you could be like this. You can—the Holy Spirit will help you be like Jesus.

In Paul's list of fruits of the Spirit, love is the first and most important. First there must be love. Without it, nothing else makes sense.

Love is patient and kind. Love is not jealous, it does not brag, and it is not proud. Love is not rude, is not selfish, and does not become angry easily. Love does not remember wrongs done against it. Love is not happy with evil, but is happy with the truth. Love patiently accepts all things. It always trusts, always hopes, and always continues strong.
1 Corinthians 13:4-7.

Joy

*I have learned the
secret of being
happy at any time
in everything
that happens.
Philippians 4:12.*

Paul was in prison again. Sometimes he was chased out of town for preaching. Sometimes he was put in prison. And beaten. And threatened. But he wouldn't stop preaching. If they threw him in prison for preaching, then he'd preach to other prisoners, to visitors, to the guards. And he wrote letters.

Paul wrote a letter to the Philippians from prison. And do you know what it was about? Joy. He told his friends that they brought him joy. Praying brought him joy. Preaching brought him joy. It made him happy to hear about more people deciding to follow Jesus. It made him happy to think about being with Jesus someday in heaven.

On Paul's list of fruits of the Spirit, joy is second, right after love. Joy follows love. Paul loved Jesus. That's what made him happy. And no one could take that away.

Paul was filled with joy and he wanted his friends to have that same joy. Paul wrote to them, "Be full of joy in the Lord always" (Philippians 4:4). And then maybe he saw clearly where he was—cold and lonely, in chains, covered with bruises from the last beating. Maybe it made him pause for a minute.

But then he saw even more clearly what was to come. And the guards, the cold, the pain all melted away. He remembered that happiness doesn't depend on things. Happiness doesn't depend on circumstances. And he added, firmly and confidently, "I will say again, be full of joy" (verse 4).

Peace

Peace is third on Paul's list of fruits of the Spirit. It doesn't seem like Paul had a very peaceful life—he was always getting chased out of town and beaten and thrown into jail. But that didn't matter. Paul had peace—the peace of Jesus.

I leave you peace. My peace I give you. I do not give it to you as the world does. So don't let your hearts be troubled. Don't be afraid. John 14:27.

You can see in today's Bible text that the peace of Jesus is not the same kind of peace the world gives. The world has a different idea of how peace can be found—by daydreaming, by watching TV, by playing video games, by escaping from reality.

That peace does not last. Perhaps you have been reading a really good book, and it's such a good story, and you can't wait to see what happens next. Then there's this buzzing noise that you sort of notice but mostly ignore. And then you realize with a start that the buzzing noise is your mother and she is standing there looking stern and saying something like "Why didn't you answer me?" That peace is definitely over.

Sometimes people choose to escape into the TV or computer instead of doing their homework or chores. They try to escape reality and responsibility—or at least avoid it for a while. This kind of peace does not last. It's not real.

The peace of Jesus is real. Nothing can change it. The peace of Jesus lasts. Nothing can take it from us. The peace of Jesus is not an escape. It does not keep us from sadness or problems. This peace does not save us from trouble—but it is with us during trouble. Jesus is with us. We don't have to be afraid.

Patience

*Be patient and accept
each other with love.
Ephesians 4:2.*

A mother lion is very patient. She lets her cubs crawl on her and swat at her and bite her with their tiny teeth. She switches her tail so the cubs can try to catch it. She calmly allows her cubs to pounce on her and ambush her and growl and snarl—even though she is probably trying to take a nap.

Why does she put up with this? With one swipe of her powerful paw she could knock some sense into them and teach them to respect her. She puts up with it because she knows that it is important for her cubs to play. By learning to stalk and pounce and wrestle they are developing the skills they will need to become good hunters. They will need to learn to hunt if they are going to survive.

So she is patient. With dignity, she puts up with their nonsense. With graciousness, she suffers through their foolishness. She is long-suffering.

Patience is fourth on Paul's list of fruits of the Spirit. With all he had to put up with, Paul really needed the fruit of patience. You might need it too. Maybe there are people who drive you crazy. They won't share, they whine, they tattle—they are pests. When you are around people like that you might want to smack them.

But there's a better solution: Be patient. If you hit people who irritate you, they'll want to hit you back, and it only gets worse from there. But there's a good chance things will get better if you bear with them and love them and remember that they're having to learn how to be good too.

Patience is one of the hardest things to learn. But be patient! Keep trying!

Kindness

Do you ever rub your hands together when they are cold? Do you know why it helps warm them up? Friction. There are many things that get warm (and even hot) when they are rubbed together. It's because of their rough surfaces. When your hands move against each other, the skin is rough enough to slow down the movement. You have to work hard to move them. This work turns into heat. That is called friction.

A gentle answer will calm a person's anger. But an unkind answer will cause more anger. Proverbs 15:1.

Friction can cause trouble with machinery. When the metal pieces of an engine slide over each other, they can get so hot that they could melt. That's why engines need oil. The oil covers the surfaces of the moving pieces of the engine so that they slide over each other smoothly. Then they don't get hot.

Friction has another meaning. Sometimes we say there is friction between people. That means they're having trouble getting along. They rub each other the wrong way.

What should you do if there is friction between you and another person? Look at today's Bible text. If you keep quarreling and arguing, the friction will only get worse. Tempers will get hotter. You need some "oil" to smooth things over. A kind answer is just the thing to cool things down. You can choose to be kind.

That's easy to say but hard to do. When someone is yelling at you, it's hard not to yell back. You'll need help. The Holy Spirit will help you. Kindness is the fifth fruit of the Spirit. The Holy Spirit will help smooth out your rough edges. Kindness will help you keep cool.

Be Good

Sin rules me as if I
were its slave. I do not
understand the things
I do. I do not do the
good things I want to
do. And I do the bad
things I hate to do.
Romans 7:14, 15.

Do you know how a yo-yo
works? You loop one end of the string around your finger. When
you let go of the yo-yo, it starts spinning downward (the law of
gravity). As it falls, the string that is wrapped around its center
shaft unwinds. When the yo-yo reaches the end of the string, it
wants to keep spinning (that's because of another law of
physics). But it can't spin down anymore, so it spins up. The yo-
yo starts to rewind the string around its shaft. If you give a little
flick of your wrist, you provide the yo-yo with enough extra
power to climb the string all the way back up to your hand.

The word "yo-yo" comes from the Philippines, where the toy
was invented. We also use this word to describe things that
behave like a yo-yo. When people change their minds back and
forth, we might call it yo-yoing.

It's fun to play with a yo-yo. But it's not fun to act like a yo-
yo. Paul knew that. Look at his confession in today's Bible text.
It sounds like Paul felt as if Satan had him on a string. Paul
wanted to do good; he tried to be good, but sin always jerked
him back. Paul was being pulled in two different directions—
good and bad.

Paul needed someone to cut the string. "Who will save me?"
Paul asked. Then he answered his own question: "God will. I
thank him for saving me through Jesus Christ our Lord!"
(Romans 7:24, 25). And Paul listed goodness as the sixth fruit of
the Spirit.

You know what you need to do to be good. But that's not
enough. You can't do it without help. Jesus can cut the string
that ties you to sin. Jesus can set you free.

Faithfulness

There are some things that you need to be faithful about. Brushing your teeth, for instance, or feeding the dog. Perhaps they are little things, but it's important that you do them every day. Faithfully.

The Lord is faithful. He will give you strength.
2 Thessalonians 3:3.

When you are faithful, people can count on you. They can trust you to do what you are supposed to do. They can depend on you to do what you say you will do.

Paul's list of fruits of the Spirit already includes love, joy, peace, patience, kindness, and goodness. Now we'll add faithfulness.

This means that the Spirit goes beyond helping you to be good and kind and all the rest—the Spirit helps you to do all these things faithfully. So not only are you patient, you are faithfully patient. You aren't just kind; you are kind all the time. You never stop loving. You are faithful about it all.

Is that even possible? No, not if you try to do it on your own. But look at today's Bible text. We can be faithful because God is faithful. He is ready to help us all the time. He won't let us down.

Paul could count on God to give him love, joy, peace, and all the rest. And God could count on Paul to preach the Good News, even when it got him into trouble.

Your teacher is counting on you to do your homework. Your parents depend on you to do your chores. Your friends trust you to keep their secrets. The Holy Spirit will help you be faithful—in the little things as well as the big things.

343

Gentleness

Learn from me. I am gentle and humble in spirit. Matthew 11:29.

When you dip the wand into a bottle of bubbles, soap stretches across the little circle, forming a film that is very thin but also very strong. When you blow into the circle, the film fills with air, getting bigger and thinner. The film is sticky, so when the bubble blows away from the wand, it seals itself into a ball, holding the air inside.

Until you touch it. Then it pops. Bubbles are very delicate.

First we said the soap film is very strong—and it is. Then we said that bubbles are very delicate—and they are. Bubbles are both strong and delicate at the same time.

So to make the bubble, you must blow exactly strong enough. If you blow too soft, nothing will happen—except the soap mixture will drip onto your toes. If you blow too hard, nothing will happen—except the soap will splatter all over. To get a bubble, you must blow gently—not too hard, not too soft, just exactly strong enough.

That's what the word *gentle* means in the Bible—being exactly strong enough for the situation. Jesus was always gentle. When He blessed the children He was careful as He "took the children in his arms" (Mark 10:16). But just before that, when He had seen the disciples shooing the children away, He had been stronger. "He was displeased," and He told the disciples, "Don't stop them" (verse 14). Later, at the Temple, He was even stronger as "He threw out all the people who were buying and selling there" (Matthew 21:12). But always Jesus was gentle—exactly as strong as He needed to be.

That's what Paul meant when he added gentleness to his list of fruits of the Spirit. The Holy Spirit will help you to be as strong as you need to be in every situation.

Self-control

We have come to the end of Paul's list of fruits of the Spirit. There is one more fruit that finishes it up—self-control. The Holy Spirit will help you be in control of what you do and say.

God did not give us a spirit that makes us afraid. He gave us a spirit of power and love and self-control. 2 Timothy 1:7.

Have you ever seen a well-trained dog? The owner has taught the dog to sit, stay, or come, and the dog eagerly obeys its master's commands. A dog that is well trained is able to control itself. When its master tells it to come, it comes—even if it would rather chase that squirrel. When its master tells it to sit, it sits—even if it would rather jump up and get its muddy paws all over a visitor. The owner has taught the dog self-control. The dog is able to obey.

People also need to learn self-control. A person with no self-control is constantly making mistakes and getting into trouble. A person with no self-control does the wrong thing and then says, "I couldn't help it."

But a person who has self-control makes good choices. When you have self-control, you are able to obey and get things done and do them correctly.

Look at this list of wonderful fruit: love, joy, peace, patience, kindness, goodness, faithfulness, and gentleness. The Holy Spirit gives them to us, but we need to choose how to use them. They don't work on their own—we need to pay attention. We need to have self-control. Fortunately, the Holy Spirit will help us with that as well.

Lovely In, Lovely Out

Think about the things that are good and worthy of praise. Think about the things that are true and honorable and right and pure and beautiful and respected. Philippians 4:8.

When you push a button on the keyboard or click the mouse, the computer does what you tell it to do. If you are a creative speller, the computer screen shows the words exactly as you spelled them. If you press the delete button accidentally, the computer deletes—even if you didn't really want it to.

There is a saying about computers: Garbage in, garbage out. Basically it means that if you give the computer bad information or bad instructions you'll get bad results.

With brains, too, you can say "Garbage in, garbage out." You've got to be careful what you put into your brain. If you see something bad, it goes into your brain. Even if you try to forget it, you can never delete it. It's there, in your brain. And if you see lots and lots of bad things, it gets harder and harder to forget.

You can choose most of the things that go into your brain. You choose which books you'll read and which TV shows you'll watch and which video games you'll play. All that stuff goes into your brain, even when you aren't studying it, even when you're just playing. And all that stuff makes a difference in you. If you play a lot of violent video games, it makes you more violent. If you watch a lot of stupid television, it makes you more stupid. Garbage in, garbage out.

Look at today's Bible text. Lovely in, lovely out. If you want to be good, think about good things. Put good stuff into your brain.

Praise Him, Praise Him

Imagine the biggest, reddest, juiciest strawberry you ever saw. And take a big bite (in your imagination, of course). Did you say "yum"? Or "mmmm"? Can you imagine taking a bite of your favorite food and not saying how good it is? When food tastes good, we like to say that it tastes good. Somehow it tastes better if we say that it's good.

Have you ever seen a falling star? You probably said, "Look!" or "Ooooo!" When we see something amazing, we want to tell others about it. We want them to see it too.

Have you ever played with a bunch of puppies? And they're all furry and so happy to see you. You may have said, "Puppies!" or "Please, can't I have one?" When we see something wonderful, we have to say so—even if there's no one around to hear.

That's praise. People praise the things they think are good. When you learned to walk, your parents praised you. When your puppy learns to go outside, you praise it. When your teammate makes a goal in soccer, you give praise.

When we praise something, we show that we think it is valuable. And somehow, praising it—saying it's valuable—makes it more valuable to us. When we say we enjoy something, it makes our enjoyment complete.

And so we praise God. We thank Him. We sing to Him. We tell Him how we appreciate the wonderful things He's made for us. We praise God because we love Him.

Praise the Lord, because he is good. Sing praises to him, because it is pleasant. Psalm 135:3.

347

It All Belongs to God

Have you ever been to a potluck? It's like a big party. Everyone brings something to eat and they put it on a big table and everyone shares. It can be a lot of fun—usually some people bring salads, some bring entrées, and others bring dessert. It can be less fun if the law of averages breaks down and everyone decides to bring a can of olives.

At a potluck people often talk about the food. They'll say such things as "Did you have some of Ethel's potato salad?" or "Try some of my banana surprise."

We say it is Ethel's potato salad because Ethel made it and Ethel brought it to the potluck. Even if Ethel gives it all away and doesn't have any left over to take home, we still think of it as Ethel's potato salad—because she made it.

Who made our world? God did. He made the world and everything in it. And then He gave it to us to take care of.

He gave it to us. He made it and brought it to the potluck and gave it to us.

But look at today's Bible text. It all belongs to Him. Even though He gave it to us, this is God's world—because He made it.

So it doesn't make much sense for us to get possessive about things. We say such things as "This is my house" or "This is my bike." But really, we just got them off the big potluck table. We didn't make them or bring them to the potluck. God did. He wants us to have them—He brought them for us. But it's important to remember where they came from and to whom they really belong.

Party!

Imagine that one morning you find a surprise: a huge basket filled with your favorite foods. What will you do? A. Put it in the freezer. B. Pull up a chair and start eating as much as you can. C. Call up your friends and invite them over for a party.

And then, that night, what will you be left with? If you choose A, you will have a bunch of frozen food. If you choose B, you will have either a lot of leftovers or a tummyache. If you choose C, your house will be a big mess with paper plates lying around everywhere. There won't be any food left. You will be tired. You will be happy.

The Bible says, "It is more blessed to give than to receive" (Acts 20:35). "Blessed" means "happy." Giving will make you happier than taking or keeping. This idea doesn't make sense to a lot of people. They count what they have. They add up the things they get. The way they see it, the more they get, the more they have.

But Jesus isn't counting things when He talks about giving. Jesus wants us to know that the more we give, the more we become. We become more loving. We become more unselfish. We become more like Him.

Jesus knows about giving. He gave us this world. He gave us everything we own. He gave His life to save us. Jesus knows how blessed it is to give.

He wants us to be blessed, too. Choose C. Invite others to the party. Share what God has given to you.

Give, and you will receive. You will be given much. It will be poured into your hands—more than you can hold. You will be given so much that it will spill into your lap. The way you give to others is the way God will give to you. Luke 6:38.

Boomerang

Do good things everywhere you go. After a while the good you do will return to help you.
Ecclesiastes 11:1.

Have you ever played with a boomerang? You hold it by one end and throw it with a twist of your wrist to send it spinning through the air. People who have had lots of practice and know just what to do are able to throw a boomerang so that it curves back toward them as it flies through the air. They can make the boomerang return to them.

Some people can make a Frisbee return too. Maybe you know how to spin a ball so that when you roll it on the floor, it will roll back to you. Or maybe you know how to play with a yo-yo so that it actually comes back up the string into your hand. This idea of making things come back to you is big in the world of toys.

It is an important idea in other ways as well. Have you ever heard the saying "What goes around comes around"? Yes, it sounds like nonsense. It means that your actions make a difference in the things that happen to you later. What you do will "come around" again. The way you behave will "boomerang" in the way people treat you.

In another version, today's Bible text is translated, "Cast thy bread upon the waters: for thou shalt find it after many days" (KJV). That really sounds like nonsense.

But think about what would happen if you took that advice. If you always share with your brother, how do you think he will feel about sharing with you? If you speak politely to your teacher and always stick up for your friends, what do you think they will say about you? If you obey, what are the chances that you will get into trouble?

Casting your bread upon the waters makes a lot of sense after all.

Making Waves

One of the best things about the beach is playing in the waves. You can dive into the waves or let them knock you over or try to catch a ride on them. No matter how full of energy you are, you always get tired before the waves do. They never stop rolling.

You can make waves. Just toss a stone into a pond. The stone makes ripples that spread wider and wider, in a circle. Ocean waves move the same way these ripples do.

There are other ways you can make waves. Sometimes when we talk about "making waves" we are talking about people instead of water. We say that people are "making waves" when they try to make a difference.

Just like a ripple in a pond, the things you do keep expanding. Your smiles keep spreading. Your helpfulness grows. Your kindness travels in wider circles.

Everything you do makes a difference. If you do something mean, that makes waves too. When you are mean, it makes other people feel mean. But when you are nice, chances are other people will pass that niceness along.

Jesus made waves. He showed us how to love. He asks us to keep those waves rippling. He asks us to follow His example. He asks us to give of ourselves to help others. He'll help us.

How many waves are in the ocean? More than you can count. What difference can you make? More than you can imagine.

The Son of Man did not come for other people to serve him. He came to serve others. Matthew 20:28.

351

Rock, Paper, Scissors

Rock, paper, scissors is a fun game because it is totally balanced. Rock crushes scissors. Scissors cuts paper. Paper covers rock. None of them has all the power. You never know what the other guy is going to choose. He never knows what you are going to choose. There is no sure thing.

Dynamite is not one of the choices. It would destroy the balance of power.

Some people don't like this idea of balance, of sharing power. They want to win every time. They want to tell everyone else what to do. They are bossy.

You might know someone who is bossy. What can you do? You can tell them you don't like to be bossed around. You can try to stay out of their way. Unfortunately, when people bring dynamite into the game, you can't always stop them.

However, you can at least make sure that you are not a bossy person. Try to be fair. Remember that you can't have your way all the time. Ask Jesus to help you do your part. Jesus can help us work together. Jesus can bring balance.

Is there balance in your home? Are some people doing more than their share of the work? Is there balance in your classroom? In a group project, do you do your fair share? When you make a mistake, do you take your share of the responsibility?

The secret of balance is thinking about others. "Do all these things; but most important, love each other. Love is what holds you all together in perfect unity" (Colossians 3:14). With dynamite, no one wins. With love, everyone wins.

Time Allowance

Do you get an allowance? Some parents give their children a certain amount of money every week. An allowance is supposed to teach you the value of money.

There is a right time and a right way for everything. Ecclesiastes 8:6.

Some people get a big allowance. Some don't get any allowance at all. That's the way it goes with money. It'll be the same when you grow up. Some people will earn more money than you, and some will earn less. Money isn't spread around evenly.

But money isn't everything. God gives us plenty of gifts besides money.

Time, for instance. Time is an important gift. In some ways it is like money. You can waste it. You can spend it.

But time is different in other ways. You can save your money, but you can't save your time. You can't put time in the bank. You can only spend it.

And time is measured evenly. It is the same for everyone. Rich people and poor people have the same-sized day. Everybody's hours are exactly 60 minutes long.

So what will you do with your time? You get to choose.

You might argue that you don't get to choose: you have to be in school for the next hour, and you have to study math. No choice about it.

Well, actually, there is. You can choose how to spend that assigned time. You can spend it finishing your assignment quickly and accurately. Or you can draw a silly picture on your arm.

Your next hour is worth as much as anybody's. Spend it well.

Jesus Builds a Bridge

We can enter through a new way that Jesus opened for us. Hebrews 10:20.

Imagine that you are exploring in the woods when you come to a stream. You look around and see that a tree has fallen over the stream. What do you do? Well, of course you walk across on the log. This is the kind of thing that makes exploring so much fun.

A log is a perfect bridge for crossing a stream in the woods. But it won't work in other places where a bridge is needed. Cars can't drive across a log. So we build other kinds of bridges. A suspension bridge hangs (or suspends) from cables that are strung between two towers. The cables kind of swoop down in the middle and back up again.

People build bridges over rivers and canyons and between islands. People build bridges to connect things. So sometimes we use the idea of bridges to talk about other things that need to be connected. For instance, if people or countries have disagreements they are trying to solve, we might say they are building a bridge.

Sin has come between us and God. God would like to be with us, and we would like to be with God, but sin keeps us apart. How can we get together? We need a bridge.

Jesus is the bridge.

When Jesus came to earth, He brought God to us. He showed us what God is like. He opened up the way to God.

Now Jesus is in heaven. He brings us to God. He introduces us as part of the family. "These are Your children," He says. "These are My brothers and sisters."

Judged

ere's the best way to make a peanut butter and jelly sandwich. You take two pieces of brown bread. On one, spread a thick layer of creamy peanut butter. On the other, spread a lot of strawberry jam, clear to the edges. Put the two pieces together. Cut the sandwich in half so it makes two rectangles. You'll also need milk to drink.

God will judge everyone through Christ Jesus. Romans 2:16.

Wait a minute. You may disagree. You may think only white bread will do. You may prefer crunchy peanut butter to creamy, or grape jelly to strawberry jam. You may think it's disgusting to use so much peanut butter. You may cut your sandwich in triangles instead of rectangles, or just use one piece of bread and fold it over.

When it comes to peanut butter and jelly sandwiches, you just have to be tolerant. You have to accept that your way is not the only way, that some people use jam even though the name of the sandwich specifically says "jelly." It's a free country.

Someone else's sandwich is pretty easy to tolerate—after all, you don't have to eat it. But it's not always easy to be tolerant. Sometimes people have the strangest ideas and the weirdest ways of doing things. What do you do?

Look at today's Bible text. It's not your job to decide whether someone else is wrong or right. God will take care of that. Don't worry about it. Think about this instead: Jesus says, "You will be judged in the same way that you judge others" (Matthew 7:2).

We need to be tolerant. When you accept others and refuse to judge them, you are treating them with love and patience. This is how Jesus wants you to treat others. This is how you want others to treat you. This is how Jesus treats us all.

355

Justified

All people have sinned and are not good enough for God's glory. . . . They are made right with God by being made free from sin through Jesus Christ. Romans 3:23, 24.

Maybe you've noticed it when you are reading a book or magazine. The words on the left side of the page almost always line up and start the same distance from the edge.

But the right side can be different. Words are not all the same length, so the end of one line of words will probably be a different length than the end of the next line of words. However, there is a way to insert spaces here and there along the line to make the right side line up evenly too. When the words are spaced so that the lines come out even at both edges, we say that the margins are justified.

When you look up and down a page with justified margins, the words are lined up with the edges of the paper. When you look across the page from left to right, the words are spaced to make the lines come out even.

The word *justify* is in the Bible, too. People become justified when they choose to follow Jesus and become a child of God. Satan says, "These people are sinners." Jesus says, "I paid for their sins." God says it comes out even.

You aren't justified by being good. You aren't justified by obeying all the rules. You aren't justified because of who *you* are. You are justified because of who *God* is. God loves you. He wants to be with you.

When we are justified, our lives are full. The future is lined up. It all comes out even. Like the lines of a paragraph with justified margins.

God Is Fair

Have you ever been at the playground when there was someone there who didn't take turns? For instance, you are waiting in line to go down the slide, and someone cuts in front of everybody and scampers up the ladder. Don't you just hate that?

Have you ever been around someone who is selfish? For instance, when there are cookies and one kid takes a lot more than everyone else? Doesn't that make you mad?

It's no fun to play with people who won't take turns or share. We want people to be fair. Taking turns and sharing are rules that help us get along. When everybody follows the rules, people are happy. They feel that they are being treated fairly.

We all like it best when things are fair. But lots of times that's not the way it is. Lots of times life isn't fair. It's not fair that some people are hungry. It's not fair that some people don't have a place to live. Or warm clothes. Or any toys.

Sometimes when people see so many things that aren't fair, they say that it is God's fault. But that doesn't make sense. God wants things to be fair. God is the one who gave us the rules. If everyone followed the rules, everything would be fair.

God is fair. He let's everyone choose. You can choose if you want to follow God's plan. You can decide if you want to believe that Jesus saved you from sin.

We get to decide. And someday God will decide. God will decide who has chosen to follow Him. God is fair. He knows who wants to be with Him and who doesn't. God will always do the right thing.

You're With Jesus

He went into heaven itself. He is there now before God to help us. Hebrews 9:24.

If you've ever gone to an amusement park, you've probably been too excited to notice the sign that said something like this: "Children under 14 must be accompanied by an adult." The company that owns the park wants you to be safe. They want someone to be responsible for you. So they won't let you in unless you're with an adult.

But that's OK, because it's more fun to go with someone else anyway—especially if that person is paying for your ticket and your ice cream and your souvenirs.

That adult might also come in useful if you decide to watch the parade. Unless you get there an hour early, there will probably be people already lining the parade route, standing in front of you. Chances are you won't be able to see the parade because, well, you're short. All you can see are the backsides of the people in front of you.

If you really are too short to see, and if you are not too sticky, and if the adult with you is strong enough and is a good sport, they might be willing to pick you up and put you on their shoulders. Then you will be able to see everything. You'll have the best seat in the house. It doesn't matter that you aren't tall. You're with someone who is.

Sometimes people worry that they won't be able to go to heaven because they make mistakes. They worry that they aren't good enough. You don't need to worry about that. Everyone makes mistakes. No one is good enough. We can't get into heaven by being good. That's not how it works.

We get into heaven because of Jesus. If we are with Jesus, He will take us in with Him. It doesn't matter if you're not perfect. You're with Someone who is.

Christmas Is Coming

Have you been getting ready for Christmas? There's a lot to do. Maybe you got a Christmas tree. Maybe you baked cookies. Or bought some presents. Or helped decorate the house with candles or wreaths or Christmas stockings.

I am coming soon.
Revelation 3:11.

A lot of the fun of Christmas is the getting ready part. While we are wrapping presents or hanging ornaments on the tree, we can think about the happiness that is coming, and we will be happy just thinking about it.

Of course, you know why we have Christmas. We're celebrating Jesus' birth. It's the happiest story there ever was. We're so glad Jesus came to earth to save us from sin. So every year we get ready for Christmas and remember that special story.

Christmas is a good time to remember the first time Jesus came to our world. It also is a good time to remember that He is coming back. Just as we get ready for Christmas, we also need to get ready for Jesus to come again. How do we do that? We get to know Jesus. We choose to follow Him. We take care of each other.

Getting ready for Jesus can be even more wonderful than getting ready for Christmas. While we are learning more about Jesus and learning to love each other, we can think about the happiness that is coming, and we will be happy just thinking about it.

Jesus promised, "I will come back. Then I will take you to be with me so that you may be where I am" (John 14:3). Christmas is coming. Jesus is coming. Isn't it wonderful? Let's get ready.

Picture-perfect

Through Christ, God decided to bring all things back to himself again—things on earth and things in heaven. Colossians 1:20.

Do you like to do jigsaw puzzles? They can be a lot of fun. Many people follow their own special plan when they put together a puzzle. They like to do all the edges first, or they have to turn all the pieces right side up first, or they sort the pieces into piles according to color or shape.

God is following a plan to put the puzzle of our world back together.

When God created the world, it was perfect. Then sin came along and ruined the perfect picture. God had a plan to put the pieces back together.

First God promised to send a Redeemer to rescue people from sin. He chose the Israelites to help Him tell the world about this plan. God kept His promise. He sent Jesus to be our Redeemer. When Jesus died on the cross, He took the punishment for our sin.

Then Jesus asked the people who believed in Him to share the good news about God's plan. We are all working together to help complete the puzzle. You know that it's even better to do a jigsaw puzzle with other people; if you get stuck on a certain piece, your friends will help you find it.

The next step in the plan is for Jesus to take us home to heaven. In heaven everything will be perfect, as it was in the beginning. God will make everything new. When we are in heaven, God's plan will be complete. All the pieces will be back together. He will make the picture perfect again.

I Will Come Back

The disciples were curious about the future. They asked Jesus how they would know when it was time for Him to come again. Jesus talked to them about what would happen, but He did not tell them when He would be coming back. "No one knows when that day or time will be," Jesus told them. "Only the Father knows" (Matthew 24:36).

Jesus knew it would be better if we didn't know when He was coming back. What if Jesus had told the disciples that it was going to be at least 2,000 years? Do you think they would have worked so hard to spread the gospel? Probably not. They might have felt there was no hurry. They might have given up in discouragement.

So Jesus didn't tell them when. He told them, "Always be ready" (verse 42).

Jesus didn't tell us when He would be coming back. But He told us how to live until He does come back. We have a job to do while we wait for Jesus to come take us to heaven. Jesus doesn't want us to put it off. He doesn't want us to get lazy. He doesn't want us to forget that He is coming back.

Because He is coming back. He promised. We know that He will come back and take us to heaven. At the Last Supper with His disciples Jesus promised, "I will come back to you" (John 14:18). And as the disciples watched Him disappear into the sky, the angels reminded them, "He will come back" (Acts 1:11).

We don't know when Jesus will come. But we know that He will come.

You, too, must be patient. Do not give up hope. The Lord is coming soon. James 5:8.

Why Jesus Went Away

I am going there to prepare a place for you. After I go and prepare a place for you, I will come back. Then I will take you to be with me so that you may be where I am.
John 14:2, 3

At the Last Supper Jesus told His disciples, "I will be with you only a little longer" (John 13:33). The disciples were worried and confused. What would they do without Jesus?

Jesus gave them words of comfort. "Don't let your hearts be troubled. Trust in God. And trust in me" (John 14:1). Jesus gave them words of hope. He promised them that He would come back.

Then He explained why He was going away and why He was coming back.

Look at today's Bible text. Jesus went to heaven to get things ready for all the people who choose to live with Him. Jesus wants to be with us. He wants to be with us even more than we want to be with Him. Jesus is coming back to take us to heaven so that we can be together.

That's the next part of His plan. Jesus loves us so much that He redeemed us from sin. And He loves us so much that He wants to be with us. He is coming back to get us so that we can be together.

This is our hope. Someday we will be with Jesus. This is what we look forward to. In heaven we will be with Jesus.

Jesus is in heaven right now, getting things ready for us.

Don't Be Afraid

For a lot of people, thinking about getting a shot is worse than actually getting it. The shot itself hurts for only a second, just as the doctor promises. But worrying about it can last from the time you find out you have to get one until you finally get it.

Don't be afraid. These things must happen before the end comes. Matthew 24:6.

You have to get shots. If you didn't get them, you could catch some horrible disease. But it's no fun. And worrying about getting them is no fun either.

Some people worry about the end of the world. They look for signs. They try to figure out when it will happen. When the disciples asked Jesus about the end of the world, He didn't tell them when it would happen. Maybe He knew we would worry about it, just as we worry when we have to get a shot.

Jesus did say that things would get tough for the people who obeyed God. But He also said something else very important: "Don't be afraid." All the bad and sinful things must stop happening before all the good and perfect things of heaven can happen. The end of the world has to happen before we can begin to live forever in heaven.

Jesus wanted His disciples to think about the good things, not the bad things. He wanted them to remember that He was coming again. He wanted them to know that everything will work out all right. In the end, Jesus will win—and we are on His side.

Jesus doesn't tell us when the world will end, but He tells us the important stuff about it. He tells us, "Don't be afraid. It won't last long; it will be OK; I will be with you." The same things your mom says to you before you get a shot.

Telling the Future

Now I have warned
you about this
before it happens.
Matthew 24:25.

Have you ever wondered what you will look like when you grow up? Scientists and detectives have invented a computer program that can "age" a photo. If they scanned your photo into the computer, they could show you what you might look like in 10, 20, or 30 years. But the computer is only guessing. And it can't show you stuff like what your job will be. A computer can't tell the future. But we still like to wonder about it.

When Jesus' disciples asked Him about the future, He didn't tell them when He would return, but He did give them some answers. He told them to always be ready. He told them what to do while they waited. And He gave them some things to watch for.

Jesus told them that there would be wars and earthquakes and other troubles. These terrible things are happening now—but they have been happening ever since sin entered the world. Jesus isn't saying that these things mean that the end of the world is coming right away. He is warning us that they will happen before He comes back.

Jesus also warns us that some people might try to trick us. Someone might say that Jesus is in the desert. Or someone might even come up to you and claim that he is Jesus. Jesus warns us, "Don't believe it" (Matthew 24:26). Jesus promises that He won't come back that way. When He comes back everyone will see Him.

Jesus gave us some hints about the future so that we won't be tricked. But the best way to get ready for the future is to become good friends with Jesus. The better we know Him, the less likely someone will be able to fool us.

A Hint

The Good News about God's kingdom will be preached in all the world, to every nation. Then the end will come. Matthew 24:14.

Here is a mystery to solve: What is going to happen very soon?

Here are some clues. The sun is going down early now. The weather is colder. We celebrated Thanksgiving a few weeks ago. The stores in the mall are covered with red and green decorations. People are making lists. Everyone keeps singing "Jingle Bells."

Can you guess from these hints? Of course. Christmas!

Would you like to know when Jesus will come again? Jesus didn't tell us exactly, but He gave us one really big hint. Look at today's Bible text.

God wants everyone everywhere to hear the good news. He wants everyone everywhere to know that He loves them. God wants everyone everywhere to have a chance to choose Him.

Then He will come again.

We can help that happen. How will everyone everywhere hear the good news? We can help tell them. How will everyone everywhere know that God loves them? We can show God's love by the way we love others. How will everyone everywhere get the chance to choose God? We can let them know that they have that choice; we can give them that chance.

Every day that Jesus waits gives us one more day to preach the good news in all the world, one more day to help each other, one more day to work for Him.

Mirrors

*Now we see as if we
are looking into a dark
mirror. But at that
time, in the future, we
shall see clearly.*
1 Corinthians 13:12.

Perhaps one day, when you were supposed to be scrubbing behind your ears, you looked into the mirror and wondered how it worked. You wondered how a mirror is different from regular glass. You wondered why you can see yourself so well in a mirror.

Here's the secret: a mirror is a piece of glass that has a very thin coat of aluminum on the back. The metal makes the glass reflect light very well and show the image of whatever is in front of it.

Other things act like mirrors. Have you ever seen yourself in a puddle on a sunny day? Have you ever looked at the stuff in the display window of a store and seen yourself looking back? These things reflect light too.

We are drawn to things that reflect light. There are other kinds of things and ideas that reflect a different kind of light—the light of knowledge and truth.

People have always wanted to see God—but we can't. He is too holy. But we want to know Him. And He wants us to know Him, so He holds up mirrors that show what He is like. He gave us the Bible—the more you read the Bible, the clearer His reflection is in the mirror. He sent Jesus—Jesus came to "show us the Father" (John 14:9).

Look at today's Bible text. Someday we will be with God. In heaven we won't have to try to see God through a mirror. We will be able to see clearly. We will understand. It'll be the real thing—no more mirrors.

It's About Time

It seems as if time would be exact. For instance, one day is 24 hours long, the time it takes for the earth to spin once. But it's not that simple. A scientist named Albert Einstein said that time is relative—time seems different, depending on what's happening to you.

When you are holding your breath, 30 seconds can be a long time. However, if your mom says, "Bedtime," and you ask for just a little longer and she says you can have an extra 30 seconds—then you will find that 30 seconds can go by very quickly indeed.

God sees time differently. Look at today's Bible text. Peter was worried that people might get discouraged waiting for Jesus to come back. So Peter tried to explain that time is relative. "The Lord is not slow in doing what he promised—the way some people understand slowness" (2 Peter 3:9). And why is God waiting? "God is being patient with you. He does not want anyone to be lost" (verse 9).

It seems like we are waiting a very long time for Jesus to come again. But things look different to God. We only see our little bit of time. God can look back, to the beginning of our world and beyond. He can look forward, to the beginning of our time in heaven, when we can be together with Him—forever.

We are holding our breath—and it seems to be taking forever. When will Jesus come? God is holding His breath— hoping, hoping that more will choose Him. He does not want anyone to be lost.

To the Lord one day is as a thousand years, and a thousand years is as one day.
2 Peter 3:8.

Life Comes From God

*God raised the Lord
Jesus from death.
And God will also raise
us from death.
1 Corinthians 6:14.*

Afuneral is a very sad thing. At a funeral people get together for a ceremony to honor someone who has died. They meet together and talk about what they liked best about their friend who is no longer with them. They pray and read comforting texts from the Bible and sing favorite songs. They cry because they are going to miss their friend.

When someone dies, the people who knew him or her are sad. But the person who dies is not sad. The person who dies does not cry. The person who dies does not feel lonely. A person who is dead doesn't know anything or do anything or feel anything.

When a person is born, God gives him or her life. When people die, they are not alive anymore. But Jesus does not forget about them. When someone chooses to become a friend of Jesus, that is a relationship that nothing can break—not even death.

When Jesus comes again, He will give people back their lives. Jesus will call the people who chose to follow Him. They will be alive again. And Jesus will take them to heaven.

The Bible says, "God will destroy death forever. The Lord God will wipe away every tear from every face" (Isaiah 25:8).

We are sad at funerals because we will miss our friends who have died. But we are comforted because we know that we will see them again when Jesus comes. And we know that in heaven we will always be together.

Wake Up!

Some families open Christmas presents on Christmas Eve. Some open them on Christmas morning. Both ways work just fine, but most families are firm about keeping their particular tradition.

Let's say a family opens presents on Christmas morning. What would happen if one of the children overslept? (Yes, yes, it's highly unlikely. But just for the sake of argument.) Would his brothers and sisters just let him sleep? Would they start without him? No! They'd drag him out of bed. They aren't going to let him miss anything.

The Christians who lived in Thessalonica were worried. They expected Jesus to come soon, and they could hardly wait. But they were worried that their friends who had already died would miss out on the wonderful, glorious excitement when Jesus returned.

So Paul wrote them a letter. He assured them that they didn't need to worry. Their friends wouldn't miss anything. They would get to see Jesus when He comes.

Look at today's Bible text. When Jesus comes He will "wake up" the dead people who believed in Him. Everyone who loves Jesus gets to see Him coming to take them to heaven.

Paul says that first the believers who have died will rise up to meet Jesus. Then the believers who are still alive "will be gathered up with them." All the believers will see Jesus come. All the believers will go to meet Him. None of them will miss out.

Those who have died and were in Christ will rise first. After that, those who are still alive at that time will be gathered up with them.
1 Thessalonians 4:16, 17.

Advent

So Christ was offered as a sacrifice one time to take away the sins of many people. And he will come a second time, but not to offer himself for sin. He will come again to bring salvation to those who are waiting for him. Hebrews 9:28.

Do you know what people are referring to when they talk about "the First Advent"? Here's a hint: we are celebrating it today. It's Christmas!

Advent means "coming" or "arrival." The First Advent was Jesus' coming to earth as a baby to save us from sin. People looked forward to the coming of the Messiah with hope. And when the moment arrived, the angels sang with joy.

What do you suppose people mean when they talk about the Second Advent? It's another arrival. The Second Advent will be Jesus' coming again, strong and mighty, to take us to be with Him in heaven. People are looking forward to this Second Coming with hope. And when it arrives, the angels will again sing with joy.

When Jesus came to earth the first time, He took on the body of a human baby. This is whom we sing about in all our Christmas lullabies.

And when Jesus comes to earth the second time, what body will He take up? What body will He gather to Himself? The body of the church. "The church is Christ's body" (Ephesians 5:23).

What do you suppose an "Adventist" is? It's someone who celebrates the First Advent with joy and looks forward to the Second Advent with hope.

Today we celebrate Christmas with joy and hope.

When Jesus Comes

Jesus told the disciples that when He comes back, everyone in the world will know about it. Everyone will see—it will be big, with angels and bright clouds of glory. Everyone will hear—it will be loud, with trumpets and shouting. You won't be able to miss it.

He will come with great power and glory. Matthew 24:30.

The believers who have been waiting and hoping for this day will go up to meet Jesus in the clouds. And in that moment everything will be changed. In an instant, we will all be changed. The old world will be over—we will no longer think about our old life and its problems. Our new life will begin. We will be happy.

But not everyone will be happy to see Jesus come. The people who decided they didn't want to follow God's plan will not go to meet Jesus. The Bible says they will try to hide "in caves and behind the rocks on the mountains" (Revelation 6:15). The people who didn't believe God will be afraid.

But Jesus says, "When these things begin to happen, don't fear. Look up and hold your heads high because the time when God will free you is near!" (Luke 21:28).

We won't be afraid. We won't try to hide. This is what we have been hoping for. We will hold our heads high. We will meet Jesus in the air.

We may wish we knew more about the Second Coming. But we do know the most important fact: "And we will be with the Lord forever" (1 Thessalonians 4:17). All the rest is details. This is what we have been waiting and hoping for. We will be with Jesus. We will be together.

Summer Vacation

God showed some Bible writers a little of what heaven will be like, and they had a hard time describing it. The Bible doesn't tell us much about what will be in heaven.

However, it does say what won't be in heaven. "There will be no more death, sadness, crying, or pain. All the old ways are gone" (Revelation 21:4). The old ways are the ways of sin. In heaven there will be no sin. Once the old ways are gone, God's way will make everything good again. Heaven will be wonderful—too wonderful for words.

What do you like best about summer vacation? Maybe you like the weather. It's so nice not to be cold, not to have to wear a coat, to be able to play outside. Or maybe your favorite thing about summer is no school. You get to sleep in. There's more time to goof off and do what you want to do. Or maybe you like swimming or picnics or going barefoot. Camping. Watermelon. Oh, summer is so wonderful it almost makes you cry.

About 100 years ago God gave a prophet named Ellen White a vision of what heaven will be like. Mrs. White says that heaven will be like summer vacation. She wrote that on earth our lives are cold and full of trouble. "The time spent here is the Christian's winter," she says. But when Jesus comes, the sadness will be over. "Then will be the Christian's summer" (*The Upward Look,* p. 311).

You like the watermelon here? Just wait. You think swimming is fun? Can you imagine what it will be like in heaven? You like having a little extra free time? Imagine having a lot. All the best parts of summer, only a whole lot better. Heaven will be our forever summer vacation.

The New Earth

When John the disciple was very old, God gave him a vision. God showed him what it would be like when Jesus came back and what heaven would be like. In the last book of the Bible, John tells us about the messages of that vision.

Amen. Come, Lord Jesus! Revelation 22:20.

John says that Jesus is coming back for two reasons. First, God wants to be with us. This has been God's plan all along. He told the Israelites, "I will walk with you and be your God. And you will be my people" (Leviticus 26:12). Jesus prayed, "Father, I want these people that you have given me to be with me" (John 17:24). In John's vision of heaven, he heard a voice say, "Now God's home is with men. He will live with them, and they will be his people. God himself will be with them" (Revelation 21:3).

There is another reason Jesus is coming back. John says He saw God sitting on His throne and God told him, "Look! I am making everything new!" (verse 5). John saw that God's people will stay in heaven for 1,000 years, and then everything sinful will be destroyed and the earth will be re-created—our tired old world will be made new. We will come home to live on the new earth.

John tries to describe it—but you get the feeling it's too wonderful for words. He says he saw a city made of gold and jewels—and big enough for everyone. He saw a crystal-clear river and an amazing tree. There won't be any night. And there will be joy. In this old earth we are busy going to school, doing our chores, paying bills. We don't have much time for joy. In the new earth there will be joy. We will be with God.

It Sounds Like Heaven to Me

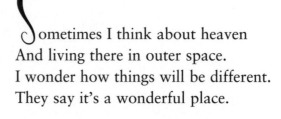

No one has ever
imagined what God
has prepared for those
who love him. 1
Corinthians 2:9.

Sometimes I think about heaven
And living there in outer space.
I wonder how things will be different.
They say it's a wonderful place.

There won't be any thunder in heaven,
Or if there is, no one will care.
You won't have any nightmares in heaven
Or get chased by a lion or bear.
There won't be anything scary, you see.
It sounds like heaven to me.

There won't be any yelling in heaven.
Nobody will argue or fight.
They won't hurt your feelings in heaven
Or have wars about whose way is right.
There won't be anyone fighting, you see.
It sounds like heaven to me.

We'll all have a home up in heaven.
No one will live out in the street.
No one will go hungry in heaven.
There'll be plenty of food there to eat.
There won't be any injustice, you see.
It sounds like heaven to me.

There won't be any doctors in heaven,
'Cause no one will ever be sick.
I won't have to get shots up in heaven.

I can get used to that real quick.
There won't be hurting in heaven, you see.
It sounds like heaven to me.

Friends won't move away up in heaven
And nobody will ever die.
All the people we love, ever with us.
We won't have to keep saying goodbye.
There won't be anyone lonely, you see.
It sounds like heaven to me.

I don't know about spinach or bedtime,
Or what the status on homework will be.
But God promises we will be happy.
That sounds like heaven to me.

Resolutions

In the next few days you might hear people talking about New Year's resolutions. These are promises they make to themselves. These promises are usually about habits they want to break or things they want to change about themselves. People make resolutions on January 1, at the beginning of the new year, because it seems like a good chance to start over, to get it right. As they look to the future, they make resolutions.

Resolution has another meaning that looks to the past. It also means that something has been dealt with successfully. If someone says that a problem has reached a satisfactory resolution, they mean that the problem has been solved—it's over; we don't have to worry about it anymore. That's the way we look at the year that's just now coming to an end. It has reached resolution.

Resolution is a good word for this time of year. It looks back and finishes up the old year. And it looks forward to the promises of the new year.

Jesus is God's resolution. He is the resolution to the problem of sin. Jesus came to this earth to take our punishment for us. He saved us. And Jesus is also the kind of resolution that looks to the promise of the future. When Jesus is our friend, we will have a better life. We can do better. We can be better. And someday we can be together.

God is getting ready to bring this earth to resolution. He is getting ready to welcome us to heaven. Soon the old things will be gone. Everything will be made new.

Set to Music

Have you ever seen a baby happily banging on a pot with a spoon or pounding with both hands on the piano? The baby is not making music—it's noise. Very good noise; a joyful noise—but just noise.

Sing and make music in your hearts to the Lord. Ephesians 5:19.

Music is organized sound. Noise is sound without a plan.

People who don't understand God's plan may think that life has no plan. They think things just happen for no reason, by chance. But life is not "noise." There has been a plan from the beginning.

We are in that plan right now, and it's moving forward. Like music. Music doesn't just wander around—it goes somewhere; it moves toward the end.

We've studied the plan from the beginning to the present; from before Creation to the way God wants us to live now. We've studied God's plan for what will happen next: we know that Jesus will come to take us to heaven.

There is a definite path and a definite goal. God's plan is working.

In music, every note has a purpose. Every note is where it is for a reason. All the notes make a difference. In God's plan, each of us has a purpose. Each of us makes a difference. God has a plan for your life. You are here for a reason.

God's plan has always been "I will be their God, and they will be my people" (Jeremiah 31:33). You are a part of that plan.